The Rollie Fingers
Baseball Bible

𝕽𝖔𝖑𝖑𝖎𝖊 𝕱𝖎𝖓𝖌𝖊𝖗𝖘 & 𝖄𝖊𝖑𝖑𝖔𝖜𝖘𝖙𝖔𝖓𝖊 𝕽𝖎𝖙𝖙𝖊𝖗

VOL. II of
THE ROLLIE'S BASEBALL FOLLIES
COLLECTION

PUBLISHED BY CLERISY PRESS

302-306 Greenup Street
Covington, KY 41011
www.clerisypress.com

ILLUSTRATIONS BY JERRY DOWLING

COVER & INTERIOR DESIGNED BY STEPHEN SULLIVAN

EDITED BY JACK HEFFRON

Baseball cards used on the following pages appear courtesy of
The Topps Company Inc.: 51, 93, 130, 244

The photos on the following pages appear courtesy of the Library of Congress:
37, 45, 65, 110, 137, 184, 191, 209, 213, 216, 269 (Young)

The photos on the following pages are drawn from wikicommons.com:
19, 25, 53, 79, 84, 85, 121, 240, 269 (Oswalt, Bacon)

Printed in the United States of America
Distributed by Publishers Group West
First edition, first printing

This book is dedicated to all the people who have ever had
a window broken as the result of
neighborhood kids putting a baseball through it.

TABLE OF
Cont

ents

𝕭𝖆𝖘𝖊𝖇𝖆𝖑𝖑:

1. An extraordinary game of dominance
involving eighteen to twenty players at any given time
in which a dangerous wooden bat is swung like an axe,
often with maximum torque,
in an effort to control a hard rubber, cloth, and leather sphere
of nearly a nine-inch circumference
that has been foisted, often with great velocity,
toward the general direction
of a batter,
in a most unfriendly manner,
often belt high,
sometimes chin high,
with the express intent to
challenge, manipulate, deceive, and/or intimidate.

2. A symmetrical bliss of athleticism, folklore, idealism,
and excellence in which two groups of diverse players
form respective alliances in an effort to become even greater
than the sum of their parts.

3. Bliss.

The Rollie Fingers Baseball Bible Glossary

By Yellowstone Ritter

Within this here book, you may run into a word from time to time that may seem a bit unusual. Therefore, I've cooked up a glossary. Of course, there may be a word or two on the list below that isn't in existence (before now), but I figure if Billy Shakespeare got to create words out of thin air, then I should be allowed to as well.

beery: *the mood created when weary people drink beer*

bridge builders: *middle relievers*

croix: *a cheap object given to recognize expensive valor*

Denise Richards: a tone-deaf actress who once semi-sang at Wrigley Field

descalpitative: *describing the whimsically comic gesture in which fans at Turner Field mime the separation of scalp from skull*

flaskers: *proactive folks with the foresight to bring concealed alcohol into public locales*

goatwash: *like hogwash, but a tad stinkier*

molotovic: *something chemically explosive in mood*

mon petit chou: *a little cute French baby*

octliminate: *to eliminate another baseball team from contention during the month of October*

permillage: *like a percentage, but one digit better!*

payshirt: *a cloth-based version of paydirt*

pigskinners: *footballers; gridironers; mudcakers*

plasticon: *an object of little value processed via polymerization*

proverbial cup of coffee: *a brief stay in the major leagues*

ricockulous: *synonym for ridiculous*

Robb Nen: *the correct spelling of Rob Nenn*

ruminant: *quadri-stomached creature prone to chewing cud*

shutups: *see sitdowns*

sitdowns: *a catchy synonym for strikeouts that never really caught on, probably because I just made it up*

stalactiting: *object featuring a downward trickle of liquid that forms into a hard spike; seen often in caves and in beards*

stopgappers: *hurlers who enter the game with runners on base*

sublime: *baseball*

swabbies: *sailors or tube shaped plasticons with cotton on the ends*

thunderiffic: *something with a propensity for great excitement; this book*

1

A Century of Baseball Icons

Every year, a future baseball star is born.
We now present 100 of the sport's most famous
personalities alongside the year that they
originally emerged from a dugout.

1890 – Casey Stengel
1891 – Dazzy Vance
1892 – Ray Schalk
1893 – George Sisler
1894 – Herb Pennock
1895 – Babe Ruth
1896 – Rogers Hornsby
1897 – Lefty O'Doul
1898 – Bill Terry
1899 – Waite Hoyt

1900 – Lefty Grove
1901 – Heinie Manush
1902 – Al Simmons
1903 – Lou Gehrig
1904 – Chuck Klein
1905 – Leo Durocher
1906 – Satchel Paige
1907 – Jimmie Foxx
1908 – Al Lopez
1909 – Mel Ott

1910 – Dizzy Dean
1911 – Josh Gibson
1912 – Arky Vaughan
1913 – Johnny Mize
1914 – Joe DiMaggio
1915 – Joe Gordon
1916 – Enos Slaughter
1917 – Phil Rizzuto
1918 – Ted Williams
1919 – Jackie Robinson

1920 – Stan Musial
1921 – Warren Spahn
1922 – Ralph Kiner
1923 – Bobby Thomson
1924 – Gil Hodges
1925 – Yogi Berra
1926 – Duke Snider
1927 – Tommy Lasorda
1928 – Billy Martin
1929 – Don Larsen

1930 – Earl Weaver

1931 – Mickey Mantle

1932 – Maury Wills

1933 – Rocky Colavito

1934 – Hank Aaron

1935 – Sandy Koufax

1936 – Harmon Killebrew

1937 – Brooks Robinson

1938 – Willie McCovey

1939 – Carl Yastrzemski

1940 – Joe Torre

1941 – Pete Rose

1942 – Tony Perez

1943 – Joe Morgan

1944 – Tony La Russa

1945 – Jim Palmer

1946 – Rollie Fingers

1947 – Nolan Ryan

1948 – Steve Garvey

1949 – Mike Schmidt

1950 – Ron Guidry

1951 – Dave Winfield

1952 – Fred Lynn

1953 – Jim Rice

1954 – Ozzie Smith

1955 – Robin Yount

1956 – Eddie Murray

1957 – Lee Smith

1958 – Rickey Henderson

1959 – Terry Francona

1960 – Cal Ripken Jr.

1961 – Don Mattingly

1962 – Roger Clemens

1963 – Randy Johnson

1964 – Barry Bonds

1965 – Craig Biggio

1966 – Curt Schilling

1967 – John Smoltz

1968 – Sammy Sosa

1969 – Ken Griffey Jr.

1970 – Jim Thome

1971 – Pedro Martinez

1972 – Manny Ramirez

1973 – Ichiro Suzuki

1974 – Derek Jeter

1975 – Alex Rodriguez

1976 – Alfonso Soriano

1977 – Roy Halladay

1978 – Chase Utley

1979 – Johan Santana

1980 – Albert Pujols

1981 – Josh Hamilton

1982 – David Wright

1983 – Joe Mauer

1984 – Tim Lincecum

1985 – Evan Longoria

1986 – Felix Hernandez

1987 – Justin Upton

1988 – Stephen Strasburg

1989 – Jason Heyward

2

The Derek Jeter Dossier

JETER, Derek

DOSSIER - 2

BIRTHPLACE: Born in New Jersey--28 miles from Yankee Stadium

BIRTH TRIVIA: Named for Derek Sanderson--a famous hockey player his father greatly admired

PARENTAL TRIVIA: Prior to becoming a doctor, Jeter's father was a shortstop for the Fisk University baseball squad

CHILDHOOD INSPIRATION: Dave Winfield

HIGH SCHOOL YEARS: Kalamazoo, Michigan

HIGH SCHOOL HONORS: Named USA Today's High School Baseball Player of the Year in basketball, the 6' 3" Jeter was named All-State honorable mention

COLLEGE: Briefly attended the University of Michigan before turning pro

DRAFTED: Was the 6th pick in the 1992 June draft

PROS DRAFTED AHEAD OF HIM: future All-Stars Phil Nevin and Jeffrey Hammonds

MINOR LEAGUE GAMES PRIOR TO MLB DEBUT: 447

JETER, Derek   DOSSIER - 2
_____

MOST FREQUENT MINOR LEAGUE HOME: Columbus, Ohio

AN EARLY ACCOMPLISHMENT: Named USA Today's 1994
Minor League Player of the Year

MLB DEBUT YEAR: 1995

AGE AT DEBUT: 20

EARLIEST NY YANKEE TEAMMATES INCLUDED:
Wade Boggs, David Cone, Rick Honeycutt,
Steve Howe, Don Mattingly, Jack McDowell, and
Darryl Strawberry

TRIVIA: Derek Jeter, Andy Pettitte, and Mariano
Rivera all made their major league debuts
within 30 days of one another

IRONIC FACT: After his sophomore season, Jeter won
the Rookie of the Year Award

PRIMARY MANAGER: Joe Torre

TOTAL MANAGERS PLAYED FOR: 3

JETER'S GOOD LUCK RITUAL: Often rubbed the bald
head of Don Zimmer

JETER, Derek

DOSSIER - 2

TOTAL SEASONS IN THE MAJOR LEAGUES
THRU 2009: 15

NUMBER OF LOSING SEASONS: 0

REGULAR SEASON STATS THUS FAR:
.317 BA   224 HR   1,068 RBI   305 SB

YANKEE REGULAR SEASON WINNING PERMILLAGE
IN GAMES IN WHICH JETER PARTICIPATED: .608

YANKEE REGULAR SEASON WINNING PERMILLAGE IN
GAMES IN WHICH JETER DID NOT PARTICIPATE
(SINCE HIS DEBUT ON MAY 29, 1995): .586

MAJOR LEAGUE AFFILIATIONS: New York Yankees
(100%)

POSITIONS PLAYED DURING HIS GAMES (rounded):
SS   99%
DH   14 games
PH   5 games

INJURY AND/OR REST RATE: 13%

BEST SEASON (1999):
.349 BA   24 HR   102 RBI   19 SB

JETER, Derek   DOSSIER - 2

MOST FREQUENT OPPONENT: Baltimore Orioles

HOME AWAY FROM HOME: Tiger Stadium
.360 BA, 2 HR, 11 RBI in 22 games

THREE MOST FREQUENT FOES:
Tim Wakefield--109 plate appearances
(.301 BA, 3 HR, 10 RBI, 5 BB, 15K)

Roy Halladay--100 plate appearances
(.242 BA, 0 HR, 5 RBI, 7 BB, 24K)

Pedro Martinez--99 plate appearances
(.256 BA, 3 HR, 6 RBI, 11BB, 22K)

THE PITCHER HE HOMERED MOST OFTEN AGAINST:
Sidney Ponson (5)

THE PITCHER HE OWNED: Hideo Nomo
.600 (12 for 20) with 5 RBIs, 5 BB, and OK.

THE PITCHER WHO OWNS HIM: Scott Kazmir
.111 (4 for 36) with 1 HR, 4 RBIs, 3 BB, and 11K)

THE PITCHER HE STRUCK OUT MOST OFTEN AGAINST:
Roy Halladay (24)

BATTING CHAMPIONSHIPS: 0

JETER, Derek

LEAGUE MVP: 0

DOSSIER - 2

GOLD GLOVES: 4

FIELDING PERMILLAGE: .976

ALL-STAR TEAMS: 10

ALL-STAR STATS:
.429   1 HR   3 RBI   1 SB

PLAYOFF RECORD: 87-51

HIS 138 PLAYOFF GAMES CONSTITUTE: 5% of his major
league total

MOST FREQUENT TEAMMATES:
Jorge Posada--15 seasons
Mariano Rivera--15 seasons

CLOSEST STATISTICAL TWIN: Barry Larkin

HALL OF FAME CALIBRE RATING: 193%

WORLD SERIES RINGS: 5

3

The Decade of the 2000s

A Series of Mini-Chapters Devoted to this
Historic Ten-Year Period

◇◇

It was the decade when the Red Sox and White Sox both
ended their lengthy droughts. It was a time that spelled the
end for the Montreal Expos and the rebirth of baseball in
the nation's capital. Despite the harsh shadow cast by
steroids, baseball hit new attendance records.
It was the decade of the 2000s.

THE FIVE MOST DOMINANT TEAMS

1

The New York Yankees

2 WORLD CHAMPIONSHIPS / 4 PENNANTS / 9 PLAYOFF APPEARANCES / 1,017 TOTAL WINS

ICONS: Joe Torre, Joe Girardi, Robinson Cano, Roger Clemens,
Jason Giambi, Derek Jeter, Hideki Matsui, Mike Mussina, Andy Pettitte,
Jorge Posada, Mariano Rivera, Alex Rodriguez, Gary Sheffield,
Alfonso Soriano, Mike Stanton, Bernie Williams, George Steinbrenner,
Brian Cashman, Michael Kay, Phil Rizzuto, Bobby Murcer, Ken Singleton,
Paul O'Neil, Bob Sheppard

2
The Boston Red Sox

2 WORLD CHAMPIONSHIPS / 2 PENNANTS / 6 PLAYOFF APPEARANCES / 954 TOTAL WINS

ICONS: Terry Francona, Josh Beckett, Johnny Damon, Nomar Garciaparra, Derek Lowe, Mike Lowell, Pedro Martinez, Trot Nixon, David Ortiz, Jonathan Papelbon, Dustin Pedroia, Manny Ramirez, Curt Schilling, Mike Timlin, Jason Varitek, Tim Wakefield, Kevin Youkilis, Grady Little, John Henry, Theo Epstein, Jerry Remy

3
The St. Louis Cardinals

1 WORLD CHAMPIONSHIP / 2 PENNANTS / 7 PLAYOFF APPEARANCES / 946 TOTAL WINS

ICONS: Tony La Russa, Albert Pujols, Chris Carpenter, David Eckstein, Jim Edmonds, Jason Isringhausen, Matt Morris, Edgar Renteria, Scott Rolen, William DeWitt Jr., Walt Jocketty, Al Hrabosky, Joe Buck, Jack Buck

4
The Philadelphia Phillies

1 WORLD CHAMPIONSHIP / 2 PENNANTS / 3 PLAYOFF APPEARANCES / 868 TOTAL WINS

ICONS: Charlie Manuel, Jimmy Rollins, Chase Utley, Cole Hamels, Ryan Howard, Pat Burrell, Ryan Madsen, Bobby Abreu, Brad Lidge, Mike Lieberthal, Brett Myers, Larry Bowa, Terry Francona, Bill Giles, Pat Gillick, Harry Kalas

5
The Anaheim/Los Angeles Angels

1 WORLD CHAMPIONSHIP / 1 PENNANT / 6 PLAYOFF APPEARANCES / 921 TOTAL WINS

ICONS: Mike Scioscia, Garret Anderson, Darin Erstad, Chone Figgins, Troy Glaus, Vladimir Guerrero, Adam Kennedy, John Lackey, Troy Percival, Francisco Rodriguez, Tim Salmon, Scot Shields, Rex Hudler, Bill Stoneman, Arte Moreno

A TIMELINE OF THE DECADE

2000 Superstar Ken Griffey Jr. is traded to his hometown of Cincinnati. Pacific Bell Park (San Francisco), Comerica Park (Detroit) and Enron Field (Houston) open for business. A 1909 Honus Wagner baseball card sells for $1.1 million. Cleveland and San Francisco sell out every home game. Boston's Nomar Garciaparra and Colorado's Todd Helton both win batting titles after hitting .372.

The season ends up as history's high-water mark for home runs. Derek Jeter picks up MVP awards during both the All-Star game and the World Series. The New York Yankees defeat the crosstown Mets to secure their fourth championship in five seasons.

2001 Alex Rodriguez begins his unprecedented ten-year $252 million contract with the Texas Rangers. Miller Park (Milwaukee) and PNC Park (Pittsburgh) open for business. Manny Ramirez joins the Red Sox just as Mike Mussina joins the Yankees. Lenny Harris tops Manny Mota to become history's top pinch hitter with 151. Barry Bonds surpasses Mark McGwire's single-season HR record and ends with 73. Bonds also slugs .863, besting Babe Ruth's single-season record. Rickey Henderson surpasses Ty Cobb as the all-time runs leader, and the Man of Steal also surpasses Babe Ruth to become the all-time walks leader. The 9/11 terrorist attacks force the cancellation of the minor league playoffs and postpone major league baseball for six days. "God Bless America" replaces "Take Me Out to the Ballgame" during the seventh-inning stretch at numerous ballparks. Enron goes bankrupt, forcing the Astros to find a new name for their field. The Arizona Diamondbacks become World Champions in only their fourth year of existence.

2002 The legendary Ted Williams passes away at the age of eight-three. Jason Giambi joins the New York Yankees. Al Leiter becomes the first pitcher to defeat all thirty franchises. In June, the Cardinals must not only mourn the death of Hall of Fame broadcaster Jack Buck, but that of ace pitcher Darryl Kile as well. The All-Star game ends in a tie. Bob Costas refers to the period as "The Steroid Era," essentially coining the phrase in the process. The Oakland A's win twenty consecutive games. Two cities that have never won a world championship (San Francisco and Anaheim) collide in the World Series. With the help of a rally monkey and thousands of thundersticks, the Angels prevail.

2003 Cincinnati debuts the Great American Ballpark. Slugger David Ortiz and twenty-eight-year-old GM Theo Epstein both join the Boston Red Sox. Top free agent Jim Thome starts his run with the Philadelphia Phillies. Barry Bonds steals his 500th base. Seventy-two-year-old Jack McKeon takes over the 16-22 Florida Marlins. Despite their low payroll, "Trader Jack" McKeon leads the Marlins past the mighty Yankees to win their second world championship in seven years.

2004 Citizens Bank Ballpark (Philadelphia) and PETCO park (San Diego) debut. Alex Rodriguez joins the Yankees. Vladimir Guerrero joins the Angels. The Red Sox trade Nomar Garciaparra to the Cubs during the season. Ichiro Suzuki sets the all-time single-season record for hits with 262. Barry Bonds hits his 700th home run and also draws his 2,191st walk (surpassing Rickey Henderson) to become the all-time leader. Bonds wins his seventh and final league MVP award. Roger Clemens wins his seventh and final Cy Young Award. The Expos play their final game in Montreal. The Boston Red Sox come back from an 0-3 deficit in the ALCS to win their first world championship since 1918.

2005 Congress summons a number of superstars to testify about steroid usage. Top free agent Carlos Beltran joins the New York Mets. Roger Clemens comes out of retirement to play for the Houston Astros. There, Roger the Rocket posts a 1.87 earned run average to win the NL's ERA crown. MLB begins suspending players for steroid usage. The Giants franchise becomes the first to win 10,000 games. The Chicago White Sox come back from being 15 games under .500 to win the World Series (their first since 1917).

2006 Twins legend Kirby Puckett passes away at the age of forty-five. The World Baseball Classic debuts, and Japan comes out on top. The Cardinals begin playing in the new Busch Stadium. Jimmy Rollins' hitting streak is snapped at 38. His teammate Chase Utley puts together a 35-game hitting streak. Miguel Tejada plays in his 1,000th consecutive game. Trevor Hoffman surpasses Lee Smith to become the all-time saves leader. Kenny Rogers pitches 23 consecutive scoreless innings. For the first of three consecutive seasons, the Yankees field the three highest paid players (Alex Rodriguez, Derek Jeter, and Jason Giambi). The St. Louis Cardinals win the World Series, despite having won only 83 games in the regular season.

2007 Roger Clemens comes out of retirement (again) to play a partial season for the New York Yankees and reaches 350 career victories. The Philadelphia Phillies become the first franchise to lose 10,000 games. Brandon Webb pitches 42 consecutive scoreless innings. Barry Bonds surpasses Hank Aaron's storied "755" mark to become baseball's all-time home run champion. Greg Maddux wins his seventeenth Gold Glove. Sixty-eight-year-old umpire Bruce Froemming retires after thirty-seven seasons in the major leagues.

2008 The New York Mets acquire Johan Santana from the Minnesota Twins. Instant replay debuts on a limited basis. President George W. Bush throws out the first pitch at Washington D.C.'s brand new Nationals Park. South Korea wins the Gold Medal in baseball at the Olympics. Omar Vizquel plays his 2,584th game at shortstop, surpassing Luis Aparicio as the all-time leader. Greg Maddux reaches 350 wins. Kenny Rogers becomes the career pickoff leader with 92. The Rockies and Padres play a 22-inning game. Manny Ramirez is swapped to the Los Angeles Dodgers. Kevin Youkilis surpasses Steve Garvey's record by playing his 193rd consecutive game at first base without an error. Thirty-nine-year-old Mike Mussina wins 20 games for the first time in his career and retires at season's end. Francisco Rodriguez sets the single-season saves record with 62. Sophomore Dustin Pedroia wins a Gold Glove, a Silver Slugger and a league MVP award. The Cubs reach the century mark since they won their last championship. The World Series pits the losingest team in baseball history (the Phillies) against the franchise with the worst lifetime winning percentage (Tampa Bay). The Phillies prevail.

2009 Japan successfully defends its crown at the second World Baseball Classic. Both the Mets and Yankees open up brand new ballparks. New President Barack Obama throws out the ceremonial first pitch at the All-Star game. Andy Pettitte surpasses Kenny Rogers to become baseball's all-time pickoff leader. Ivan Rodriguez catches his 2,275th game behind the plate, surpassing Carlton Fisk to become the all-time leader. Derek Jeter surpasses Lou Gehrig to become the all-time Yankees hit leader. Tony La Russa reaches 2,500 managerial victories. For the third consecutive season, a tiebreaker game is needed to determine the eighth playoff spot. The Metrodome in Minneapolis hosts its final baseball game. For the second time, the Yankees christen a new ballpark in the Bronx with a World Championship.

2000-2009 OVERVIEW

Multiple Cy Young Award Winners
Randy Johnson – 3
Roger Clemens – 2
Johan Santana – 2

Multiple MVP Award Winners
Barry Bonds – 4
Albert Pujols–3
Alex Rodriguez – 3

The Ten All-Star Games
American League – 9 victories
National League – 0 victories
One tie

Most All-Star Selections
Manny Ramirez – 9
Alex Rodriguez – 9
Ichiro Suzuki – 9
Derek Jeter – 8
Albert Pujols – 8
Mariano Rivera – 8
Vladimir Guerrero – 7
Alfonso Soriano – 7

Most Regular Season Wins By a Manager
Joe Torre – 952
Tony La Russa – 913
Mike Scioscia – 900

Highest Regular Season Home Attendance
New York Yankees – 37,781,051
Los Angeles Dodgers – 34,497,148
Chicago Cubs – 30,339,604

FROM 2000 THROUGH 2009...

~ Curt Schilling was the only player to win
three World Series championships

~ Barry Bonds was the only two-time NL batting champion.

~ Only five of the decade's eighty-eight big-league managers helmed teams for ten
consecutive seasons (Bruce Bochy, Bobby Cox, Tony La Russa,
Mike Scioscia, and Joe Torre).
However, only Joe Torre guided his teams to the postseason
each of the ten years.

~ The New York Yankees and St. Louis Cardinals
both played in five league championship series.
However, not once did they concurrently advance
to oppose one another in the World Series.

~ Andy Pettitte won more games than any other pitcher, despite the fact that he never
once led his league in wins.

~ Only the Oakland A's, Florida Marlins, and Seattle Mariners produced more than
one rookie of the year (The A's and Fish had three apiece, and the M's had two).

~ Only Bobby Cox and Lou Piniella managed to win more than one manager of the
year award (two apiece).

~ Despite missing 39 percent of the decade to injury, rest, or forced retirement,
Barry Bonds still drew 90 more walks
than the next closest player (Bobby Abreau).

~ Jimmy Rollins led everyone in triples with 95.

~ Only four players hit 200 home runs and stole 200 bases.
(Bobby Abreau, Carlos Beltran, Mike Cameron,
and Alfonso Soriano).

~ Jason Marquis was the only player whose teams made it to the postseason
every year of the decade.

THE REVOLVING DOOR
FRESH BLOOD

2000	Johan Santana and Michael Young
2001	Albert Pujols and Ichiro Suzuki
2002	Carl Crawford and Francisco Rodriguez
2003	Miguel Cabrera and Mark Teixiera
2004	Matt Holliday and David Wright
2005	Jonathan Papelbon and Hanley Ramirez
2006	Russell Martin and Dan Uggla
2007	Ryan Braun and Tim Lincecum
2008	Evan Longoria and Brad Ziegler
2009	Andrew Bailey and Chris Coghlan

NOTABLE FINALES

2000	Will Clark and Dwight Gooden
2001	Tony Gwynn, Cal Ripken Jr.
2002	Chuck Finley and Tim Raines
2003	Rickey Henderson and Jesse Orosco
2004	Roberto Alomar and Barry Larkin
2005	Kevin Brown and Rafael Palmiero
2006	Bernie Williams and Tim Salmon
2007	Craig Biggio, Barry Bonds, Roger Clemens, Roberto Hernandez, Jose Mesa, Mike Piazza, Curt Schilling, Sammy Sosa
2008	Tom Glavine and Greg Maddux
2009	Troy Percival and Randy Johnson

PITCHING (2000-2009)
THREE OF THE DECADE'S GREATEST PITCHERS

Randy Johnson (*Diamondbacks, Yankees, Giants*)
- Nicknamed the "Big Unit"
- Lanky 6'10" mullet aficionado with omnipresent scowl
- Possessed a devasting slider and a triple-digit fastball
- Notched more lifetime strikeouts than any other southpaw
- Raised in suburban Northern California
- College teammate of Mark McGwire
- Highest strikeout ratio in history among starters
- Was eventually tutored by his idol, Nolan Ryan
- Pitched effectively into his mid-forties
- From 2000-2009, went 143-78 with 12 shutouts, 2,182 strikeouts and a 3.34 ERA

Mariano Rivera (*Yankees*)

- Born and raised in a fishing village in Panama
- Worked as a commercial shrimper
- Righthanded
- Known for his calm and serene demeanor
- Master of the cut fastball (also known as "the buzzsaw")
- Switch-hitters often hit righty against Rivera to prevent getting jammed on their fists
- His cutter once shattered 3 bats during a lone plate appearance
- Widely considered the MVP of the late 1990s Yankee dynasty.
- Devout Christian
- Pitched 34.1 consecutive scoreless postseason innings
- Was left unprotected by the Yankees in the 1992 expansion draft but went untouched by Colorado and Florida
- From 2000-2009, posted 397 saves, 45 victories, 669 strikeouts and a 2.08 ERA in his 651 appearances

Johan Santana (*Twins, Mets*)

- Born and raised in Venezuela
- Lefthanded
- As a kid, started out as a center fielder
- Snatched away from the Astros in a Rule V draft
- Owner of a deadly three-punch (fastball, circle changeup, and slider)
- His changeup is nicknamed "the Bugs Bunny" as a testament to how cartoonishly strange it moves
- From 2000 through 2009, went 122-60 with a 3.12 ERA and 1,733 strikeouts

MORE OF THE DECADE's TOP PITCHERS
(with their regular-season statistics from 2000 to 2009)

SP **Roger Clemens** (*Yankees, Astros*) (8 seasons)
107-50, 1 shutout, 3.34 ERA, 1,346K in 1,454.1 innings

SP **Roy Halladay** (*Blue Jays*)
139-69, 14 shutouts, 3.40 ERA, 1,400K in 1,883.1 innings

SP **Pedro Martinez** (*Red Sox, Mets, Phillies*)
112-50, 6 shutouts, 3.01 ERA, 1,620K in 1,469 innings

SP **Roy Oswalt** (*Astros*) (9 seasons)
137-70, 6 shutouts, 3.23 ERA, 1,473K in 1,803.1 innings

SP **Andy Pettitte** (*Yankees, Astros*)
148-89, 3 shutouts, 1,441K in 1,882 innings

SP **Curt Schilling** (*Phillies, Diamondbacks, Red Sox*) (8 seasons)
117-63, 7 shutouts, 3.54 ERA, 1,545K in 1,569.1 innings

RP **Trevor Hoffman** *(Padres, Brewers)*
23 wins, 363 saves, 2.77 ERA, 523K in 533 innings

RP **Joe Nathan** *(Giants, Twins)* (9 seasons)
39 wins, 246 saves, 2.53 ERA, 664K in 594.2 innings

RP **Jonathan Papelbon** *(Red Sox)* (5 seasons)
14 wins, 151 saves, 1.84 ERA, 346K in 298 innings

RP **Francisco Rodriguez** *(Angels, Mets)* (8 seasons)
26 wins, 243 saves, 2.53 ERA, 660K in 519.2 innings

RP **Takashi Saito** *(Dodgers, Red Sox)* (4 seasons)
15 wins, 83 saves, 2.05 ERA, 297K in 245.1 innings

RP **Billy Wagner** *(Astros, Phillies, Mets, Red Sox)*
23 wins, 284 saves, 2.40 ERA, 698K in 580.2 innings

Most Pitching Victories
Andy Pettitte—148
Randy Johnson—143
Jamie Moyer—140

Lowest ERA
(810 innings minimum)
Pedro Martinez—3.01
Johan Santana—3.12
Roy Oswalt—3.23

Most Strikeouts
Randy Johnson—2,182
Javier Vazquez—2,001
Johan Santana—1,733

Most Seasons Leading League in Victories
Curt Schilling—2
Brandon Webb—2

Most ERA Crowns
Pedro Martinez—3
Johan Santana—3
Randy Johnson—2
Jake Peavy—2

Most Seasons Leading League in Strikeouts
Randy Johnson—4
Johan Santana—3
Tim Lincecum—2
Pedro Martinez—2
Jake Peavy—2

Most Appearances
Dave Weathers—712
LaTroy Hawkins—654
Mariano Rivera—651

Most Saves
Mariano Rivera—397
Trevor Hoffman—363
Jason Isringhauen—284
Billy Wagner—284

Lowest ERA
(162-inning minimum)
Jonathan Papelbon—1.84
Takashi Saito—2.05
Mariano Rivera—2.08

Most Seasons Leading League in Saves
Francisco Rodriguez—3
Mariano Rivera—2
Jose Valverde—2

Most Offensive Pitchers
Livan Hernandez collected 157 hits and 59 RBIs
Carlos Zambrano smashed 20 home runs
Micah Owings tallied a .547 slugging percentage
Greg Maddux stole 7 bases
Tom Glavine put down 92 sacrifice hits

Fewest Earned Runs Surrendered
Los Angeles Dodgers—6,360
Atlanta Braves—6,398
Oakland A's—6,533

IRONIES AND ODDITIES

2000 Though the first game of the regular season takes place in Tokyo, the "World Series" ends up being played by two teams from the very same place (New York City). Numerous sluggers, most notably Barry Bonds, begin launching moon shots into the San Francisco Bay. The bobbing souvenirs are retrieved by an array of kayakers, yacht captains, swimmers, and trained Portuguese water dogs.

2001 A fraction of a second after delivering to the plate, Randy Johnson drills a bird that had the misfortune of crossing the path of his fastball, resulting in an explosion of feathers. A leadoff hitter (Ichiro Suzuki) wins the AL MVP award. His team, the Seattle Mariners, wins a record 116 regular season games, yet fails to win the pennant.

2002 Joaquin Benoit records a seven-inning save. Kevin Millar is rewarded with a ground-rule double after hitting a fly ball that lodges in the catwalk grid of Tropicana Field. Jose Rijo wins his first game in seven years.

2003 The Astros use six pitchers to no-hit the Yankees. The Expos play twenty-two of their home games in Puerto Rico. The Detroit Tigers lose 119 games. Eric Gagne converts all 55 of his save opportunities for the Dodgers, and yet blows one in the All-Star game.

2004 Cincinnati Red Adam Dunn literally hits a home run that lands in Kentucky. Barry Bonds is intentionally walked 120 times (he ends the season with a .609 on-base percentage). Eric Gagne's streak of consecutive save conversions tops out at 84. The Boston Red Sox find the best possible time to string together an eight-game winning streak.

2005 A pitcher (Dontrelle Willis) is slotted seventh in his team's batting order. Every team in the NL East finishes with at least 81 victories. The Astros beat the Braves 7-6 in an eighteen-inning postseason game. The Angels play three games on successive nights in three different cities (traveling 4,700 miles within thirty-two hours to do so).

2006 Ninety-four-year-old Buck O'Neil bats in a Northern League All-Star game. Cory Sullivan triples twice in the same inning. A catcher (Joe Mauer) wins a batting title. The Red Sox post $51.1 million in a sealed bid auction for the exclusive right to negotiate with a Japanese superstar (Daisuke Matsuzaka). It later surfaces that the second-closest suitor had only offered $38 million.

2007 Former pitcher Rick Ankiel makes his way back to the Cardinals as a slugging outfielder. Ichiro Suzuki hits an inside-the-park home run at the All-Star game. A pitcher (Trever Miller) somehow appears in seventy-six games without getting a single decision. The Colorado Rockies win fourteen out of their final fifteen games to just barely push their way into the playoffs.

2008 A preseason game is played in China. After sixty years, the Dodgers vacate their spring training camp in Vero Beach. The Tampa Bay franchise exorcises the "Devil" from their name to become known as the "Rays." The Dodgers and Red Sox draw 115,300 fans to the LA Coliseum for an exhibition game. The Cincinnati Reds bat out of order. Due to a hurricane, the Astros and Cubs play two games in Milwaukee. Slugger Adam Dunn hits exactly 40 home runs for the fifth consecutive season. Roger Clemens doesn't come out of retirement for the first time in four years.

2009 Alan Embree wins a game without so much as throwing a pitch (he picked off a runner). Jayson Werth steals three bases after a lone at-bat. The Yankees go eighteen games without a fielding error. Carl Crawford swipes six bases in one game. The Pittsburgh Pirates suffer through their seventeenth consecutive losing season. The Red Sox sell out their five hundredth consecutive game at Fenway Park.

THE GOLF STREAM?

When the new Yankee Stadium debuted in 2009, folks quickly took notice that home runs were being launched with far greater frequency. This phenomenon seemed especially mystifying since the outfield dimensions of the new park were identical to that of its predecessor. It was quickly determined that wind patterns unique to the modern structure were the culprit. However, upon further examination, it appears that the "golf stream" effect has been somewhat exaggerated. Here is why.

During the final year of the original Yankee stadium, the park yielded 160 home runs. The following season, the new place yielded 237. Now, that's a whopping 48 percent increase, but it fails to take into account two significant factors.

Firstly, we can determine from road totals that Yankee hitters became far more adept at hitting home runs in 2009 as compared to the year prior (in part, due to the addition of Mark Teixiera).

Secondly, we can determine that Yankee pitchers became less effective at keeping the ball in the park—no matter what stadium they were in. As it turns out, the 2008 Yankees (hitters and pitchers combined) saw 163 homers during their games away from the Bronx, but in 2009, that aggregate total ticked upward to 188.

So, when crunching the numbers, it can be determined that the true home run differential between the old Yankee Stadium and the new Yankee Stadium (at least from 2008 to 2009) was (+ 28.4 percent).

What does this all boil down to? Basically, this means that a slugger who put up a fifty-homer season while playing his home games at the old Yankee Stadium could expect to hit fifty in the new one (and probably more if he was especially prone to hitting balls out to right field).

By contrast, the "true home run differential" between Shea Stadium and Citi Field was merely nominal (-2.4 percent).

HITTING (2000-2009)
THREE OF THE GREATEST BATS FROM THIS DECADE

Todd Helton (*Rockies*)
- Nicknamed "The Toddfather"
- Scruffy, calm, intense, likable demeanor
- All-time Colorado Rockies leader in hits, home runs, RBIs, runs, walks, and games played.
- 6' 2" lefthanded first baseman.
- Knoxville native who once passed for 2,722 yards as a high school quarterback.
- Also played QB for the University of Tennessee, where he was briefly slotted ahead of Peyton Manning
- Through 2009, has hit .294 on the road with 1,576 total bases and 531 walks.

- His #17 uniform is a nod to fellow first baseman Mark Grace
- In the decade, he hit .331 with 1,756 hits, 1,001 walks, 260 homers, 1,017 runs, and 981 RBIs
- Led the majors in doubles in the decade with 431.

Albert Pujols (*Cardinals*)

- Righthanded first baseman and three-hole hitter known for terrifying managers and pitchers alike
- Born and raised in the Dominican Republic but played his high school baseball in Independence, Missouri
- Tried out for the Tampa Bay Devil Rays, but the brass was unimpressed with him. The scout who arranged the tryout quit in protest.
- Made his major league debut early as a result of a hamstring injury to Cardinal third baseman Bobby Bonilla
- Upon the signing of third baseman Scott Rolen in 2002, Pujols moved to leftfield.
- Once had 7 assists in a game (as a first baseman)
- Never hit lower than .314 across his first nine seasons
- Never hit fewer than 32 homers and 103 RBIs across his first nine seasons
- Three-time MVP
- Launched a foundation to support people with Down's Syndrome
- Active in trying to bring a major league soccer franchise to St. Louis
- From his debut in 2001 through 2009, hit .334 with 1,717 hits, 1,071 runs, 366 homers and 1,112 RBIs.

For a more extensive look at Albert Pujols, check out our first book, Rollie's Follies

Alex Rodriguez (*Mariners, Rangers, Yankees*)

- Nicknamed "A-Rod"
- Born in Manhattan, raised in part in the Dominican Republic and attended high school in Miami
- 6' 3" righthanded shortstop with speed and power
- As a kid, was an avid fan of the New York Mets and of Keith Hernandez in particular
- The University of Miami tried to recruit him as a QB
- Debuted in the majors at the age of eighteen
- Strained, cool, and cautious demeanor
- Became the highest paid player of all-time
- The Yankees only sought A-Rod as means to replace third baseman Aaron Boone, who seriously injured himself playing pickup basketball.
- Became the youngest player (thirty-two) to reach 500 homers.
- Four-time Hank Aaron Award winner
- From 2000 to 2009, hit .304 with 1,740 hits, 1,190 runs, 435 homers, 1,243 RBIs, and 179 steals.

MORE OF THE DECADE's TOP HITTERS
(with their regular season statistics 2000-2009)

LF Barry Bonds *(Giants)* (8 seasons)
.322 BA, 925 hits, 772 runs, 317 HR, 697 RBIs, 54 SB

1B Carlos Delgado *(Blue Jays, Marlins, Mets)*
.286 BA, 1,416 hits, 863 runs, 324 HR, 1,045 RBIs, 9 SB

RF Vladimir Guerrero *(Expos, Angels)*
.323 BA, 1,751 hits, 929 runs, 315 HR, 1,037 RBIs, 147 SB

1B Ryan Howard *(Phillies)* (6 seasons)
.279 BA, 750 hits, 465 runs, 222 HR, 640 RBIs, 10 SB

SS Derek Jeter *(Yankees)*
.317 BA, 1,940 hits, 1088 runs, 161 HR, 727 RBIs, 219 SB

C Joe Mauer *(Twins)* (6 seasons)
.327 BA, 844 hits, 419 runs, 72 HR, 397 RBIs, 34 SB

DH/1B David Ortiz *(Twins, Red Sox)*
.283 BA, 1,365 hits, 831 runs, 307 HR, 1,016 RBIs, 9 SB

LF/RH/DH Manny Ramirez *(Indians, Red Sox, Dodgers)*
.317 BA, 1,562 hits, 933 runs, 348 HR, 1,106 RBIs, 10 SB

2B/LF Alfonso Soriano *(Yankees, Rangers, Nationals, Cubs)*
.279 BA, 1,505 hits, 859 runs, 289 HR, 759 RBIs, 257 SB

RF/DH Sammy Sosa *(Cubs, Orioles, Rangers)* (7 seasons)
.282 BA, 995 hits, 634 runs, 273 HR, 726 RBIs, 10 SB

CF/RF Ichiro Suzuki *(Mariners)* (9 seasons)
.333 BA, 2,030 hits, 973 runs, 84 HR, 515 RBIs, 341 SB

1B/DH Jim Thome *(Indians, Phillies, White Sox, Dodgers)*
.271 BA, 1,255 hits, 877 runs, 368 HR, 986 RBIs, 3 SB

HIGHEST BATTING AVERAGE
(800 plate appearance minimum)

Albert Pujols — .334 / Ichiro Suzuki — .333 / Todd Helton —. 331

Most Hits
Ichiro Suzuki—2030
Derek Jeter—1940
Miguel Tejada—1860

Most Runs
Alex Rodriguez—1,190
Johnny Damon—1,115
Derek Jeter—1,088

Most Home Runs
Alex Rodriguez—435
Jim Thome—368
Albert Pujols—366

Most Runs Batted In
Alex Rodriguez—1,243
Albert Pujols—1,112
Manny Ramirez—1,106

Most Games Played
Miguel Tejada—1,581
Bobby Abreau—1,574
Orlando Cabrera—1,533

Most Stolen Bases
Juan Pierre—459
Carl Crawford—362
Ichiro Suzuki—341

Most Batting Titles
Joe Mauer—3
Barry Bonds—2
Ichiro Suzuki—2

Most Seasons Leading League in Home Runs
Alex Rodriguez—5
Ryan Howard—2
Sammy Sosa—2

Most Sacrifice Hits
Omar Vizquel—113
Juan Pierre—110
Luis Castillo—102

Most Sacrifice Flys
Orlando Cabrera—76
Mike Lowell—76
Carlos Lee—75

Most Intentional Walks
Barry Bonds—390
Vladimir Guerrero—213
Albert Pujols—198

Most Times Drilled
Jason Kendall—159
Jason Giambi—138
David Eckstein—134

Most Runs Scored
New York Yankees—8,834
Boston Red Sox—8,647
Texas Rangers—8,468

EXPOSITION

In late 2001, speculation ran rampant through baseball that major changes were on their way. Fans in Miami, Minneapolis, Montreal, and Tampa were nervous that their beloved ballclubs would either fold or relocate. Even the world champion Arizona Diamondbacks began to wonder if they would be forced to play in the American League to balance things out following a contraction.

Rumors were plentiful. Would the owner of the Marlins abet the folding of his team if he could own the Angels instead? Would the owner of the Expos allow the same thing to happen if he could become owner of the Devil Rays? Would the Marlins relocate to Washington D.C.? No one knew for sure how it would all play out.

On November 6, baseball owners voted twenty-eight to two in favor of eliminating two teams. As it turned out, the two unlucky ballclubs on the chopping block (and the ones who had opposed the vote) were the Minnesota Twins and the Montreal Expos. Commissioner Bud Selig stated that he had every intention of moving forward with the contraction for the greater good of the sport.

Immediately, the player's union and select members of Congress vehemently opposed the idea. However, they did not have sufficient leverage to stop it. All the same, members of Congress began to talk about legislation that could reverse baseball's anti-trust exemption.

Things looked bleak for longtime Expos and Twins fans. However, the plan to kill them off was thwarted when a judge in Minnesota ruled that the Twins had to legally fulfill the final years of their lease with the operators of the Metrodome.

Commissioner Selig and the owners fought this decision, as did the owner of the Twins, Carl Pohlad, who stood to make a payday from having his team bought and folded, but this time, it was they who didn't have the sufficient leverage to get the decision reversed. Since MLB scheduling requires an even number of teams, the Montreal Expos were saved by the Minnesota court ruling as well.

By early 2002, all the major league ownership groups formed a special partnership for the purpose of purchasing the Montreal Expos away from art dealer Jeffrey Loria, who had purchased the Florida Marlins away from commodities trader John Henry, who had purchased the Boston Red Sox. Ipso facto, the commissioner's office began running the Montreal Expos.

Eventually, the idea for contraction came completely off the table when new developments occurred. A new ownership strategy emerged in Minnesota that was far more amenable to increasing every possible revenue stream, such as drawing plans for a new stadium.

In addition, the idea of moving the Expos to Washington D.C. began to appeal more to owners and congressmen alike. Besides, the very notion of baseball in the Beltway put to rest the idea of Congress introducing legislation that would repeal baseball's anti-trust exemption. The slow process to relocate the Expos had begun, and at the end of the 2004 season, the Expos finished out their three-year term as wards of the commissioner's office and were forced to bid a painful adieu to Ville-Marie.

Que sera sera.

But with every door that closes, a window opens, and 2005 marked the return of the national pastime to the nation's capital after a thirty-three-season absence. Manager Frank Robinson made the jump from Montreal as did twenty-five of his forty-six players from the previous season.

Despite fielding an average team (81-81) and even though they played in a nearly obsolete ballpark (RFK Stadium), the franchise saw their home attendance more than triple. The move was deemed successful and prospective ownership groups began to show interest in purchasing the ballclub.

In 2006, the partnership of baseball owners sold the Washington Nationals to Lerner Enterprises (a local real estate business) for $450 million. Champagne corks popped from coast to coast since the selling price was significantly higher than the $120 million the owners originally pooled together to buy the Expos.

One must wonder if the owners felt at least a little bit of gratitude to the judge back in Minnesota who had made the windfall possible.

Que Sera Sera.

FIELDING (2000-2009)

Fewest Unearned Runs Surrendered
Seattle Mariners—514
Minnesota Twins—529
Los Angeles Dodgers—541

Fewest Errors
Philadelphia Phillies—906
Seattle Mariners—906
San Francisco Giants—935

Most Baserunners Caught Stealing
Jorge Posada—302
Jason Kendall—295
Ramon Hernandez—280

Most Infield Assists
Miguel Tejada—4,665
Orlando Cabrera—4,203
Jimmy Rollins—3,883

Most Outfield Assists
Bobby Abreau—96
Carlos Beltran—89
Pat Burrell—86

Most Defensive Innings
Miguel Tejada—13,577.2
Bobby Abreau—13,336.0
Orlando Cabrera—13,164.1

Most Gold Glove Awards
CF Torii Hunter—9
RF Ichiro Suzuki—9
CF Andruw Jones—8
P Greg Maddux—8
3B Eric Chavez—6
CF Jim Edmonds—6
3B Scott Rolen—6
C Ivan Rodriguez—5
P Kenny Rogers—5

THE IRONMEN OF THE DECADE

Jason Kendall caught 84 percent of his team's innings
Miguel Tejada played 94 percent of his team's innings
Derek Jeter played ninety-three postseason games and eight All-Star games
in addition to his 1,500 regular season games.
Livan Hernandez led all pitchers with 332 starts, 2,201 innings
and 35,079 pitches thrown.

MILESTONE CLUBS

THE 300 WINS CLUB
Roger Clemens (2003)
Greg Maddux (2004)
Tom Glavine (2007)
Randy Johnson (2009)

THE 500 HOME RUN CLUB
Barry Bonds (2001)
Rafael Palmiero (2003)
Sammy Sosa (2003)
Ken Griffey Jr. (2004)
Alex Rodriguez (2007)
Jim Thome (2007)
Frank Thomas (2007)
Manny Ramierez (2008)
Gary Sheffield (2009)

THE 500 SAVES CLUB
Trevor Hoffman (2007)
Mariano Rivera (2009)

THE 600 HOME RUN CLUB
Barry Bonds (2002)
Sammy Sosa (2007)
Ken Griffey Jr. (2008)

THE 3,000 HIT CLUB
Cal Ripken Jr. (2000)
Rickey Henderson (2001)
Rafael Palmiero (2005)
Craig Biggio (2007)

THE 3,000 STRIKEOUT CLUB
Randy Johnson (2000)
Greg Maddux (2005)
Curt Schilling (2006)
Pedro Martinez (2007)
John Smoltz (2008)

THE 4,000 STRIKEOUT CLUB
Roger Clemens (2003)
Randy Johnson (2004)

FINAL REGULAR SEASON STANDINGS
(FOR THE TEN COMBINED SEASONS)

American League

AL EAST	WINS	LOSSES	PCT.	GB
NEW YORK YANKEES	965	651	.597	--
BOSTON RED SOX	920	699	.568	46.5
TORONTO BLUE JAYS	805	814	.497	161.5
BALTIMORE ORIOLES	698	920	.431	268
TB DEVIL RAYS/RAYS	694	923	.429	271.5

AL CENTRAL	WINS	LOSSES	PCT.	GB
MINNESOTA TWINS	863	758	.532	--
CHICAGO WHITE SOX	857	764	.529	6
CLEVELAND INDIANS	816	804	504	93
DETROIT TIGERS	729	891	.450	133.5
KANSAS CITY ROYALS	672	948	.415	190.5

AL WEST	WINS	LOSSES	PCT.	GB
ANAHEIM/LA ANGELS	900	720	.556	--
OAKLAND ATHLETICS	890	728	.550	9
SEATTLE MARINERS	837	783	.517	63
TEXAS RANGERS	776	844	.479	124

National League

NL EAST	WINS	LOSSES	PCT.	GB
ATLANTA BRAVES	892	726	.551	--
PHILADELPHIA PHILLIES	850	769	.525	42.5
NEW YORK METS	815	803	.504	82
FLORIDA MARLINS	811	807	.501	86
EXPOS/NATIONALS	711	908	.439	181.5

NL CENTRAL	WINS	LOSSES	PCT.	GB
ST. LOUIS CARDINALS	913	706	.564	--
HOUSTON ASTROS	832	787	.514	81
CHICAGO CUBS	807	811	.499	105.5
CINCINNATI REDS	751	869	.464	162.5
MILWAUKEE BREWERS	741	878	.458	172
PITTSBURGH PIRATES	681	936	.421	231

NL WEST	WINS	LOSSES	PCT.	GB
LA DODGERS	862	758	.532	--
SF GIANTS	855	762	.529	5.5
AZ DIAMONDBACKS	804	815	.497	57.5
COLORADO ROCKIES	769	852	.474	93.5
SAN DIEGO PADRES	769	852	.474	93.5

NOTES:

• During the decade of the 2000s, the Montreal Expos posted a .454 winning permillage as compared to the .424 put up by the Washington Nationals.

• The division with the best winning permillage was the AL West (.525) (which happens to be the least competitive division in that it only includes four ballclubs).

• The division with the worst winning permillage was the NL Central (.487) (which happens to be the most competitive division in that it includes six ballclubs).

• Somewhat unfairly, on average, an AL West team stands a 31.8 percent chance of gaining a playoff spot under this bracketing while an NL Central team has only has a 23.1 percent chance.

• This means that if the Texas Rangers and Houston Astros were always of equal caliber, the Rangers could expect to make the postseason one additional time every 11.5 years due to their bracketing advantage.

• As for the teams in five-team divisions, those in the American League stand a 27.3 percent chance of reaching the postseason, and those in the National League stand a 26.2 percent chance.

• This means that if the New York Mets and New York Yankees were always of equal caliber, the Yankees could expect to make the postseason one additional time every eighty-nine years due to their slight bracketing advantage.

ELITE POSTSEASON HITTERS (2000-2009)

In ten games, Seattle's **Ichiro Suzuki** hit .421 with 5 walks

In ten games, **Carlos Delgado** of the Mets slugged .757
with 4 homers, 6 walks, 8 runs, and 11 RBIs

In sixteen games, **B.J. Upton** of the Rays slugged .652
with 7 homers, 5 walks, 16 runs, 16 RBIs, and 6 stolen bases

In twenty-one games, **Troy Glaus** slugged .797
with 9 homers, 9 walks, 18 runs, and 16 RBIs

In twenty-two games, **Carlos Beltran** slugged .817
with 11 homers, 18 walks, 8 steals, 31 runs, and 19 RBIs.

In forty-eight games, **Alex Rodriguez** hit .304, slugged .575
with 12 homers, 29 walks, 34 runs, 34 RBIs, and 6 steals

In 56 games, St. Louis' **Albert Pujols** slugged .578
with 13 homers, 36 walks, 39 runs, and 36 RBIs

In 59 games, **Manny Ramirez** slugged .604
with 16 homers, 44 walks, 41 runs, and 52 RBIs.

In 66 games, **David Ortiz** of the Red Sox slugged .520
with 12 homers, 41 walks, 39 runs, 47 RBIs, and 3 walk-off hits.

In 93 games, the Yankees' **Derek Jeter** hit .307
with 16 homers, 42 walks, 64 runs, and 43 RBIs.

ELITE POSTSEASON PITCHERS (2000-2009)

In four games, **Kenny Rogers** went 3-0 with a 0.00 ERA
along with 22K in 24.1 innings.

In five games, **Cliff Lee** of the Phillies went 4-0 with a 1.56 ERA
along with 2 complete games and 33K in 40.1 innings.

In nine games, **Manny Corpas** of the Rockies went 1-0 with an 0.87 ERA
and 5 saves along with 7K in 10.1 innings.

In ten games, **Adam Wainwright** of the Cardinals went 1-0 with an 0.51 ERA
and 4 saves along with 22K in 17.2 innings.

In thirteen games, **John Smoltz** went 3-0 with a 1.98 ERA
and 3 saves along with 26K in 27.1 innings.

In fourteen games, **Josh Beckett** went 7-3 with a 3.07 ERA
along with 99K in 93.2 innings.

In fifteen games, **Curt Schilling** went 10-1 with a 2.12 ERA
along with 3 complete games and 92K in 102 innings.

In twenty-two games, **Alan Embree** went 1-0 with a 1.13 ERA
along with 8K in 16 innings.

In twenty-six games, **Andy Pettitte** went 12-5 with a 3.41 ERA
along with 113K in 161 innings.

In fifty-seven games, **Mariano Rivera** of the Yankees went 4-1 with a 0.94 ERA
and 26 saves along with 68K in 86 innings.

THE DECADE'S MOST ENDURING IMAGE

uring the tide-turning ALCS in 2004 that pitted archrivals New York against Boston, Red Sox starter Curt Schilling took it upon himself to make his team's nickname literal.

Despite being on the mend from an ankle surgery in which doctors had to sew up a torn ankle tendon, Schilling took the mound anyway. As he pitched during Game Six, the sutures ripped. Had this been a regular season game, there's little doubt he would have been removed. But the Red Sox were on the brink of elimination, and so Schilling remained in the game.

At first, a dot of blood appeared on his sock. Then, seemingly with every pitch, the dot got a little larger. Eventually, blood had soaked all the way through.

But despite this plasmic leakage, Schilling surrendered only one run in seven innings and picked up the victory.

Schilling's performance helped force a pivotal Game Seven and the Bloody Sox won that one as well.

THE WORLD CHAMPIONS

2000 – New York Yankees
2001 – Arizona Diamondbacks
2002 – Anaheim Angels
2003 – Florida Marlins
2004 – Boston Red Sox
2005 – Chicago White Sox
2006 – St. Louis Cardinals
2007 – Boston Red Sox
2008 – Philadelphia Phillies
2009 – New York Yankees

4

Cap and Nap

◇◇◇

1852 **Adrian Constantine Anson** is born in a small town in Iowa, 247 miles away from both Minneapolis and Kansas City.

1862 Besides billiards, **Anson's** favorite pastime is baseball. He practices these skills intensely, even inside a barn during winter.

1866 **Anson** is characterized as a hard case. Summarily, he is packed off to a boarding school on the campus of Notre Dame. Baseball turns into one of the teenager's more wholesome pursuits.

1869 Still prone to vice and mischief, **Anson** is sent to the University of Iowa to get straightened out. However, after just one semester, the school tells the incorrigible teenager to pack his bags and hit the road.

1870 **Adrian Anson** winds up playing baseball alongside his father and brother for their hometown team. His budding skills impress an opposing pitcher barnstorming through town (Albert Spalding).

1871 The first professional baseball league begins play (the National Association), and **Adrian Anson** is aboard as the third sacker for the Rockford Forest Cities. They are an eleven-man squad who play their home games at the Agricultural Society Fairgrounds. Anson earns the princely sum of $66 per month (equal to about $1,175 in today's currency). Unfortunately, with their 4-21 record, Rockford skids to a ninth- (and last-) place finish.

1872 **Anson** is lured away by a winning team, the Philadelphia Athletics. The twenty-year-old becomes their top hitter with a .415 batting average (98 points higher

ANSON

ADRIAN C. ANSON.
ALLEN & GINTER'S
RICHMOND. Cigarettes. VIRGINIA

LAJOIE

than the team's average). Off the field, he crosses paths with Virginia Flegal, the thirteen-year-old daughter of a Philly bar owner. Though it may now seem distasteful for a twenty-year-old man to become romantically linked to a thirteen-year-old gal, in Anson's defense, Virginia only looked eleven.

1874 A baby of French-Canadian descent is born in Rhode Island, fifty miles away from the future site of Fenway Park. The *mon petit chou* is given the name **Napoleon Lajoie**.

Displaying utility value, **Adrian Anson** moves over to play shortstop for the Athletics. During the offseason, he joins other players on a tour of Great Britain, where they play exhibition baseball for the natives. On occasion, they even take to the cricket fields. Despite most of the Americans having no experience at cricket, they handily defeat their British counterparts all the same.

1875 The versatile **Anson** tops himself by playing five different positions for Philadelphia. They include catcher, center fielder and the role he will be best remembered for, first baseman. Anson's annual salary reaches $1,800 (about $35,000 in current funds) In a sign of times to come, Anson is handed the managerial reigns for eight games.

Great change is in the air. The National Association's star pitcher, Albert Spalding, secretly signs a contract with an upstart league in midseason and sets about coaxing other superstars like **Adrian Anson** to jump as well.

1876 The National League (as we now know it) makes its debut. With no small amount of reluctance, Anson gives in to Al Spalding and leaves Philadelphia to go "out west" to play for the Chicago White Stockings. A mass exodus to this newly formed league occurs and dooms the National Association. The union of **Anson** and Spalding is highly successful and their team wins the very first NL pennant. During the offseason, Anson returns to Philadelphia and takes Virginia as his wife.

1879 Anson becomes the captain-manager of Chicago and soon becomes better known by the moniker **"Captain Anson."** He runs his team with military precision. Learning from his own past, he staunchly forbids smoking and drinking. But on the field, he is colorful, aggressive, and a fan favorite. Often, he antagonizes umpires simply to give his pitcher more time to rest and/or warm up, and the home fans adore him for it.

1880 "Cap" Anson begins a historic run that will see his ballclub win five of the next seven pennants.

1880-1886 Cap gains widespread recognition for his many innovations to the game. He installs a third base coach, sends coded signals to his batters and baserunners, teaches his fielders to back up each other, and even implements a "rotation" of two starting pitchers to keep his ace from flaming out. His ideas end up being copied by every other team. Cap is also an early proponent, if not the earliest, of "hit and run" baseball, and his teams steal oodles of bases.

1881 Cap notches the best batting average in the entire sport (.399).

Young **Napoleon's** father passes away unexpectedly, and the Lajoie family is thrown into financial disarray.

1883 In an exhibition game against the Toledo Blue Stockings, **Cap** refuses to put his team on the field *if* Toledo insists on playing their African-American catcher. However, upon hearing that he would have to forfeit his share of the gate revenue *unless* his team played, Cap backtracks and takes part in the game—proving that green isn't one of the colors he's prejudiced against.

1884 **Cap Anson** leads the league in RBIs for the first of three consecutive seasons. In the offseason, his ambitions lead him to attend business college. This choice ends up as money poorly spent.

1885 Al Spalding and **Cap** decide to hold spring training in a warm Southern climate. The innovative idea catches on...to say the least. Off the field, Cap's skills as a billiard player add to his citywide popularity.

At the age of eleven, **Napoleon** leaves school to help support his family as a janitor in a textile mill. However, his passion is for baseball despite the fact that his mother forbids him from playing. But love finds a way, and young Napoleon competes with other kids under a false name.

1886 The Chicago White Stockings win their final NL pennant.

1888 Cap hits .344 for his second and final batting title. With greater frequency, offers are made for him to make public appearances, even outside of the Windy City. He is baseball's first crossover superstar.

1889 With a 13 percent stake, **Cap** becomes a minority owner of the Chicago White Stockings.

1890 **Cap Anson's** team officially changes their nickname to the "Colts." This is a reflection on the squad having to make due with young players after so many of their seasoned veterans bolted for the short-lived Players League. Cap is seen as even more of a father figure and given the nickname of "Pop." Despite his relatively advanced age of thirty-eight, "Pop" Anson leads the league in games played with 139.

1890 Yet another one of **Cap's** business ventures ends in misfortune as his bottles of ginger beer show a disturbing tendency to spontaneously explode. (It happens to the best of us—or so I've been told). Reacting to sportswriters' criticisms that he is getting too old, Anson plays an entire game wearing a white wig and long beard. Ultimately proving them wrong, "Anse" goes on to lead the league in RBIs for the eighth time.

1894 **Cap Anson** becomes the first player to reach 3,000 hits.

Napoleon Lajoie blossoms into a top player for his hometown semi-pro team. He is of such quality that he rents out his services as a ringer to other teams when their games are especially crucial. However, Nap's primary occupation is giving taxi rides to the public in his horse-drawn carriage, and he becomes well known locally as the "Slugging Cabby."

1895 Cap appears on Broadway in *The Runaway Colt*—a baseball vehicle designed specifically for him by a leading playwright. The show bombs.

1896 **Napoleon** leaves his $7.50 per week job driving his hack for a $25 per week job playing baseball for a Class B team in Fall River, Massachusetts. However, Nap only lasts there until August as he is spotted by a scout from the Phillies and offered a contract. Before the year is out, the twenty-one-year-old Nap is playing first base in the major leagues.

On September 5, **Nap** and **Cap** play on the same field for the first time when the first-place Phillies play the Colts. Nap's team wins this initial horserace 10-5.

1897 On September 10, **Nap** and **Cap** play their final game against each other with Anson's Colts taking the game 8-6. But it is a rough season for both teams, as they finish in ninth and tenth place respectively. On the bright side, Nap Lajoie posts a .569 slugging percentage, tops in the league.

1898 Before the season can begin, **Anson** is let go by Al Spalding after an internal power struggle. His twenty-seven-year career as a player (a record that still stands) is finished, as is his nineteen-year run as the club's skipper. The Chicago ballclub, now without "Pop" around, changes its name to the Chicago "Orphans." This nickname will stick for five seasons before the ballclub finally takes on its most famous name: the Chicago Cubs. For a curtain call, Cap briefly manages the New York Giants. However, he leaves in midseason when the owner refuses to relinquish the degree of control Cap requires.

The graceful **Nap Lajoie** is moved to second base, the position where he will become legendary. It is remarked that he fields the toughest of plays with the ease of someone casually picking fruit.

1899 **Nap's** reputation as a great hitter grows by leaps and bounds. On top of being able to reach numerous pitches outside of the strike zone, he literally tears the cover off of the ball on three separate occasions.

Cap fails in an attempt to purchase a majority share of the Orphans. His life focuses on a series of get-rich schemes, most of which fail. He does manage to open up a somewhat successful billiards hall and bowling alley in downtown Chicago.

1900 Cap puts out the first baseball autobiography. He also attempts to organize an opposition baseball league but the venture folds before it can even begin.

1901 The American League makes its debut. Just like Cap Anson twenty-five years earlier, **Nap Lajoie** jumps to a new league, to a team that calls itself the Philadelphia Athletics. He becomes their leading hitter and helps a new major league establish credibility. At season's end, Nap hits an amazing .426—an American League record that stands to this day. Nap more than earns his $6,000 salary (about $150,000 in current funds).

Cap picks up some scratch umpiring amateur games, some of which even have African-Americans as participants, a sign that his racism may have mellowed with age.

1902 Legal trouble strikes **Nap** when his former team, the Phillies, win an injunction from the Pennsylvania Supreme Court preventing him from playing for any other ballclub. Nap's manager, Connie Mack, is especially perturbed. However, Lajoie's legal side discovers that the ruling is only enforceable within the state of Pennsylvania. Summarily, American League brass intervenes and moves Nap to the Cleveland Bronchos. Nap proves to be an immediate drawing card and Cleveland is instantly smitten with its new superstar.

1903 Due to his popularity, **Lajoie's** team renames itself the Cleveland Naps. Late in the season, the Pennsylvania injunction is lifted so he is once again allowed to play road games in Philadelphia and Pittsburgh.

1904 Napoleon Lajoie is suspended after throwing chewing tobacco into the eye of an umpire. However, the incident does less than nothing to curtail his popularity with fans, many of whom wish they could do the same thing.

1905 Ever popular, even in retirement, **Cap Anson** is elected City Clerk of Chicago.

Lajoie is appointed the captain-manager of the Naps. However, his status as the game's greatest hitter is suddenly challenged by the arrival of a kid in Detroit by the name of Ty Cobb. During a game, **Nap** is spiked. Blue dye from his socks gets into the wound that leads to a serious case of blood poisoning, nearly forcing doctors to amputate his leg. He ends up missing eighty-nine games of the season.

1906 Napoleon marries a woman named Myrtle Smith, and together they move to a small farm outside of Cleveland.

1907 Cap purchases a semi-pro baseball team in Chicago. In an effort to boost attendance, the fifty-five-year-old places himself at first base. However, the move fails to yield profits. Anson fails in his political campaign to become sheriff of Chicago.

1908 Thirty-four-year-old **Nap** comes as close to the postseason as he ever will when his team finishes a half game behind the pennant-winning Detroit Tigers.

Cap organizes a local football team and calls them "Anson's Colts." Despite winning the city championship, the team fails to turn a profit. Cap declares bankruptcy.

1909 Cap is forced to sell his billiards hall and bowling alley due to financial troubles.

After seven hundred games at the helm, **Nap Lajoie** relinquishes the reigns of the team, feeling that the managerial duty has taken a toll on his contributions as a player.

1910 Nap wins his fifth and final batting title in a most controversial fashion. His opponents go easy on him on the final day of the season, allowing him to surpass Ty Cobb's batting average of .383. A fury erupts, in part because the hitting champ had been promised a new Chalmers automobile, as part of a marketing plan by the car maker. When all is said and done, Cobb and Lajoie both end up with new wheels.

Cap loses his longtime home to mounting debt. However, he bounces back with his own vaudeville show comprised of material written by Broadway legend George M. Cohen. The skit is a hit.

1912 Nap is presented with an astounding gift by Cleveland fans—a giant horseshoe decorated with a thousand silver dollars.

1914 Cap Anson finally gains company in the 3,000 hit club when both Nap Lajoie and Honus Wagner join him.

1915 After 13 seasons in Cleveland, **Nap Lajoie** finally packs his bags. He returns to play for Connie Mack's Philadelphia Athletics, though they are hardly the same caliber of team they were when he left.

1916 Cap's beloved wife, Virginia, passes away. Together, they had seven children, four of which survived infancy. Two of his daughters accompany him on the vaudeville circuit.

At the age of forty-one, **Nap Lajoie** walks away from the major leagues. He played twenty-one seasons and compiled a .338 lifetime batting average. To this day, many still consider him to be the greatest second baseman of all time.

1917 **Napoleon** marks time as the player-manager for Toronto in the International League. Against diminished competition, he hits .380 and leads the team to a pennant.

1918 **Nap** becomes the player-manager for Indianapolis in the American Association. He leads them to a third-place finish before the season is called off due to World War One. Suddenly idle, the forty-three-year-old offers his services to the draft board, but they respectfully decline his offer.

1918-1925 Like **Cap** before him, **Nap** runs for the sheriff of his local area but fails to win. To keep busy, he spends time as the commissioner of a minor baseball league, sells truck tires, and sets up a small company that manufactures brass.

1921 Winding down physically, **Cap Anson** retires from the vaudeville circuit. Despite not having any source of income, he proudly refuses a pension from Major League Baseball.

1922 **Cap** is hired to be the general manager of a golf course in Chicago. However, three days shy of his seventieth birthday, he passes away.

1925 **Nap Lajoie**, financially shrewd and comfortable, retires to Florida with his wife.

1937 **Nap Lajoie** is inducted into Cooperstown.

1939 **Cap Anson** is inducted posthumously into Cooperstown.

1954 **Napoleon**'s beloved wife, Myrtle, passes away.

1959 **Nap** passes away in Florida at the age of eighty-four.

1999 *The Sporting News* lists **Nap Lajoie** as the twenty-ninth best player of all-time.

Ten Cent Beer

(A poem by Yellowstone Ritter)

◇◇

JUNE 4, 1974

Long before the days of the Jake
tragedy struck the mistake by the lake.
Circumstances most Erie
made the fans oh so beery
that THIS story just might take the cake!!

The Indians were hosting the Rangers
unaware of impending dangers.
Crowds in town had been sparse
so in the spirit of farce
the Tribe set out to lure strangers.

An idea burst forth at the time
that lacked both reason and rhyme.
But the notion *seemed* clever,
a most creative endeavor:
Beer would sell FOR A DIME.

The folks—they flocked to the park!
Many were there on a lark.
They sloshed down those brews
while the flaskers drank booze
and then the proceedings turned dark.

Of his Rangers, Billy Martin was proud,
so he ignored the crowd's taunts oh so loud.
But the mood was corrupting,
fistfights were erupting,
so Billy blew kisses to the crowd.

From the stands, a fan stormed on the field,
her breasts no longer concealed.
Chaos bounced through the air
all the players did stare
and the fate of the night had been sealed.

The situation grew ever more hairy,
as the mob grew more and more merry.
More mayhem was beckoned
when a fan SLID NUDE into second
earning himself a most painful strawberry.

As booze was wildly consumed
the air was marijuana perfumed.
The Rangers played on that grass
fearing they might lose their sass
since civility was all but entombed.

The bright moon shined FULL on this night
bathing the many stoned fans in loon light.
Two men stood up PROUD
then full mooned the crowd
causing many to regret having sight.

The folks they did sure like their suds!!
Be it Strohs, Heineys, or Buds.
That buzz they did feel
was a pleasure most real
for it transforms all men into studs.

One dude plopped HIMSELF to the ground
and snatched Burroughs' cap WITH NO SOUND.
When Jeff turned to confront
he tripped and fell blunt
leaving teammates to think he'd been crowned.

Liquid courage was uncorked and unsealed
The right of way—soon no one would yield.
Billy Martin called his troops,
who ran with bats and loud WHOOPS
toward the riot that had come out of left field.

In the smell of brew, firecrackers and pot,
that nice family atmosphere? ALL BUT SHOT!!
As Hargrove neared first base
a jug whizzed by his face
MORE Cleveland fans were about to get fought!

Hargrove snared a trespasser at first
and pummeled him like he was cursed.
The fan's skull did soon chafe.
For him, NO BASE was safe.
His injuries would require they be NURSED.

In left field, fans hurdled the wall
forcing all of the baseball to stall.
They darted on the green
in that mausoleum so mean
looking for Rangers to brawl.

Few pranksters were part of *this* mix
for they wielded sharp knives, chains, and sticks.
The Rangers were surrounded,
in danger of being pounded
in this most bizarre of conflicts.

The Tribe took notice from their dugout
and ran toward the scrum to help out.
Led by Ken Aspromonte,
whose mood was ANYTHING but jaunty,
they helped to save Texas, no doubt.

Brawling teams became friends in a flash.
Together, they fled this monster mash.
Through the tunnel they flocked,
beyond doors that got locked
as the rioters continued their bash.

Politeness had been more than repealed
as full fury hit the diamond unconcealed.
The rampage was so swollen
that the bases were stolen
for the field could yield no shield.

'Twas a night of spit, wieners, and jugs,
puffs of smoke, dime beer, and thugs.
As the field got mauled,
a forfeit was called
leaving no fan in the mood to give hugs.

But amidst that violent commotion
and despite the angry emotion,
the night delivered a surprise
making Indians and Cowboys ALLIES
—all thanks to a fire-brewed potion!!

6

Ten Little Known Facts About Joe Torre

Joe Torre...

...though born and raised in Brooklyn, grew up rooting for the Giants.

...made his major league debut at the age of twenty.

...won a Gold Glove, a batting title, and a league MVP award.

...amassed career numbers comparable to Hall of Famers Gary Carter and Ryne Sandberg.

...was a teammate of Hank Aaron for nine seasons.

...spent 41 percent of his career as a catcher, 36 percent as a first baseman, and 23 percent as a third baseman.

...drew Ferguson Jenkins as his most frequent foe, who he hit .294 against despite striking out twenty times.

...spent the bulk of his career hitting cleanup.

...is the brother of first baseman Frank Torre, a seven-year major league veteran.

...is a big fan of thoroughbred horse racing.

...once hit into four double plays in a single game.

...had 33 hits in 64 at-bats against Ken Holtzman.

...managed only 1 hit in 29 at-bats against Al Downing.

…hit .350 and slugged .620 off of Juan Marichal.

…managed to hit only .220 off of Sandy Koufax.

…was chosen for the All-Star game six times as a catcher, three times as a third baseman, and once as a first baseman.

…hit .363 with 230 hits, 24 homers, and 137 RBIs in 1971.

…played his final game at the age of thirty-six.

…was briefly a player-manager, but hung his cleats up after eighteen games to concentrate on managing.

…already had 894 career victories (and over eleven years of major league managerial experience) before he took over the Yankees. The three teams he played for
(Braves, Cardinals, Mets) turned out to also be the first three franchises he managed.

…managed 123 Yankee postseason games

… played eighteen seasons and managed another twenty-eight. Here are the teams he spent those forty-six years as a player or manager with (thru the 2009 season and including postseason games):

New York Yankees—2,065 games (33 percent)

St. Louis Cardinals—1,624 games (26 percent)

Atlanta Braves—884 games (14 percent)

New York Mets—745 games (12 percent)

Milwaukee Braves—639 games (10 percent)

Los Angeles Dodgers—340 games (5 percent)

TOTAL—6,297 games

…never made the postseason as a player. (Hank Aaron's only postseason appearances were right before Torre joined the Braves and the year after Torre had been traded away).

…was originally offered by the Braves to the Mets, but they didn't want to part with Amos Otis. Torre was instead traded to the Cardinals for Orlando Cepeda. Because of the presence of catcher (and future broadcaster) Tim McCarver, Torre was shifted to first base.

…didn't manage a ballclub from 1985 through 1990. During that interim, he worked as a broadcaster for the California Angels.

…was in a broadcast booth in Candlestick Park during the

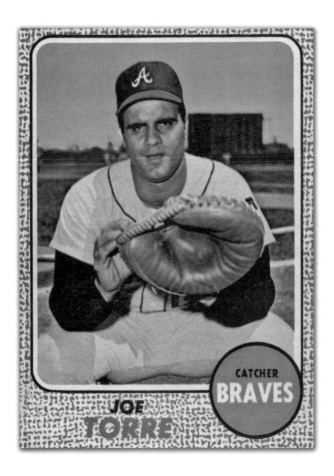

major earthquake that interrupted the 1989 World Series.

...caught Warren Spahn's 350th victory.

...managed Roger Clemens' 350th victory.

...was, upon being hired by the Yankees, immediately tagged by the press as "Clueless Joe." However, before the year was out, he took manager of the year
honors and guided the Yankees to their first world championship in eighteen seasons.

...was the only man to manage ten consecutive teams into the postseason from 2000 through 2009.

The Great Dominican Pipeline

or decades, baseball has been referred to as the "Great American Pastime." However, with each passing year, the term becomes more and more of an understatement.

Though baseball certainly took bloom in America, its impact became global. Not only are games played worldwide, but nearly four dozen of the world's nations have now produced major league players. China is on that hallowed list as are other major population centers like Indonesia, Russia, and Australia.

Yet oddly enough, the one place that has produced the greatest number of exports to America is the relatively tiny nation of the Dominican Republic. But the reasons why they have been so important to baseball are not nearly as surprising.

Right after the American Civil War ended in 1865, a large number of sailors from the USA found themselves ported in Cuba. There, they helped to liberate mass quantities of sugar from its homeland. When they weren't laboring away for Uncle Sam's sweet tooth, the swabbies would occasionally blow off steam by playing baseball. The Cubans saw all the fun and wanted in.

It wasn't long before the natives also felt the joy of clubbing a ball a few hundred feet, the thrill of striking out a hitter, the rush of a diving catch, and the exhilaration of stealing a base. Soon enough, the Cubans were well past the point of tutoring, and indigenous pickup games began to be played all across the island nation.

But in 1878, a bloody war began that would last ten years. Numerous Cuban families were forced to sail away from their beloved homeland for a safe haven, one of which was the Dominican Republic a few hundred miles to the

southeast. The refugees brought with them all the traditions they held most dear, and baseball made the short list.

Soon, the Cubans began playing their old game in their new homeland in front of Dominican spectators. After seeing all the fun there was to be had, they wanted in as well.

During the 1890s, their sport evolved to the point that organized leagues were formed. The game was in an incubation period, and it was just a matter of time before it would take over the Caribbean.

Few Americans know all that much about the Dominican Republic. To them, it is perhaps best known for its lovely beaches, year-round golf courses, and for the thousands of kids with makeshift gloves who dream of playing in the major leagues.

But the D.R. is, in fact, an eclectic locale that possesses lagoons, swamps, sugar plantations, smoky industrial centers, and even mountain ranges.

It is a nation that's about twice as large as the state of Vermont, but with fifteen times the people (and significantly less maple-syrup-scented snow). However, the Dominicans do produce quite a bit of sugarcane, coffee, cocoa, tobacco, and bananas—so it isn't like they are without their own treats. But for many Dominicans, the most addictive treat of all is baseball, and it is now one that has been passed down for generations.

Back in 1906, the "Tigres el Licey" officially came to play in the city of

Santo Domingo. Impressively, that same team is still active today. These Tigers were so dominant for so long that in 1921, three of their competitors united to form a super team in hopes of ending the Tigres' dominance. This fused trio was the equivalent of the Red Sox, Athletics, and Tigers joining forces to take on the dominant Yankee teams of the Babe Ruth era. They became known as "the Lions of the Chosen One."

During the remainder of the 1920s, as the Tigers and Lions fiercely battled, the sport's popularity escalated to the point that key players began to be taken not only by competing teams but by other Caribbean countries. People couldn't get enough of the sport, and unlike in America, where cold weather pretty much dictated an April–October season, in the D.R, they got to play year-round.

In 1930, baseball in the Dominican Republic received yet another boost when the nation fell under the control of a fierce dictator named Rafael Trujillo. In some ways, he was a lot like George Steinbrenner, except that when he fired people, it had a slightly different meaning.

Trujillo happened to be a major baseball fan, and as such, he supported its progress at every turn. Numerous venues were upgraded, and the sport was thoroughly promoted throughout the entire culture. Winning was important, and lucrative offers were even made to American stars to play in the winter league. Satchel Paige was among these ringers, and in 1937 Satchel led his Dominican team to a championship.

During the decade of the 1950s, two events transpired that embedded baseball even deeper into the Dominican culture.

In 1955 fans saw the opening of a beautiful 14,000-seat stadium in Santo Domingo. It was so modern that it even had lights installed for night baseball. No longer would games in the D.R. have to rest when the sun did.

Then, in 1956, something even more culturally significant occurred. An athlete named of Ozzie Virgil was chosen by the New York Giants to play third base. Virgil instantly became a national hero in his homeland and provided proof that Dominicans could play ball with the best players in the world.

Virgil not only played nine seasons in the majors, he opened the door for fellow countrymen like Juan Marichal and the three Alou brothers to make the journey to America. The Giants franchise was on to something big, and the rest of baseball started to awaken that they too should be mining the same land.

Consequently, major leagues clubs began investing extensive time and energy into the D.R. With every subsequent decade, more and more scouts scoured the island, combing impoverished barrios and rural areas alike looking for the next top prospect. Eventually, every major league organization installed at least one academy there to help nurture, develop, and integrate their top finds.

To date, the Dominican Republic has already produced nearly five hundred major league players, four big league skippers, and even one general manager. These numbers, in time, will only notch higher.

*To see our all-time 25-man Dominican Republic team,
check out chapter on page 263.*

Follies Factoids

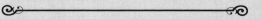

★ The Dominican Republic is geographically closer to Miami than is Washington D.C.

★ Luis Silviero only played in the major leagues for eight games. But during his 14 plate appearances for the 1978 Kansas City Royals, he hit .545 with three singles, two doubles, a triple, a stolen base, and eight runs scored.

★ In the classic 1980 comedy *Airplane*, one of the phrases Ted Striker hears in his own mind is *"Pinch hitting for Pedro Borbon...Manny Mota...Mota...Mota."* This dialogue was historic for it marked the first time in Hollywood film history that two major league baseball players of Dominican descent were referenced in the same sentence by the subconscious mind of a hallucinating ex-fighter pilot with a drinking problem *who didn't* have fish for dinner.

8

The
Andre Dawson
Dossier

DAWSON, Andre

DOSSIER - 8

UPBRINGING: Raised by his mother and grandmother in Miami, Florida

HIGH SCHOOL: Southwest Miami

NICKNAME: "Hawk"
Given for his tendency to stare at things like they were rodents about to be eaten

HIGH SCHOOL FOOTBALL: Played free safety

INJURY and AFTERMATH: Suffered ripped cartilage and ligaments during an accidental blindside, prompting surgery. The doctor knifed out the cartilage, a primitive technique that prevented the knee from ever being rehabilitated.

SCOUTED: by the Kansas City Royals who took a pass, prompting Dawson to play college baseball instead

COLLEGE: Florida A & M University

FELLOW RATTLER ALUMNI INCLUDE: Hal McRae, Vince Coleman, Marquis Grissom

DRAFTED: The Montreal Expos made him the 250th pick in the 1975 June amateur draft

DAWSON, Andre   DOSSIER - 8

PROS DRAFTED AHEAD OF HIM IN '75 INCLUDED:
Clint Hurdle, Lee Smith, Carney Lansford,
Lou Whitaker

MINOR LEAGUE GAMES: 189

MOST FREQUENT MINOR LEAGUE HOME: Denver, CO

MINOR LEAGUE ACCOMPLISHMENTS: Hit .339 and
slugged .609, prompting a callup to the major
leagues less than two years after being drafted

DEBUT YEAR: 1976 (as a late-season call up)

OTHER PLAYERS WHO DEBUTED IN 1976 INCLUDED:
Mark Fidrych, Jim Gantner, Dennis Martinez,
Dale Murphy, Bruce Sutter, Garry Templeton,
Willie Wilson

PLAYERS WHO RETIRED IN 1976 INCLUDED:
Hank Aaron, Jim Brewer, Bill Freehan, Tommy
Harper, Tony Oliva, Frank Robinson, Billy Williams

AGE AT DEBUT: 22

IN 1977: Won the NL Rookie of the Year award

DAWSON, Andre

DOSSIER - 8

EARLIEST TEAMMATES INCLUDED:
Gary Carter, Tim Foli, Joe Kerrigan, Steve Rogers,
Andre Thornton, Ellis Valentine

FINAL SEASON: 1996

FINAL TEAMMATES INCLUDED: Kevin Brown, Luis Castillo, Livan Hernandez, Robb Nen, Gary Sheffeld

PRIMARY MANAGER: Dick Williams

TOTAL MANAGERS PLAYED FOR: 15

TOTAL SEASONS IN THE MAJOR LEAGUES: 21

NUMBER OF WINNING SEASONS: 7

CAREER STATS: .279 BA
2,774 HITS, 438 HR, 1,591 RBI, 314 SB

REGULAR SEASON WINNING PERMILLAGE
IN GAMES IN WHICH DAWSON PARTICIPATED: .494

MAJOR LEAGUE AFFILIATIONS:
Montreal Expos (55%)
Chicago Cubs (33%)
Boston Red Sox (7%)
Florida Marlins (5%)

DAWSON, Andre   **DOSSIER - 8**

POSITIONS PLAYED (rounded):
RF 51%   CF 41%   DH 7%   LF 1%   PH 1%

INJURY AND/OR REST RATE: 6%

TRIVIA: Slugged .481 at home and .483 on the road

BEST SEASON: (1978)
.315 BA   46 HR   139 RBI

GOLD GLOVES: 8

SILVER BATS: 4

MOST FREQUENT TEAMMATE: Steve Rogers--10 seasons

THREE MOST FREQUENT FOES:
Bob Forsch--140 plate appearances
(.323 BA   6 HR   19 RBI   9 BB   17K)

Rick Reuschel--125 plate appearances
(.311 BA   2 HR   11 RBI   4 BB   16K)

Steve Carlton - 118 plate appearances
(.291 BA   4 HR   14 RBI   14 BB   21K)

DAWSON, Andre

THE PITCHER HE OWNED: Mark Grant
.571 (12 for 21) with 3 HRs, 9 RBIs, 1 walk,
and 0 strikeouts.

THE PITCHER WHO OWNED HIM: John Smoltz
.074 (2 for 27) with 1 HR, 1 RBI, 0 walks,
and 9 strikeouts.

THE PITCHER HE STRUCK OUT MOST OFTEN AGAINST:
Nolan Ryan (25)

THE PITCHER HE HOMERED MOST OFTEN AGAINST:
Bob Knepper (7)

HIS RECORD AGAINST HALL OF FAME PITCHERS:
429 AT-BATS
.247 BA   24 HR   70 RBI   116K

LEAGUE HOME RUN CHAMPION: 1 time

LEAGUE MVP: 1 time

MOST FREQUENT OPPONENT: Philadelphia Phillies

HOME AWAY FROM HOME:
Atlanta Fulton County Stadium
.276 BA   26 HR   75 RBI

DAWSON, Andre   DOSSIER - 8

ALL-STAR TEAMS: 8

ALL-STAR STATS: 20 AT-BATS
.200 BA   1 HR   1 RBI

TRIVIA: Played in the major leagues concurrently
with both Henry Aaron and Derek Jeter

PLAYOFF RECORD: 2 postseasons, 15 games
59 AT-BATS
.186 BA   0 HR   3 RBI
2 divisional titles, 0 pennants

CLOSEST STATISTICAL TWIN: Billy Williams

HALL OF FAME CALIBRE RATING: 103%

9

A Side Effect of World War II

◇◇◇

In December of 1941, the United States formally entered a global war to combat tyranny. Eventually, millions of brave Americans left their homes to fight (and hundreds of professional baseball players were among them).

For a time, it was thought that major league baseball might be suspended indefinitely, but words from Franklin Delano Roosevelt citing the sport's impact on the nation's morale kept that from happening. Consequently, over the course of the next four seasons, the national pastime continued, although it didn't play out how it otherwise would have.

Numerous plans on the books had to be scuttled immediately. The deal to install lights at Chicago's Wrigley Field was put off.

In addition, baseball's expansion to the West Coast was scrapped when the St. Louis Browns were forced to cancel their 1942 relocation to Los Angeles—one of America's coastal cities that was bracing for catastrophic air raids.

Even before the start of the '42 season, players of all skill levels jumped at the chance to serve their country. Bob Feller and Hank Greenberg were among the many who urgently swapped their baseball uniforms for military ones, sometimes without so much as asking their teams for permission

By the time the '43 season rolled around, even more superstars were missing from ballparks. Joe DiMaggio had jolted, as had Johnny Mize, Pee Wee Reese, Warren Spahn, and Ted Williams. To replace them, major league rosters had to be filled out by athletes who otherwise would not have been in the Show.

Nearly everyone associated with the sport began to contribute to the

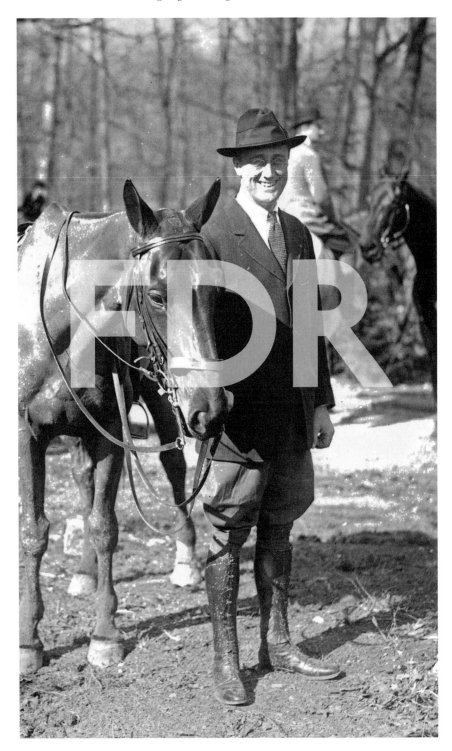

war effort in one way or another. Numerous players donated portions of their paychecks. Night games became less frequent so that electricity could be conserved. Fans even donated kitchen grease and scrap metal at the ballparks to aid the military in the manufacture of explosives.

Even players past their prime were chipping in. Though in their late thirties, future Hall of Famers Bill Dickey and Charlie Gehringer valiantly made their way to the Pacific Theatre of Operations. So did the legendary Mickey Cochrane, even though he had retired from baseball years earlier.

Youngsters who had yet to make their major league debuts were also filling out the ranks. Larry Doby, Ralph Kiner, Jackie Robinson, and Duke Snider were all in the service, as was Yogi Berra, who spent ten of the longest days of his life off the coast of Normandy during and after D-Day. Berra was one of the luckier ones. There's no doubt that this war prevented more than a few budding stars from having the chance to live out their dream.

Back in the US, the game rolled on. Adults chowed down hot dogs, and star-struck children watched games through knotholes. Filling other voids, lesser-known athletes such as Mort Cooper, Hal Newhouser, Bill Nicholson, Vern Stephens, and Dizzy Trout grew to become fan favorites.

Yet, for even the successful teams, the mood was bittersweet. Attendance dipped 14 percent in 1942 and declined another 11 percent in '43. All of the sixteen ballclubs could make excuses for how they were making due without key players, but the truth is that some clubs were far more depleted than others.

When President Roosevelt first declared war, the Brooklyn Dodgers were the reigning NL champs. In 1942, despite losing their third baseman to military service, they still remained a powerhouse as they posted a lofty .675 winning percentage. But with the 1943 exodus came the loss of two pitchers from their rotation and three more everyday players. From 1943 through '45, the average Dodger winning percentage dipped down to a mediocre .501 and postseasons in Brooklyn became a thing of the past.

One could speculate that when World War II finally came to an end, the widespread celebration may have been just a little bit sweeter in the vicinity of Ebbets Field. After all, the reassembled Brooklyn Dodgers in 1946 posted a .615 winning percentage, and in 1947 they completely returned to form by playing their way back into the postseason.

However, the team that collapsed the most during World War II was the Boston Red Sox. They opened the 1942 season without their catcher and shortstop but still managed to win a highly respectable ninety-three games.

But in '43 they found themselves without Ted Williams, Dom DiMaggio, three additional position players, and two of the six hurlers who had logged triple-digit innings for them the previous year. Even though the Bosox were facing other depleted teams, their downward spiral was particularly acute. From '43 through '45, the normally dangerous club averaged only seventy-two victories.

But once the gang reunited in 1946, they ran away from the rest of the league with 104 victories and nabbed their first pennant since 1918.

Of course, not every team won fewer games during the war years. The Pirates and Indians both gave the appearance of improvement and even the normally average Cubs put together a magical year that ended with them in the 1945 Series. But the one city that has to be the recipient of the silver-lining award during those incredibly challenging times is St. Louis, Missouri.

No ballclub during World War II upped their average victory total by thirteen games like the St. Louis Browns did. Although the Brownies were losers both prior to and immediately after the war, they managed to put together three winning seasons during it and even secured a pennant. They probably would have won it all in 1944 had they not run into the team that BEST dominated the war years—and that team happened to be their ball-park mates, the St. Louis Cardinals.

From 1942 through '45, the Cards won 411 regular season games, three pennants, and two world championships. This run is remarkable for the fact that the Cards went into the '43 season without their number two starting pitcher, their second baseman, and two-thirds of their starting outfield. But the Cardinals were more than a little fortunate when a young superstar emerged by the name of Stan Musial.

The 1943 season was tremendous for Stan. At the tender age of twenty-two, he played his first of twenty-four All-Star games and also took home the first of three league MVP awards. However, time waits for no man and neither did this war. Musial was inducted into the service by his Uncle Sam and missed the entire 1945 season.

As a testament to the greatness of Stan Musial, the Cardinals won the World Series in both '44 and '46 with him in the lineup, but failed to do so the year he was gone. But that is as it should have been, for Musial was helping to secure that infinitely more important victory for the Allied Forces and that, more than any other reason, is why Stan is the Man.

Follies Factoids

★ During World War II, the **United States Navy** could boast of having three of the greatest catchers of all time: Mickey Cochrane, Bill Dickey, and Yogi Berra. Other World War II swabbies included: Larry Doby, Bob Feller, Charlie Gehringer, Billy Herman, Ralph Kiner, Bob Lemon, Lee MacPhail, Johnny Mize, Stan Musial, Pee Wee Reese, Phil Rizzuto, and Duke Snider.

★ The **United States Army** could brag about how they once had a trio of Hall of Fame outfielders within their ranks: Monte Irvin, Joe DiMaggio, and Enos "Country" Slaughter. Other GIs during WWII included Luke Appling, Nestor Chylak, Leon Day, Bobby Doerr, Hank Greenberg, Larry MacPhail, Robin Roberts, Jackie Robinson, Red Ruffing, Red Schoendienst, Warren Spahn, and Early Wynn.

★ As for the few and the proud, their elite ranks included the likes of Ted Lyons, Bill Veeck, and Ted Williams.

★ The 1943 New York Yankees were the least star-studded Yankee championship team of all-time. Only three members of that team reside in Cooperstown (Bill Dickey, Joe Gordon, and manager Joe McCarthy).

★ The 1945 World Champion Detroit Tigers were greatly aided by the mid-season return of Hank Greenberg, who not only smashed 13 homers, but ended up driving in a club-leading 7 RBIs in the World Series

★ The depletion of baseball's ranks during World War II had little impact on the two perennial last-place teams in Philadelphia From 1942 to 1945, the Athletics and Phillies combined to finish in last place six out of a possible eight times.

★ In the five years from 1948 through 1952, only three people were born who would enter the Hall of Fame (Goose Gossage, Mike Schmidt, and Dave Winfield). However, from 1943 through 1947, thirteen people were born who made it in.

★ Instead of moving to Los Angeles in 1942, the Browns eventually relocated in 1954 to Baltimore, where they remain to this day as the "Orioles."

★ As for Los Angeles, their long wait for a major league franchise ended in 1958 with the arrival of the Dodgers.

★ As for Wrigley Field in Chicago, they eventually got those light standards (and night baseball) in 1988.

10

Name That Player

**NAME THE FOLLOWING BASEBALL PERSONALITY
BASED ONLY ON THESE CLUES**

He was born eight miles outside of Toronto.

While playing American Legion baseball,
this young outfielder led the nation in hitting at that level.

He was originally signed by Kansas City.
Ironically, the Royals became one of the two opponents
he battled most frequently over the course of his long career.

His teammates over the years included Darrell Evans,
Dave Kingman, and Mickey Lolich.

At one point, he was better known as a starting pitcher.
In 37 major league starts, he had 2 shutouts, 4 complete games
and a 4.32 earned run average.

In 1972, he hit a career high .316 to go along with a .474 slugging percentage.

He briefly wore the uniform of the Boston Red Sox.

Lifetime, he amassed a Yankee Stadium batting average in excess of .300 to
go along with a 1.39 ERA.

Who is this player?

The answer can be found on p. 276.

11

The Great White Hunter

◇◇

OCTOBER 2, 1977

Not a drop of suspense was in the air. But there was some rain. Despite the inclement weather, 7,365 loyal fans trickled into Busch Stadium to root on their Cardinals—even though it was the final game of the season and well after their beloved team had been eliminated from contention.

In the visitor's dugout, taking cover from the rain, were Joe Torre's New York Mets. This was a team so woeful that they had actually been knocked out of the pennant race the previous August. For the hometown fans, the prospect for excitement seemed remote.

But despite the precipitation and low stakes, small puddles of Cardinal fans gathered by the railings, some without umbrellas, to catch their last glimpses of Lou Brock, Keith Hernandez, and their other heroes that season. Some wondered if the game would be cancelled. Others wondered, with far greater concern, if the prizes for Fan Appreciation day would still be given away in case the game was scrapped.

Intermittently, the blue umps stared up into the gray skies, puzzling it out, looking for a clear opening to get the game in. It would not be happening any time soon.

In the meantime, most of the St. Louis ballplayers retreated to the inner sanctum of the clubhouse. There, some of the athletes gamely played cards while other players enjoyed other games. But two of the youngest Cardinals, Rick Bosetti and Butch Metzger, sat perched in the dugout, like two birds on a bat. There, they took in the same bittersweet sights as the increasingly wet fans in attendance.

Stationed near Bosetti and Metzger were a few proud members of the Marine Color Guard in full uniform. They were on hand to perform clean-hand drills for the crowd with their M-1 semi-automatic rifles. Since Bosetti had rifle experience while in the Air Force ROTC, he decided to strike up a friendly conversation with one of the Marines.

In no time, the two gun experts began talking shop. Inevitably, Bosetti asked if he could check out the USMC's weapon of choice. Only blanks were loaded in the chamber, and so the Marine thought nothing of letting the ballplayer handle the deadly weapon.

Meanwhile, in a booth high above the field sat legendary broadcaster Jack Buck. Though the game was far from starting, Buck stayed on the airwaves, regaling his audience with anecdotes and giving updates as to when the tarp might finally be rolled up.

While inspecting the powerful firearm, Bosetti got an amusing idea for a prank. He would storm into the clubhouse, rifle in hand, act psychotic, aim it at star shortstop Garry Templeton, and squeeze the trigger. Seeing Templeton have his life flash before his eyes would surely be an unforgettable memory for both of them!

However, as one might expect, the Marine interjected some much needed common sense. Although he liked the idea on an artistic level, he told Bosetti that opening fire with an M-1 in such a closed space could do irreparable harm to eardrums—and to players far more popular than Templeton.

Bosetti's grand idea had been scrubbed. He looked over at Metzger with wily disappointment. But his defeat was only temporary, for the cogs in his practical-joke wheelhouse began spinning. Within seconds, Bosetti concocted a secondary plan that promised to be even more fun than the first.

He and Metzger put the finishing touches on their new scheme. This was a most novel idea. Even the Marine was looking forward to seeing their plan come together. As Jack Buck continued broadcasting whatever ballpark minutia he could find, Bosetti and Metzger took their positions in the St. Louis dugout.

Their time was at hand.

Metzger sprinted out with frantic speed. Once past the infield dirt, he began cutting back and forth, serpentine style, as though he were trying to duck enemy fire. Jack Buck couldn't help noticing Metzger's unusual behavior and began relaying the strange event to the masses.

It was then that Bosetti emerged from the dugout, calm and proud, like the proverbial great white hunter on safari in Africa.

As Metzger reached right-center, Bosetti nonchalantly perched his foot up onto the rolled-up tarp as though it were a felled tree, precisely surveyed his quarry, and peeled off a blast. Right on cue, Metzger dropped to the ground like dead weight.

A hush fell over the stunned crowd.

With triumphant aplomb, Bosetti trotted over to the fallen body and placed his foot upon Metzger as though it was the proudest kill of his career.

The thousands in attendance stood aghast at the sight, save for some members of the St. Louis Metropolitan Police Department who drew their handguns and stealthily began to make their way toward Bosetti. Noticing that the natives were more than a little restless, the great hunter thought it best to break the charade and chided Metzger to quickly get to his feet.

But wanting to make his "assassin" look bad for as long as possible, Metzger whispered "NO" and continued to lay motionless on the turf. It was at that point, that Rick Bosetti began to see his own life flashing before his eyes.

Reacting quickly, Bosetti did his best to look disarming in as many ways as possible. But like a pack of lions, the police continued to close in until it finally became obvious that the murder had only been a prank.

Never one to miss details, the alarmed Buck had reported the event as it happened. He even managed to identify Metzger as the victim. One of the thousands of listeners hanging onto Jack Buck's every syllable that day was Butch Metzger's wife, who was at home putting on a little makeup before driving out to the ballpark. As you might imagine, when she learned the truth, she was slightly less amused by the prank than her husband was.

Wives…are just funny like that.

Follies Factoids

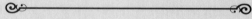

★ Butch Metzger and his wife later divorced.

★ Butch Metzger never played another day for the Cardinals. He spent 1978 with the last-place New York Mets.

★ After the prank, the Cardinals not only swapped Rick Bosetti to the last-place Toronto Blue Jays, they essentially exported him to an entirely different country.

★ In 2009, Rick Bosetti and Butch Metzger crossed paths again when Metzger, a regional scout for the Texas Rangers, visited Coach Bosetti's Simpson University baseball team (in Redding, CA) to scout one of his top ballplayers.

To read about another elaborate practical joke that Rick Bosetti cleverly perpetrated on thousands of fans, check out our first book, Rollie's Follies.

12

The Braves' New World

(1991–2005)

◇◇◇

A series of mini-chapters devoted to this
historic fifteen-year period

At the end of the 1990 season, all the Atlanta Braves cleaned out their lockers and went home for the winter. Their mood was somber, as it should have been. After all, it was the third consecutive year they had finished in last place. Even fan favorite Dale Murphy had been traded away earlier that season, meaning Braves nation had less to root for than ever.

It would have been a very good time to place a bet on the team's chances of winning the 1991 pennant.

During the offseason, manager Bobby Cox and general manager John Schuerholz rolled up their sleeves and began planning for what would be their first full season running the team together. Interestingly enough, the two had crossed paths before at a time when the stakes were extremely high. It was Schuerholz's Royals who had come back from a three-game deficit to defeat Cox's Blue Jays in the 1985 ALCS—a game that turned out to be his swan song in Toronto.

Both men were known as architects who could build winning organizations from scratch. In addition, few were their equals when it came to evaluating talent. But despite their many gifts, neither could have known that they were on the verge of launching (and maintaining) a ballclub that would win fourteen consecutive divisional titles.

Just stop and let that accomplishment sink in for a couple seconds. The odds of a team winning fourteen straight division titles back then were even greater than twelve million to one. In fact, the only thing that kept the Braves out of the postseason during those years was the 1994 player's strike—and even then, they were in first place for the wild card spot when that season was halted.

But even though the Bravos' rise to power seemed instantaneous, it was anything but. A lot of the groundwork had already been laid due to Bobby Cox's previous incarnation as the team's general manager. In hindsight, many of his decisions ended up looking brilliant.

In 1987, Cox traded away thirty-six-year-old Doyle Alexander straight up for a twenty-year-old prospect named John Smoltz. In 1989, he took a chance on a relatively unknown minor league pitching coach (Leo Mazzone). In 1990, Cox used the number one draft pick to choose an eighteen-year-old infielder by the name of Larry "Chipper" Jones.

These moves may have been all ice cream and syrup, but the sundae still needed a cherry on top of it. Following the credo of "If you want something done right, do it yourself," Cox fired the Braves skipper in midseason of 1990 and installed himself in the dugout. Realizing he would be spread too thin if he were both the skipper and the GM, he handed the keys to the front office at the end of the season to his old nemesis John Schuerholz.

Schuerholz wasted no time. His first major move was to sign free agent Terry Pendleton to play third base. The transaction didn't exactly send shockwaves through the sport in that Pendleton was coming off a year in which he only hit .230 with 58 RBIs for the Cardinals. But Schuerholz saw far more potential in the castoff than did his previous employers.

These instincts paid off handsomely. Terry Pendleton not only ended up hitting .319 with 86 RBIs for the Braves, he took home the National League MVP trophy as well. But to be fair, Terry Pendleton had an advantage over most of the other players up for the award because he never once had to face the NL's best pitcher that year: Tom Glavine.

From '90 to '91, Glavine not only doubled his win total from 10 to 20, he also also managed to lower his ERA from 4.28 all the way down to 2.55. Within the space of one offseason, Glavine somehow became a Hall of Fame caliber pitcher.

Seemingly, all of the throwers Mazzone worked with that season were seeing sizable results. More and more, Braves pitchers began targeting outside locations and throwing fastballs to set up breaking pitches. Bucking the conventional wisdom, starters even began throwing twice in between starts (as opposed to once) to build up arm strength.

But despite giving the fans loads to cheer about, the year of 1991 didn't end perfectly for these Braves as they were dumped in the World Series by another "worst to first" team (the Minnesota Twins). But all things considered, Atlanta had come an incredibly long way in a short time.

It's been said many times that as hard as it is to win a pennant, it's even harder to repeat. However, in 1992 the Braves made it look easy. Yet, once again, they got thumped in the Fall Classic, and the team that took them apart was none other than Bobby Cox's previous organization, the Toronto Blue Jays.

Ironically, some of the credit for Toronto's world championship that year should have gone to the skipper in the opposing dugout. After all, Cox spent 1982 through 1985 engineering Toronto's own rise from the ashes, transforming them from a last-place squad into a divisional winner.

It must have been bittersweet for Cox to see some of his old Blue Jay players do so well for themselves in that '92 Series. After all, two of the Jays' starting pitchers, their closer, and two of the their starting infielders were acquired on Bobby Cox's watch, as was their catcher, Pat Borders, who hit a blistering .450 against the Braves that year en route to taking the World Series MVP award.

Though they had been the cream of the National League for two years running, the Braves were still desperate to improve. As such, they went out and signed Greg Maddux, the only pitcher who managed to finish ahead of Tom Glavine in the 1992 NL Cy Young Award balloting. This pair of aces was to be joined in the rotation by a fireballer, John Smoltz, who was coming off of an All-Star season of his own. Atlanta was on the verge of something big.

From 1993 through 1999, Tom Glavine, Greg Maddux, and John Smoltz became the best one-two-three punch that baseball had ever seen. During those seven seasons, each member of the trio won at least one Cy Young Award, each held the honor of being the opening day starter, and all three were selected to the All-Star game on multiple occasions. Combined, they went 340-166, hurled 4,603 1/3 innings, and posted an aggregate ERA of 2.92. Also, each and every year, they played well into October.

But even though the trio came apart in 2000 (when Smoltz was forced to miss the season due to injury), Bobby Cox's Braves still found a way to win. In 2001, the legendary trio of pitchers were briefly reunited in the rotation, but after just five starts by Smoltz, it was determined that he would better serve the club as its new fireman.

This decision fueled yet more winning dividends for the Bravos. Curiously, during this fifteen-year period of Braves dominance, Smoltz not only was one of the club's three best starters, but hands down, the best closer as well.

But as remarkable as these three hurlers were, perhaps the most fascinating aspect of their unprecedented run was how well Cox and Schuerholz kept replacing key position players. All in all, twenty-six Braves players were selected to All-Star games during the fifteen-year dynasty. The legendary pitching trio notwithstanding, the Braves were essentially a revolving door of high-caliber talent.

As proof, we present below a list of the players who logged at least one hundred games at any given position during the Braves stretch of dominance.

CATCHER
Javy Lopez—1,106 games
Eddie Perez—357
Greg Olson—302
Johnny Estrada—251
Damon Berryhill—190
Henry Blanco—131
Charlie O'Brien—112

FIRST BASE
Fred McGriff—629 games
Julio Franco—339
Brian Hunter—307
Sid Bream—295
Andres Galarraga—281
Adam Laroche—223
Ryan Klesko—124
Wes Helms—122
Robert Fick—115

SECOND BASE
Mark Lemke—891 games
Marcus Giles—499
Keith Lockhart—352
Tony Graffanino—186
Bret Boone—151
Quilvio Veras—149
Jeff Treadway—138

SHORTSTOP
Jeff Blauser—791 games
Rafael Furcal—777
Rafael Belliard—531
Walt Weiss—267
Ozzie Guillen—166
Mark Derosa—114

THIRD BASE
Chipper Jones—1,205 games
Terry Pendleton—585
Vinny Castilla—290
Mark DeRosa—102

LEFT FIELD
Ryan Klesko—625 games
Chipper Jones—356
Ron Gant—293
Gerald Williams—176
Lonnie Smith—134
B.J. Surhoff—129
Otis Nixon—107
Danny Bautista—103

CENTER FIELD
Andruw Jones—1,334 games
Marquis Grissom—294
Otis Nixon—239
Ron Gant—171
Deion Sanders—166
Kenny Lofton—122

RIGHT FIELD
David Justice—665 games
Brian Jordan—442
Gary Sheffield—280
Michael Tucker—220
J.D. Drew—138
Andruw Jones—115

All in all, the Braves posted a .606 regular season winning percentage from 1991 through 2005. However, as almost every baseball fan knows, their fate in the postseason was usually a different story. There, they could only manage to post an okay 63-62 record. Among their fourteen postseason appearances, the Braves advanced past the first round on nine occasions, won the National League pennant six times, and managed to win one world championship (in 1995).

Aside from the Braves, the National League was awash in parity through those years. During that span, no other team reached the playoffs half as many times as the Braves, nor did any win as many as two pennants.

All told, in the "Warpath Era" the Braves battled thirteen different NL opponents during their various postseasons—with only the Brewers and Expos/Nationals failing to make it to those October battlefields.

The Atlanta Braves were so good during this run that they never even had a traditional rival. Perhaps the Houston Astros were the closest thing to one, because the clubs clashed in the postseason five times, but it was hardly the stuff of the Yankees-Red Sox rivalry. The Astros were, however, a thorn as they were the only NL team to eliminate the Braves twice during this time frame.

But the Braves managed to octliminate the Astros on the other three occasions. As killer as the Killer Bees were, no one exterminated them quite like the Braves.

The Philadelphia Phillies were another notable pest. No other team beat the Braves as many times during this era as the Phillies (97 wins). They also had the pleasure of octliminating them in 1993 en route to their own pennant. Overall, however, Atlanta dominated Philadelphia. The Phillies suffered 124 losses at the hands of the Braves and were likely prevented from winning the NL East title on at least two occasions because of them.

But 2006 marked the end of the trail. It would be hard to identify the single biggest reason why the Braves failed to fifteen-peat, but it can be theorized that it had a lot to do with how the New York Mets added both Carlos Delgado and Billy Wagner to their roster. It probably didn't help matters that both shortstop Rafael Furcal and pitching coach Leo Mazzone bolted Atlanta for other organizations at the conclusion of 2005.

But all in all, it had been a most impressive run. We now present a twenty-five-man team of the most prolific members of the Atlanta Braves from 1991 through 2005 along with their statistics from those fifteen glorious seasons.

THE 25-MAN WARPATH TEAM
(1991–2005)

MANAGER
Bobby Cox

PITCHING STAFF
(The top five pitchers in games started and the top six
pitchers in relief appearances)

STARTERS

	Won-Loss	ERA	Strikeouts
Tom Glavine	209-102	3.15	1,731
Greg Maddux	194-88	2.63	1,828
John Smoltz*	145-93	3.27	1,912
Steve Avery	69-51	3.67	740
Kevin Millwood	75-46	3.73	840

* statistics only include games in which Smoltz started

MIDDLERS

	Won-Loss	ERA	Strikeouts
Mike Remlinger	25-10	2.65	315
Greg McMichael	18-14	2.96	302
Mike Stanton	18-17	3.86	189
Kerry Ligtenberg	12-12	3.04	256

CLOSERS

	Won-Loss	ERA	Saves	Strikeouts
John Smoltz**	4-6	2.35	154	280
Mark Wohlers	31-22	3.73	112	437

** statistics only include games in which Smoltz relieved

POSITION PLAYERS
(The top fifteen Braves in plate appearances)

Position		AVG	HR	RBI	SB
3B / LF	Chipper Jones	.303	331	1111	123
CF / RF	Andruw Jones	.267	301	894	129
C	Javy Lopez	.287	214	694	8
SS	Rafael Furcal	.284	57	292	189
SS	Jeff Blauser	.269	85	54	46
2B	Mark Lemke	.248	32	263	11
RF	David Justice	.274	131	441	20
LF / 1B	Ryan Klesko	.281	139	449	26
1B	Fred McGriff	.293	130	446	23
3B	Terry Pendleton	.287	71	322	24
2B	Marcus Giles	.292	61	234	50
RF	Brian Jordan	.277	68	313	28
LF / CF	Ron Gant	.262	85	302	92
CF / LF	Otis Nixon	.278	3	80	186
2B	Keith Lockhart	.248	26	166	10

Follies Factoids

★ No single player played every season for the Braves during the Warpath Era. However, John Smoltz managed to play in fourteen of them. Tom Glavine, Andruw Jones, Chipper Jones, and Javy Lopez were all next in prolificacy with twelve seasons apiece.

★ The famed tomahawk chop, the favorite forearm gesture of Braves fans everywhere, is believed to have come from Braves outfielder Deion Sanders, whose college football alma mater, the Florida State Seminoles, favor a similar descalpitative gesture.

★ Upon Leo Mazzone's departure from the Braves after the 2005 season, the team ERA rose from 3.98 all the way to 4.60. However, Mazzone's new team in 2006, the Baltimore Orioles, also saw their ERA balloon from 4.56 up to 5.35, taking some of the luster off of Mazzone's storied reputation as a guru.

★ The 1997 All-Star game featured seven Atlanta Braves.

★ The most frequent Brave All-Star from 1991 through 2005 was Tom Glavine with eight appearances. Greg Maddux and John Smoltz were next, each with six appearances.

★ The New York Yankees did extremely well during the same era, having won thirteen consecutive playoff berths from 1995 through 2007. They also were the only team to defeat the Atlanta Braves twice in World Series play.

★ An unusual number of Atlanta Braves wound up playing for Joe Torre's Yankees. This long list includes Kyle Farnsworth, Chris Hammond, David Justice, Steve Karsay, Kenny Lofton, Denny Neagle, Luis Polonia, Gary Sheffield, Mike Stanton, Mike Wohlers, and Jaret Wright.

★ Atlanta's home attendance in 1993 (3.88 million) had nearly quadrupled from what it had been in 1990 when Bobby Cox took over as manager.

★ The two hitters Glavine, Maddux, and Smoltz collectively pitched to most often during the course of their careers were Craig Biggio and Barry Bonds.

★ The two pitchers Andruw Jones, Chipper Jones, and Javy Lopez collectively faced most often over the course of their careers were Al Leiter and Steve Trachsel.

★ The Braves' 1995 world championship marked the first time that a franchise had reached the pinnacle for three different cities (Boston, Milwaukee, and Atlanta).

13

The Cathedrals—New & Old

◇◇

Of the thirty current major league stadiums, what year was
your favorite one completed? Here's a handy guide to let you
know for sure (along with, when applicable, the facility's
original name when it first hosted baseball)

1912 Fenway Park, Boston
1914 Weeghman Park / Wrigley Field, Chicago
1962 Dodger Stadium, Los Angeles
1966 Anaheim Stadium / Angel Stadium of Anaheim
1966 Oakland-Alameda County Stadium
1973 Royals Stadium / Kaufman Stadium, Kansas City
1987 Joe Robbie Stadium / Landshark Stadium, Miami
1989 SkyDome / Rogers Centre, Toronto
1990 Tropicana Field, St. Petersburg
1991 Comiskey Park (II) / U.S. Cellular Field, Chicago
1992 Oriole Park at Camden Yards, Baltimore
1994 Jacobs Field / Progressive Field, Cleveland
1994 The Ballpark in Arlington / Rangers Ballpark in Arlington
1995 Coors Field, Denver
1996 Turner Field, Atlanta
1998 Bank One Ballpark / Chase Field, Phoenix
1999 Safeco Field, Seattle
2000 Comerica Park, Detroit

2000   Enron Field / Minute Maid Park, Houston
2000   Pacific Bell Park / AT&T Park, San Francisco
2001   Miller Park, Milwaukee
2001   PNC Park, Pittsburgh
2003   Great American Ball Park, Cincinnati
2004   Citizens Bank Park, Philadelphia
2004   PETCO Park, San Diego
2006   Busch Stadium (III), St. Louis
2008   Nationals Park, Washington
2009   Citi Field, Queens, NYC
2009   Yankee Stadium, Bronx, NYC
2010   Target Field, Minneapolis

Now, for contrast, we present the thirty structures from the past that have hosted the most seasons of major league baseball:

1. Sportsman's Park (II-III), St. Louis—99 seasons
2. Tiger Stadium, Detroit—88 seasons
3. Yankee Stadium (original), Bronx, NYC—84 seasons

4. Comiskey Park (original), Chicago—81 seasons
5. Shibe Park, Philadelphia—79 seasons*
6. Cleveland Municipal Stadium—62 seasons**
   Forbes Field, Pittsburgh—62 seasons
8. Polo Grounds (III-IV), Manhattan, NYC—59 seasons***
   Redland Field / Crosley Field, Cincinnati—59 seasons
10. League Park, Cleveland—55 seasons***
11. National League Park / Baker Bowl, Philadelphia—52 seasons
12. National Park / Griffith Stadium, Washington—51 seasons
13. Shea Stadium, Queens, NYC—47 seasons****
14. Ebbets Field, Brooklyn, NYC—45 seasons
15. Milwaukee County Stadium, Milwaukee—44 seasons
16. Busch Stadium (II), St. Louis—40 seasons
   Candlestick Park, San Francisco—40 seasons
18. Memorial Stadium, Baltimore—38 seasons
   National League Park / Braves Field, Boston—38 seasons
20. Harris County Domed Stadium / Houston Astrodome—35 seasons
   San Diego / Jack Murphy / Qualcomm Stadium—35 seasons

22. Riverfront Stadium / Cinergy Field, Cincinnati—33 seasons
    Veterans Stadium, Philadelphia—33 seasons
24. Atlanta Fulton-County Stadium—31 seasons
    Three Rivers Stadium, Pittsburgh—31 seasons
26. New Sportsman's Park / Robison Park, St. Louis—28 seasons
    Hubert H Humphrey Metrodome, Minneapolis—28 seasons
    Olympic Stadium, Montreal—28 seasons
29. Kingdome, Seattle—23 seasons
30. Arlington Stadium, Texas—22 seasons

* *For seventeen years, the Athletics and Phillies shared Shibe Park, which was eventually renamed Connie Mack Stadium.*

** *For eleven seasons, the Indians split their home games between Municipal Stadium and League Park, both in Cleveland.*

*** *For ten years, the Giants and Yankees shared the Polo Grounds. In addition, during the venue's final years, it was home to the Mets during their first two seasons. The third and fourth versions of the Polo Grounds shared the exact same diamond. The venue's original name when baseball debuted there was Brush Stadium.*

**** *For two years, the Mets and Yankees shared Shea Stadium.*

ABOUT SPORTSMAN'S PARK (II-III) IN ST. LOUIS

For thirty-four years, the Browns and Cardinals shared this venue.

As it happened, the original Sportsman's Park occupied the same land and is where the Cardinals franchise (then known as the Brown Stockings and later as the Browns) played their initial eleven seasons before moving across town to "New Sportsman's Field," a venue that failed to survive its namesake.

In addition, the unrelated "St. Louis Brown Stockings" played three seasons at the location, 1875–1877.

This venue was originally referred to as the Grand Avenue Ball Grounds and during its final years was rechristened as Busch Stadium (not to be confused with the 1966 concrete structure that would showcase the likes of Lou Brock, Bob Forsch, Mark McGwire, Ozzie Smith, and Bruce Sutter).

All told, 8,391 major league baseball games have been played at the NW corner of Dodier Street and Grand Avenue in St. Louis. (This total (includes twenty-seven postseason contests and three All-Star Games).

No other specific location can claim to have hosted more games of major league baseball in the world (at least until 2016–2017 when Fenway Park will surpass the number).

Follies Factoids

★ The locale that Redland Field/ Crosley Field was built upon had already hosted MLB for the previous twenty-eight seasons, so this patch of land in Cincinnati has played host to eighty-seven seasons of major league baseball.

★ The three different versions of the South End Grounds (all built on the same patch of land) served as the home for the Boston Braves for forty-four consecutive seasons.

★ Of the eighteen major league ballparks constructed between 1960 and 1980, only four are still being used by major league teams—three of which are located in California.

★ Toronto's domed stadium is already the eighth oldest facility in the majors.

★ Tropicana Field was completed in 1990, a full eight years before the city's expansion team played its first game there. At various times, five different franchises made serious overtures toward relocating there (Giants, Mariners, Rangers, Twins, and White Sox).

★ Dinosaur bones were uncovered during the building of Coors Field in Denver.

14

Previously Known As...

◇◇

Of the thirty current major league stadiums, more than a few of today's baseball clubs used to go by other names. The same holds true for manyof basball's greatest players. Here's a combined list that takes a look at some of these previous monikers.

Red Ames . . . . Leon Ames

Cap Anson . . . . Adrian Constantine Anson

Home Run Baker . . . . John Franklin Baker

Red Barber . . . . Walter Barber

Chief Bender . . . . Charles Albert Bender

Atlanta Braves . . . . Boston Beaneaters

Three Finger Brown . . . . . Mordecai Peter Centennial Brown

Chicago Cubs . . . . Chicago Orphans

Cincinnati Reds . . . . Cincinnati Redlegs

Cleveland Indians . . . . Cleveland Naps

Dizzy Dean . . . . Jay Dean

Red Faber . . . . Urban Clarence Faber

Rube Foster . . . . Andrew Foster

Los Angeles Angels . . . . . California Angels

Los Angeles Dodgers . . . Brooklyn Bridegrooms

Connie Mack . . . . Cornelius Alexander McGillicuddy

Rube Marquard . . . . Richard William Marquard

New York Yankees . . . . . . New York Highlanders

Oakland A's . . . . Kansas City Athletics

Philadelphia Phillies . . . . Philadelphia Blue Jays

San Francisco Giants . . . . New York Giants

St. Louis Cardinals . . . . . . St. Louis Perfectos

Red Smith . . . . Walter Smith

Chief Tokohama . . . . Charlie Grant

Dazzy Vance . . . . Clarence Vance

Rube Waddell . . . . George Edward Waddell

Honus Wagner . . . . John Peter Wagner

Ted Williams . . . . Teddy Samuel

*(to find the "original" names of many franchises,
check out our companion book—Rollie's Follies.)*

15

Evolution Of The Strikeout Artists

◇◇◇

A selective look at some of the flamethrowers
that led all of baseball in strikeouts.

1879 John "Montgomery" Ward of the first-place Providence Grays led baseball with 239 strikeouts.

1889 Mark "Fido" Baldwin threw 368 shutups for the sixth-place Columbus Solons of the American Association.

1899 Frank "Noodles" Hahn of the sixth-place Cincinnati Reds chucked 145 strikers.

1909 Orval Overall of the second-place Chicago Cubs bumped off 205 clodhoppers.

1919 Walter "Big Train" Johnson of the seventh-place Washington Senators steamrolled 147 palookas.

1929 Robert "Lefty" Grove of the world champion Philadelphia A's rubbed out 170 saps.

1939 Bob Feller of the third-place Cleveland Indians blew away all competitors by cutting down 240 chumps.

1949 Virgil "Fire" Trucks of the fourth-place Detroit Tigers hosed away 153 suckers.

1959 Don Drysdale of the World Champion Los Angeles Dodgers collected 242 trading stamps.

1969 Sudden Sam McDowell of the last-place Cleveland Indians fanned 279 dupes.

1979 J.R. Richard of the second-place Houston Astros smoked 313 victims (90 more K's than any other hurler that year).

1989 Forty-two-year old Nolan Ryan of the fourth-place Texas Rangers led both leagues by whacking 301 dudes.

1999 Randy "Big Unit" Johnson of the NL West division-winning Arizona Diamondbacks blew away 364 jibronis.

2009 Justin Verlander of the Detroit Tigers punched out 269 homeys.

Follies Factoids

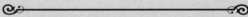

★ Matt "Matches" Kilroy of the 1886 Baltimore Orioles (of the American Association) notched 513 strikeouts, the single-season record.

★ However, the modern single-season strikeout record belongs to Nolan Ryan, who tallied 383 for the 1973 California Angels.

16

Cecil Cooper and Phil Garner: A Shared Life

◇◇◇

Both Cooper and Garner were born in the South in 1949.

Both made their major league debuts for American League clubs.

Both played in the 1975 ALCS between Boston and Oakland.

Both were reserve infielders at the 1980 All-Star game.

Both had higher career batting averages during All-Star games
than they did during the regular season.

Both hit exactly one postseason home run.

Both had World Series experience as a player.

Both are in the Texas Baseball Hall of Fame.

Both notched six hits, one homer, and three RBIs off of Tom Seaver.

Both had lengthy runs with the Milwaukee Brewers but never at the same time.

Both managed the Houston Astros for part of the 2007 season.

Both spent three seasons as a coach for the Astros before being abruptly
promoted to skipper in the middle of a season.

Both were fired by the Astros in midseason.

Both were teammates of Sal Bando, Don Sutton, Luis Tiant, and me,
Rollie Fingers.

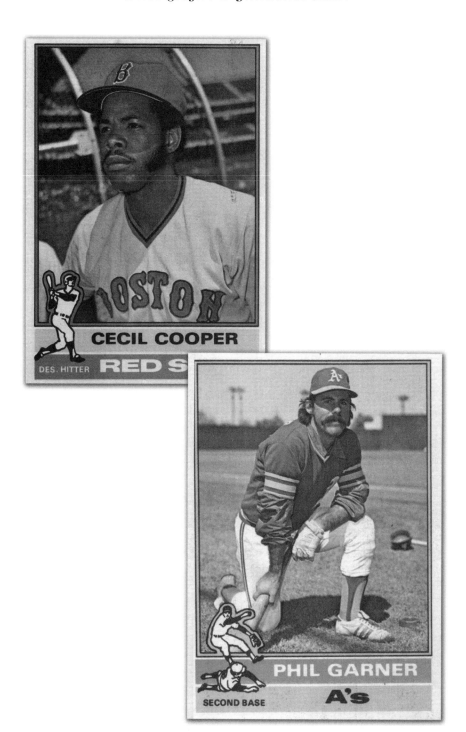

17

The Great Depression
of 1987

◇◇

In 1966, the average major league baseball player earned in the neighborhood of fifteen grand a year. Although, to be fair, they often ended up making significantly more because of all the odd jobs they were forced to pick up during the offseason.

By 1969, the per annum had risen into the neighborhood of $25,000. This was a nice increase but still a miniscule portion of the actual money the players were generating for the owners.

Then along came Curt Flood.

Curt was an All-Star Gold Glove outfielder who ended up costing himself a whole lot of green by taking a stand against the owners. In lieu of being told what team to play for, and upset that he had no leverage to court other ballclubs, Curt simply walked away from his contract, forfeiting six-figure money in the process.

Though the move shortened his career, Curt Flood's actions indirectly pumped tens of thousands of dollars into the pockets of his fellow players. It's not uncommon for a player to take one for his team, but Flood took one for *every* team.

Though he lost his case in front of the Supreme Court, he had succeeded in raising public awareness while helping to embolden other players. Free agency eventually became the law of the land, and by 1976 the average player not working for Charlie Finley was making in the vicinity of $50,000 per year. In essence, Curt was the guy who opened the floodgates.

Things seemed quite rosy for a while. Every year players got closer and closer to making their actual worth. It was the most capitalistic the game had been since before the advent of the reserve clause. But even though the players were making more money, the game prospered, no teams contracted, and exactly zero owners went bankrupt.

But in 1987, that gravy train came to a grinding halt. For no apparent reason, the salaries offered to players declined by an average of nearly $8,000. This was an especially strange time to implement a paycut since the sport was coming off an all-time attendance record. In addition, the revenue in 1986 had topped 1985's rake by over forty-one million dollars (a 15 percent increase).

But the owners were claiming poverty and their once fertile practice of signing free agents dried up faster than the dew on an Arizona summer morning. Even George Steinbrenner somehow developed a priority higher than trying to buy himself a winner.

However, the Boss may have been rewarded for that policy because when Ron Guidry became a free agent after the 1986 season, Gator received no offers, except for, of course, from the Yankees. Simply put, outside of the Bronx, no one had interest in an innings-eater coming off a two-year run in which he had notched 31 victories alongside a 3.57 ERA. The situation was more than a little depressing.

But it was around this time that a new hero emerged in the mold of Curt Flood, and his name was Andre Dawson.

Dawson was a longtime Montreal Expo who entered the free agent market that season with great optimism. All he did the season before was smash 20 homers, steal 18 bases and knock in 78 runs. But he was shocked to learn that no one wanted to sign him except, of course, his old team.

The Chicago Cubs were among the ballclubs to turn away his advances, despite the fact that Dawson had notched more total bases in 1986 than any of their three outfielders. Money was never even discussed. The Cubs simply dismissed him by citing that they doubted he could single-handedly turn them from a 71-91 team into a 91-71 team. Apparently, they were saving their money for Roy Hobbes.

But the natural grass of Wrigley Field beckoned to Dawson's thirty-two-year old knees like cupcakes to teamsters, and he showed up, uninvited, for spring training anyway. Cubs management dismissed his actions as nothing more than a "dog and pony show" and further disrespected him by refusing to so much as have a cup of coffee with him. Somewhere, Expos management was probably rejoicing.

But Dawson and his agent would not be ignored. A couple weeks into that preseason, they let the world know that they were presenting the Cubs with a blank contract, essentially agreeing to play for them for the major league minimum, despite the fact that the Hawk was clearly a seven-figure ballplayer.

Quite brilliantly, Cubs management had been placed over a barrel. Not signing Dawson to a deal would not only infuriate their fan base, it would prove to the densest of skulls that the owners were indeed colluding. Additionally, only paying Hawk the league minimum would paint themselves to the outside world as misanthropic skinflints.

Finding *what they thought* was middle ground, the Cubs offered Dawson an incentive-laden contract that was 31 percent lower than what he had earned the season before. Surely, that would send a powerful message not only to Dawson, but also to any future ballplayers who tried to collect their fair value.

Surprisingly, Andre Dawson signed the deal.

He then hit 49 homers and went on to collect every single one of the contract's incentives, including the one that kicked in if he won the National League MVP award. The next year, a most curious thing happened. Owners started to pursue other team's free agents once again. Accordingly, the average player salary once again began to reflect fair market levels.

As for the owners, they subsequently learned the hard way that being penny-wise can be millions-foolish. The players union sued them on charges of collusion and presented evidence so strong that in 1990 the owners agreed to settle out of court for an award in the neighborhood of $280 million dollars. A small portion of that money went to pay for beer that was raised all across baseball to toast Andre Dawson and his agent, the men who were clever enough (and unselfish enough) to engineer the reversal of the great depression of 1987.

18

Gone But Not Forgotten

◇◇

Over the years, more than a few major league ballclubs
have relocated to other regions. Many more have
swapped out their nicknames.
Some clubs have gone out of business entirely.
But even so, the ancient names of these long-ago
professional franchises can still inspire magic
in those of us who enjoy uncovering their history.
We now present a list of all the defunct baseball
entities that were in existence for at least ten seasons—
along with a little bit of history for each.

Seventy-Nine Seasons Of

Washington Senators

1892–1899, 1901–1971

CROWNING ACHIEVEMENT
1924 World Champions

KEY ICONS
Walter Johnson, Frank Howard, Harmon Killebrew, Clark Griffith,
Joe Cronin, Gil Hodges, Bucky Harris, Goose Goslin, Sam Rice,
Roy Sievers, Heinie Manush, Chuck Hinton, Rick Ferrell

NOTES

There have been three different incarnations of Washington Senators.

Though the franchise officially switched their nickname to the Nationals (from 1901 to 1956), the moniker of Senators stuck with fans and sportswriters to the extent that it stayed dominant.

Only three players from the 1960 Senators played for the 1961 version. (The '60 version moved away to become the Minnesota Twins and the '61 team was an expansion team.)

Their final manager was Hall of Famer Ted Williams.

Both the Minnesota Twins and Texas Rangers have senatorial roots.

★ ★ ★ ★ ★ ★ ★ ★ ★ ★

Seventy-Four Seasons Of
New York Giants
1885–1957

CROWNING ACHIEVEMENTS
Five-time World Champions
(1905, 1921, 1922, 1933, 1954)
Champions in 1888 and 1889 as well.

KEY ICONS
Willie Mays, Christy Mathewson, Johnny Mize, John McGraw,
Mel Ott, Leo Durocher, Monte Irvin, Carl Hubbell, Bill Terry,
Frankie Frisch, Rube Marquard, Hoyt Wilhelm, Roger Bresnahan,
Iron Man Joe McGinnity, Amos Rusie, Ernie Lombardi, George Kelly,
Jim O'Rourke, Travis Jackson, George Davis, Tim Keefe, Ross Youngs,
Dave Bancroft, Roger Connor, Buck Ewing, Smiling Mickey Welch,
Ed Roush, Freddy Lindstrom, John Montgomery Ward

NOTES
1890 saw two New York Giant teams play pro baseball
(in separate leagues).

From 1900 through 1929, the New York Giants led baseball
in overall attendance.

Forty-eight members of the Hall of Fame once wore the uniform
of the New York Giants as players and/or managers.
No other franchise can claim as many enshrined.
(To date, the Yankees only have thirty-nine.)

In 1919, the baseball team sponsored a football team and christened them
"The New York Giants." However, these pigskinners didn't play a game
until 1921 and folded shortly thereafter.
In 1925, an unrelated New York football team sprung up
and took the Giant nickname as their own (today's NFL team).

The San Francisco Giants came directly from this New York ballclub.

The orange in the New York Mets uniform is a nod
to the departed New York Giants.

★ ★ ★ ★ ★ ★ ★ ★ ★ ★

Seventy Seasons Of

Philadelphia Athletics
1871–1876, 1882–1891, 1901–1954

CROWNING ACHIEVEMENT
Five-time World Champions (1910, 1911, 1913, 1929, 1930)
Champions in 1871 AND 1883 as well.

KEY ICONS
Connie Mack, Jimmie Foxx, Lefty Grove, Eddie Collins,
Mickey Cochrane, Chief Bender, Al Simmons, Nap Lajoie, Eddie Plank,
Rube Waddell, Cap Anson, Frank "Home Run" Baker, Herb Pennock,
George Kell, Wilbert Robinson

NOTES
1890 saw two Philadelphia Athletic teams play pro baseball
(in separate leagues).
Overall, there have been five incarnations
of Philadelphia Athletics.

Astonishingly, Connie Mack managed the team from 1901 through 1950. He
has 968 more career victories than any other manager.

The Oakland A's roots run all the way back to this ballclub.

Sixty-Eight Seasons Of
St. Louis Browns
1883–1898, 1902–1953

CROWNING ACHIEVEMENT
Champions in 1886, Co-Champions in 1895

KEY ICONS
Rogers Hornsby, George Sisler, Bill Veeck, Bobby Wallace,
Branch Rickey, Heinie Manush, Ken Williams, Roger Connor,
Rick Ferrell, Jimmy McAleer, Tommy McCarthy, Tip O'Neil,
Dave Foutz, Charles Comiskey

NOTES
There have been two distinct incarnations of St. Louis Browns.
Both the St. Louis Cardinals and Baltimore Orioles have Brown roots.

In 1941, the Browns were set to move to Los Angeles in time for the following season, but the bombing of Pearl Harbor and ensuing fears of
military strikes on the Pacific Coast prevented the move.

During World War II, with many of the nation's best players
fighting overseas, the Browns employed Pete Gray,
the only one-armed position player in baseball history.

Thirty-Six Seasons Of
Boston Braves
1912–1935, 1941–1952

CROWNING ACHIEVEMENT
1914 World Champions

KEY ICONS
Rabbit Maranville, Casey Stengel, Rube Marquard, Johnny Evers,
Warren Spahn, Billy Southworth, Bill McKechnie, Dave Bancroft

NOTES
The World Champion "Miracle" Braves of 1914
were in last place as late as July 18

In 1935, Babe Ruth finished his career with the Boston Braves.

The Boston Braves are ancestors of today's Atlanta Braves.

★ ★ ★ ★ ★ ★ ★ ★ ★ ★

Thirty-Six Seasons Of
Montreal Expos
1969–2004

KEY ICONS
Andre Dawson, Gary Carter, Frank Robinson, Tim Raines,
Vladimir Guerrero, Tony Perez, Larry Walker, Dick Williams,
Felipe Alou, Rusty Staub, Steve Rogers, Tim Wallach,
Pedro Martinez, Randy Johnson

NOTES
Pete Rose reached the 4,000-hit plateau as a member of the Expos.

At the time of the 1994 strike, the Montreal Expos had the
best winning percentage in all of baseball (.694).

In 2003, the Expos played twenty-two of their home games
in Puerto Rico.

The Washington Nationals are the offspring of the Expos franchise.

★ ★ ★ ★ ★ ★ ★ ★ ★ ★

Thirty-Two Seasons Of
California Angels
1965–1996

KEY ICONS
Nolan Ryan, Reggie Jackson, Brian Downing, Rod Carew,
Chuck Finley, Gene Mauch, Don Sutton, Bryan Harvey

NOTES
The Los Angeles Angels of Anaheim are but the latest of
four names that the Angels franchise has used.

The franchise almost chose Long Beach over Anaheim as its base,

but the deal fell apart because owner Gene Autry refused
the city's demand to name the franchise the Long Beach Angels.
A second opportunity to host MLB never came down the pike
for this seaside metropolis.

★ ★ ★ ★ ★ ★ ★ ★ ★ ★

Twenty-Eight Seasons Of
Brooklyn Dodgers
1911–1912, 1932–1957

CROWNING ACHIEVEMENT
1955 World Champions

KEY ICONS
Jackie Robinson, Branch Rickey, Duke Snider, Pee Wee Reese,
Roy Campanella, Sandy Koufax, Gil Hodges, Don Newcombe,
Walter O'Malley, Leo Durocher, Red Barber, Clem Labine,
Walter Alston, Larry MacPhail, Paul Waner, Joe Medwick,
Billy Herman, Hack Wilson, Al Lopez, Arky Vaughan,
Waite Hoyt, Vin Scully

NOTES
Their nicknames included "Dem Bums" and "The Boys of Summer."

The Brooklyn Dodgers are the direct ancestors of today's
Los Angeles Dodgers.

The blue in the New York Mets uniform is a nod to the
departed Brooklyn Dodgers.

★ ★ ★ ★ ★ ★ ★ ★ ★ ★

Twenty-Four Seasons Of
Boston Beaneaters
1883–1906

CROWNING ACHIEVEMENT
Champions In 1883, 1891, 1892, 1893, 1897, 1898

KEY ICONS
Hugh Duffy, Kid Nichols, "Sliding" Billy Hamilton, King Kelly,

Jimmy Collins, Fred Tenney, John Clarkson, Vic Willis, Frank Selee,
Herman Long, Tommy McCarthy, Charley Radbourn

NOTES
The Boston Beaneaters are a distant ancestor of today's
Atlanta Braves.

Hall of Famer Frank Selee was the first manager
who didn't also play on the field.

The 1898 Beaneaters had a winning percentage of .685

No team won as many nineteenth century championships.

★ ★ ★ ★ ★ ★ ★ ★ ★ ★

Twenty Seasons Of
Chicago White Stockings
1871, 1874–1889, 1901–1903

KEY ICONS
Cap Anson, King Kelly, Clark Griffith, John Clarkson,
Al Spalding, Paul Hines

NOTES
There have been three incarnations of the Chicago White Stockings.
The ballclub ceased play for two seasons due to the Great Chicago Fire
of 1871, the next incarnation eventually became the Cubs and the
final one became today's White Sox.

★ ★ ★ ★ ★ ★ ★ ★ ★ ★

Eighteen Seasons Of
Brooklyn Robins
1914–1931

KEY ICONS
Burleigh Grimes, Zack Wheat, Casey Stengel, Dazzy Vance,
Babe Herman, Wilbert Robinson, Max Carey, Rube Marquard

NOTES

The Robins are ancestors of both the Brooklyn and LA Dodgers.

The Robins nickname was a play on manager
Wilbert Robinson's last name.

The team's players were often insultingly referred to as
"The Daffiness Boys," in part because of a baserunning incident
that saw three Robins end up on third base.

★ ★ ★ ★ ★ ★ ★ ★ ★ ★

Eighteen Seasons Of
Baltimore Orioles

(the defunct incarnation)
1882–1899

CROWNING ACHIEVEMENT

Three consecutive championships in 1894, 1895, 1896

KEY ICONS

John McGraw, Willie Keeler, Wilbert Robinson, Ned Hanlon,
Hughie Jennings, Joe Kelley

KEY ICONS

Of all the dissolved franchises, this team was the winningest,
totaling 1,133 victories. They started as members of the American
Association but entered the National League in 1892.

Legendary manager Ned Hanlin relocated his entire family from
Pittsburgh to a house in Baltimore just a block away from the stadium.

★ ★ ★ ★ ★ ★ ★ ★ ★ ★

Fifteen Seasons Of
Louisville Colonels

(the defunct incarnation)
1882–1899

CROWNING ACHIEVEMENT

Champions in 1890
(in what was considered baseball's third-best league that year)

KEY ICONS
Honus Wagner, Fred Clarke

NOTES
Played in the American Association before joining
the National League in 1892.

★ ★ ★ ★ ★ ★ ★ ★ ★ ★

Thirteen Seasons Of
Kansas City Athletics
1955–1967

KEY ICONS
Catfish Hunter, Hank Bauer, Lou Boudreau, Vic Power, Norm Siebern

NOTES
Reggie Jackson, Roger Maris, and Satchel Paige all spent
a small portion of their careers with KC.

Direct ancestors of today's Oakland A's.

From 1955 through 1960, through lopsided trades, this franchise
unofficially served as a feeder system for the New York Yankees.

★ ★ ★ ★ ★ ★ ★ ★ ★ ★

Thirteen Seasons Of
Milwaukee Braves
1955–1967

CROWNING ACHIEVEMENT
1957 World Champions

KEY ICONS
Hank Aaron, Warren Spahn, Eddie Mathews, Joe Torre, Lew Burdette,
Joe Adcock, Phil Niekro, Bud Selig, Del Crandall, Red Schoendienst,
Johnny Logan.

NOTES

Direct ancestor of today's Atlanta Braves.

Never had a losing season.

Led baseball in attendance every year from 1953 through 1958.

★ ★ ★ ★ ★ ★ ★ ★ ★ ★

Twelve Seasons Of
Cleveland Naps
1903–1914

KEY ICONS

Cy Young, Nap Lajoie, Shoeless Joe Jackson, Addie Joss, Elmer Flick

NOTES

A distant ancestor of today's Cleveland Indians.

The fans named the team the Naps as a nod
to the captain (and eventual manager) Nap Lajoie.
On occasions when the team played poorly, they were instead
called the Napkins "because they fold up so easily."

★ ★ ★ ★ ★ ★ ★ ★ ★ ★

Eleven Seasons Of
Cleveland Spiders
1889–1899

KEY ICONS

Bobby Wallace, Jesse Burkett, Cy Young, Patsy Tebeau, Cupid Childs

NOTES

After six consecutive winning seasons, the club fell apart in 1899
and went 20-134—a mark that still ranks as the worst in history.
That year they averaged only 179 fans per game.

Eleven Seasons Of
New York Highlanders
1903–1912

KEY ICONS
Jack Chesbro, Clark Griffith, Wee Willie Keeler

NOTES
This direct ancestor of the New York Yankees
played in Manhattan, walking distance from the home field
of the New York Giants and less than a mile from the future site of
Yankee Stadium (across the Harlem River in the Bronx).

In 1904, Jack Chesbro won 41 games, a record that still remains.

★ ★ ★ ★ ★ ★ ★ ★ ★ ★

Eleven Seasons Of
Tampa Bay Devil Rays
1998–2007

KEY ICONS
Carl Crawford, Scott Kazmir, Aubrey Huff, Joe Maddon, Lou Piniella

NOTES
Direct ancestor of the Tampa Bay Rays.

The team actually plays across the bridge from Tampa
in the city of St. Petersburg.

Hall of Famer Wade Boggs hit the first home run in franchise history.

19

The Little Injuns That Could

he history of the United States of America is rife with references to the earliest Americans.

These native peoples once thrived all across the "lower forty-eight" for centuries. However, the debut of European settlers on the same stretch of land (in the form of Juan Ponce de Leon in 1513) set the stage for the beginning of an end.

This vast land mass would prove to be too small for the natives and the exploring settlers who came after them. After countless battles, skirmishes, and incidents, the so-called "Indians" eventually lost the war, and with it, so many of their previous freedoms. It was one of the most extreme makeovers of all time.

But despite this great defeat, remnants of "Native-American" culture remain an integral part of American life today, and this fact is especially evident within professional baseball. After all, nine of our thirty major league teams have Indian names somewhere within their official titles.

In the American League, you have the *Chicago* White Sox, Cleveland *Indians*, *Kansas* City Royals, *Minnesota* Twins, and *Seattle* Mariners. As for the senior circuit, their tribes include the *Arizona* Diamondbacks, the Atlanta *Braves*, the *Chicago* Cubs, the *Milwaukee* Brewers, and let's not forget that the Marlins are from *Miami*.

In addition, there have been a number of major leaguers of Native-American descent with Charles Bender, Allie Reynolds, and Jim Thorpe being chief among them. As for current players, consider that every time Yankee Joba Chamberlain squares off against Jacoby Ellsbury of the Red Sox

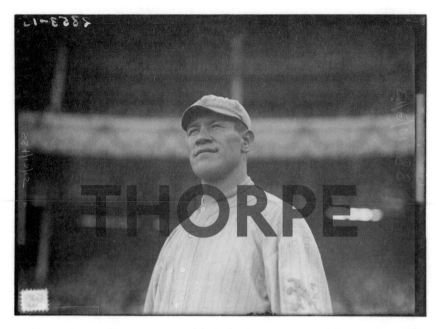

you're not just seeing a century-old rivalry between two cities, you're seeing two warriors in battle whose ancestors were living on this continent more than ten thousand years ago.

Indeed, the legacy of the earliest Americans is alive and well within baseball. But paying tribute to this great culture's influence on our national pastime wouldn't be complete without mentioning two of the mightiest Native-American legends of all: Chief Wahoo and Chief Noc-a-Homa.

It was way back in 1947 when the highly animated Chief Wahoo first made his way into the hearts of Cleveland fans. The people of the era found him to be an inviting beacon, and the Chief quickly became a symbol of city pride. His wide comic smile and playful eyes insinuated that anyone who came into his ballpark would be given a most enjoyable experience.

But as the decades passed, more and more people began finding this wahoo to be an insensitive stereotype. Accordingly, his visibility began to shrink. Although Chief Wahoo still exists, he has been pushed off of the primary real estate into less visible acreage, not unlike the Indians he was modeled after.

But to understand Chief Wahoo as he was intended, one must understand the context in which he was created. During the early part of the twentieth century, "Indians" were a favorite staple in American pop culture. They were widely represented in radio, in comics, and at the movies. They were often equated with elements of action and high drama. Some Indians were good guys, some were baddies, many were wise, but almost all were tough and resilient.

But despite the occasional evil and/or simplistic portrayals the overall adoration of the pop culture Indian reached the point that a great number of sports teams nationwide began adopting nicknames that honored them. The Washington Redskins, the Stanford University Indians, and the Hines Middle School Warriors are but three examples.

In addition, toy stores of the era were well stocked with Indian costumes, rubber bows and arrows, and other tribal paraphernalia, as many little boys preferred playing an Indian to playing a cowboy.

During the 1950s, television featured many Westerns. More Indians were making their way into the country's living rooms than you can shake a firestick at. It was during this time that someone in Milwaukee had a vision quest.

Sensing that introducing yet another Indian caricature might be passé in the age of television, the Braves came up with the idea to employ a live-action Indian to root for the home team. They even raised a teepee in the outfield bleachers from which the Indian would emerge to perform a celebratory dance when a Braves player would knock a homer.

Apropos, this hero's name was Chief Noc-A-Homa.

Oddly enough, the pun was mysteriously lost on many palefaces. Broadcaster Curt Gowdy, for instance, would instead pronounce the chief's name as Nokah-hawma—as though it were the name of a Japanese sushi shop.

The Milwaukee Braves fans took to Chief Noc-A-Homa faster than the Jamestown settlers took to tobacco. Rather quickly, the chief was all the rage, and his autograph was sought almost as much as Warren Spahn's.

But as was so often the case with Native-Americans, Chief Noc-A-Homa was eventually asked to leave his original territory. In 1966, the nomad packed up with the rest of his Braves who made their way down to the Georgia territory. But legend has it that the chief traveled well. One can surmise that all those celebratory dances he had performed for Hank Aaron's home runs had kept the chief in top physical condition.

As one might expect, Chief Noc-A-Homa became a big hit in Atlanta. He did so well that he remained a fixture for over twenty years. The chief even found companionship, first in the form of Princess Poc-A-Homa and then again with Princess Win-A-Lotta. There is absolutely no truth to the vicious rumor that he had a third squaw on the side by the name of Princess Poc-A-Lotta.

But not all good things last, and in 1986 the teepee began to unravel. Disagreements had cropped up between the chief and the executives that had been granting him his land parcel. In addition, the rising tide of political correctness was playing an ever-increasing role in sealing this Indian's, nay, this Native-American's fate. Eventually, there was only one direction for

Chief Noc-A-Homa to walk—and that was toward the great sunset.

Today, to a new generation of Braves' fans, the chief is mostly forgotten. No longer do they associate Indian culture with celebratory dances of joy, but instead with stadium-wide war chants and arm gestures that mimic the slicing off of scalps. It has become a world in which Chief Nok-A-Homa would never fit, and in that bizarre sense the trail of tears continues.

But even so, both Wahoo and Nok-A-Homa can rest assured that in their day, they created more than their share of smiles, cheers, and celebratory dances of joy.

An informal list ranking the most famous Indians in history can be found on page 273.

20

The Bird Fidrych

He was a tall and lanky plank with yellow frizzy hair and a smile reminiscent of childhood. He reminded old folks of a wonderful bygone era they had never really experienced, and to kids he was that fun-loving adult they wished all grown-ups would be.

Once in a while, a special player comes along who can innocently create frenzy. Fans will pack stadiums to cheer them on, and TV cameras will follow them around like they are rock stars. In 1976, Mark Fidrych was one of those rare birds.

Mark didn't have movie star looks. But what he did have was a friendly face that was just a tad goofy, the sort of mug toward which both toddlers and con artists naturally gravitate. If anything, he bore a slight resemblance to Sesame Street's Big Bird—appropriate since Mark shared many of same cheerfully awkward personality traits.

Mark Fidrych grew up in a rural patch of Massachusetts and for years it seemed his destiny would either play out as a farmer or as a gas pumper at the local filling station. But the highly unusual things Mark could talk a baseball into doing put these two job prospects on the back burner.

His pitching in high school caught the attention of a scout for the Tigers, and it led the farm boy into becoming a Detroit farmhand. Within two years, Fidrych was invited to spring training camp, almost on a lark. Then, against heavy odds, he made the major league squad as a mop.

Even so, no one was ready to bet the farm on the youngster's ability. In fact, he wasn't even called upon to pitch his second inning that season until May 15. But on that fateful day, his life changed. It always does in stories like these. A regular starter came down with the flu, and Mark was handed the ball in his stead.

All the frizzy mop did that day was throw seven no-hit innings before holding on for a 2-1 victory. The Tigers were more in shock than they were happy. But "cooler heads" prevailed, tabbed it as a fluke, and the rookie hurler was hurled back to his normal role.

Ten days later, he was handed the ball again, and as one might expect he didn't pitch as well. He gave up TWO runs in eight innings and lost the game. In addition, his ERA swelled to 1.50. But despite the losing effort, Tigers management knew they were onto something. It was as if they had discovered a winning Irish Sweepstakes ticket in an old forgotten jacket and in short order, they slotted Mark into the starting rotation.

For his third start, Fidrych went the distance for eleven full innings and took home the victory. For his fourth start, the he picked up yet another eleven-inning, complete-game win.

As a bonus, Fidrych's personality was as winning as his pitching record, and Detroit fans were drawn to him like Tigers to catnip. Never before or since had a Massachusetts accent been so revered in Michigan.

But there was yet another dimension to this man. He was clearly an eccentric. More and more, he began to stand out for his strange behavior.

On one occasion, Mark Fidrych quit looking at his catcher in the middle of an at-bat and instead stared at the baseball. That was odd enough, but then he began having a conversation with the white sphere as though it were a living, breathing person.

Then, he proceeded to throw this perfectly new baseball out of the game in favor of one that was more agreeable. After a quick meet and greet, he used the "friendly" ball to retire the next batter. Behavior such as this became his standard fare.

Opposing teams wondered aloud if this behavior was some sort of act, but Fidrych's Tiger teammates always set them straight. It was no charade. The Bird was the same on the field as he was in the clubhouse—friendly, energetic, polite, and a wee bit off kilter.

Fidrych also had the peculiar habit of getting down on his hands and knees in the middle of games to sculpt the pitching mound into dimensions that made him more comfortable. Just as a farmer plants crops, Fidrych was seemingly planting victories.

By June 28, Fidrych possessed a solid 7-1 record to go along with a measly 2.18 ERA. But to many, he was still unproven. However, that was all about to change.

That evening, he was slated to face the Bronx Bombers in a nationally televised game on ABC's *Monday Night Baseball*. It would be the first chance for millions to get a gander at the player that they had heard so much about.

Tiger Stadium was packed for the occasion as the powerful Yankees aimed to dismantle the phenom. This game was arguably Fidrych's toughest challenge to date. True to form, the network cameras caught him talking to the baseball just as he always did even when cameras weren't present. In the process, Mark Fidrych unwittingly made himself into an adorable spectacle to fans nationwide.

But these New York Yankees weren't fans of the Bird, and third baseman Graig Nettles decided to express those feelings. While at bat, Graig interrupted Fidrych's momentum by stepping out of the batting box. The slugger then mockingly began talking to his bat in a show of disrespect to the rookie hurler, making himself less than well liked to all those chirping fans at Tiger Stadium.

However, the mind game didn't quite register as intended with the childlike Fidrych. He merely broke into a wide smile, came off the mound, and held his arms open in playful wonder at Graig's antics. Fidrych then laughed his contagious laugh. Nettles grinned as well and retook his place in the batters box to do some real damage. But the Bird quickly found his concentration and sent the star third baseman packing with a knee-high fastball. The Tiger Stadium crowd erupted with a boom that could be heard a mile away.

Fidrych ended up earning a one-run, nine-inning, complete-game victory over the Bombers that night, but in the process he became a national icon. The wins kept coming for the one-time mop despite the fact that the Tigers weren't a very good team. During Mark Fidrych's magical 1976 season, he even managed to outduel the likes of Nolan Ryan and Bert Blyleven.

At season's end, the Bird ended up with 19 wins and a 2.34 ERA, incredible numbers considering that he barely played during the season's first six weeks. But as good as he was at collecting wins for the organization, some in Tiger management considered his true value to be as a drawing card. Why else did Fidrych have eighteen of his starts at home and only eleven on the road?

Some speculate that Fidrych, who made a mere $16,500 that season, probably made his club an additional $1,000,000 in ticket revenue. Even in relatively low drawing locales like Oakland and Minneapolis, the Bird was good for selling twenty thousand extra tickets whenever he pitched.

But throughout the media clamor, Fidrych remained a regular guy. He wore old blue jeans, lived modestly in a tiny Detroit apartment, and drove a subcompact car. He even wondered how he would be able to afford to answer all his fan mail.

During the offseason, the Tigers showed their new ace appreciation by giving him a $25,000 bonus and a three-year contract for $255,000. With his popularity zooming, he inked a book deal, showed up on network variety shows, and performed in a national commercial for Aqua Velva. The Bird was flying high, and many expected that the best was yet to come.

But it was not to be.

During spring training camp in 1977, Mark was playfully messing around in the outfield shagging flies. On one particular flyball, with carefree abandon, he tried to make a diving catch. But he landed awkwardly and injured the cartilage in his knee. Although it wasn't a career-threatening injury, it was something he began to compensate for when pitching.

Finally, during one game, his arm mysteriously went dead. The compensations had taken their toll. It wouldn't be properly diagnosed until many years later, but he had torn his rotator cuff. In 1977 season he went 6-4 with a 2.89 ERA. The following year, he only managed to pitch three times.

But despite the decline in his abilities, Fidrych always retained his positive personality. To many, he was just as much a fresh breath of charisma as he had been before. Well into his fifth season, fans continued to hope that he could somehow return to that phenomenal form he displayed in 1976.

But, on October 1, 1980, Fidrych pitched his last major league game. Fittingly, it was a victory, as the Tigers put 11 runs on the board for him. Still, it was sad—Fidrych was finished well before his time.

He returned home to Massachusetts and even spent a little time playing minor league ball for the team he had grown up admiring, the Boston Red Sox. He married his love, Ann, they had a daughter named Jessica and together, they all lived on a 107-acre farm.

Aside from granting a few interviews, the final decades of Mark's life had little to do with baseball despite the indelible mark he left on the game. Though his friends in the sport were numerous, he always felt more at home by actually being at home.

There, in the same community where he had learned to throw a baseball, Mark became a helpful neighbor—whether it was by using his ten-wheeler dump truck to haul gravel and asphalt for various construction projects or by helping out in whatever capacity was needed at his mother-in-law's diner on weekends.

Nationally, he was perceived by some as a little boy who had awakened into the body of a man who possessed an All-Star-caliber arm. But to the locals, he was something far more important—a good neighbor who offered help whenever needed.

On April 13, 2009, tragedy struck while Mark was working underneath his ten-wheeler. A portion of loose clothing got caught in the spinning apparatus of his truck's power takeoff shaft. It ended up suffocating him. He was only fifty-four years old.

Once again, he seemed to leave us far too early, but perhaps we should concentrate on the numerous joyful memories Mark Fidrych left us and how they will continue to be appreciated for years to come.

Follies Factoids

★ Mark Fidrych completed twenty-four of the twenty-nine games he started in 1976 with his average stint going in excess of 8 1/3 innings

★ Jim Leyland was Mark Fidrych's manager during parts of three different minor league seasons. All told, the Bird went 13-11 in fifty-two games for the legendary manager

★ A Detroit police officer who guarded the Tiger dugout had to wear a towel around his head to block out the thousands of deafening chirps that came from the hometown fans whenever the Bird took the mound.

21

The Top Home Run Surges in History

◇◇

We wondered which full-time players best increased their homerun output when compared to their previous season's total. The following chart shows you our findings.

Qualifier: a minimum of one hundred games played per season (to disqualify those players coming back from severe inactivity).

+38   Davey Johnson, Baltimore Orioles/Atlanta Braves (1972-1973)*

+34   Brady Anderson, Baltimore Orioles (1995-1996)

+32   Harmon Killebrew, Minnesota Twins (1968-1969)
      Greg Vaughn, San Diego Padres (1997-1998)
      Javy Lopez, Atlanta Braves (2002-2003)

+31   Lou Gehrig, New York Yankees (1926-1927)

+30   Sammy Sosa, Chicago Cubs (1997-1998)

+29   Johnny Mize, New York Giants (1946-1947)
      Andre Dawson, Montreal Expos/Chicago Cubs (1986-1987)*
      Richard Hidalgo, Houston Astros (1999-2000)*

+28   Jimmie Foxx, Philadelphia Athletics (1931–1932)
     Ralph Kiner, Pittsburgh Pirates (1946–1947)
     Carl Yastrzemski, Boston Red Sox (1966–1967)
     Rico Petrocelli, Boston Red Sox (1968–1969)
     Kevin Mitchell, San Francisco Giants (1988–1989)
     Frank Thomas, Chicago White Sox (1999–2000)

+27   Bob Cerv, Kansas City Athletics (1957–1958)
     Cito Gaston, San Diego Padres (1969–1970)
     Kirby Puckett, Minnesota Twins (1985–1986)
     Phil Plantier, Boston Red Sox/San Diego Padres (1992–1993)*

+26   Dick Stuart, Pittsburgh Pirates/Boston Red Sox (1962–1963)*
     Dusty Baker, Los Angeles Dodgers (1976–1977)
     Phil Bradley, Seattle Mariners (1984–1985)
     Ellis Burks, Colorado Rockies (1995–1996)
     Luis Gonzalez, Arizona Diamondbacks (2000–2001)
     Morgan Ensberg, Houston Astros (2004–2005)

+25   Babe Ruth, Boston Red Sox/New York Yankees (1919–1920)*
     Ripper Collins, St. Louis Cardinals (1933–1934)
     Ernie Banks, Chicago Cubs (1954–1955)
     Jim Gentile, Baltimore Orioles (1960–1961)
     Shawn Green, Los Angeles Dodgers (2000–2001)
     Adrian Beltre, Los Angeles Dodgers (2003–2004)
     Carlos Beltran, New York Mets (2005–2006)

* HR differential accomplished at two different home stadiums.

NOTES:
• None of the thirty-three players listed above made the list twice.
• Brady Anderson's manager during the season of his power surge was none other than Davey Johnson.
• The 2000s decade placed more players (eight) on the list than any other.
• The 1960s and 1990s tied for second with six apiece.
• The 1980s placed four players on the list.
• The 1970s were next with 3 players.
• The 1920s, 1930s, 1940s, and 1950s all placed two apiece.

22

The Silly Billy Goat Curse

◇◇

We all know the folklore. The Chicago Cubs have supposedly not been able to win a pennant in decades simply because they once kicked a tavern owner (and his pet billy goat) out of Wrigley Field back in 1945.

But what is lost on history is that a lot of fans at the time were quite supportive of the expulsion. The beast apparently was emitting scents and sounds *so horrific* that even Denise Richards would have complained!

Although it is unclear how the Cubs players felt about the goat's eviction, it is clear from historical records that the master of the billy goat was more than a little perturbed. Legend has it that during the humiliating exit, he pointed at the Cubs dugout while cursing the entire team in a raspy voice right before a series of thunderbolts clapped. Legend also has it that the goat's master had some choice words of his own, slamming a curse onto the franchise that, in essence, would keep them from winning another pennant.

The team, of course, has not won the National League flag since that fateful proclamation. But let us now set this record straight. This "billy goat curse" is humbug. It's hogwash. Worse than that, it's goatwash. It's nothing more than a super superstition. It is the literal application of the word scapegoat.

However, some curse-loving advocates will point out that whenever one of these bearded ruminants has been welcomed back into Wrigley Field, good luck ended up happenstancing. After all, such wry and festive goat-themed ceremonies in 1984 and 1989 *did* precede divisional wins. But if this goat magic had actually worked, then wouldn't the Cubs have ended up with AN ACTUAL PENNANT either of those two seasons?

But despite this evidence to the contrary, some Cubs fans remain true believers in the power of the goat. One such fan, back in 2007, with great stealth, managed to adorn the hallowed statue of broadcaster Harry Caray with butchered goat parts, ostensibly in an attempt to reverse the curse. Holy Goat!

But despite this gross display of voodoo carnage, the Cubs STILL FAILED to reach the Fall Classic that year. If anything, this macabre mobile of dangling goat chunks backfired, for it forever gave the world a bloody and violent connotation to the once serene phrase of "Harry Caray."

Now that we have so adequately deflated the silly theory about how a goat's expulsion from the "Unfriendly Confines" could somehow be responsible for the Chicago Cub's inability to take a National League crown...I'll let you know of an alternate curse that we've have had absolutely no luck in disproving.

In theory, *the real reason* for the Cubbies' perpetual tough sledding is simply because the team wronged the good name of a very good man oh so very long ago—and have yet to make amends for it.

It was on the 23rd of September way back in 1908. The Cubs were visiting Manhattan to play the Giants. But back then, it was the Cubs who were the goliaths, having stormed their way to the two previous pennants whereas the Giants were the plucky underdogs.

With less than two weeks to go in the season, these rivals were tied for first place, battling to eliminate the other. Every game was incredibly meaningful, especially because there were no league playoffs back then. Whoever finished first advanced directly to the World Series.

Thousands of fans jammed and crammed into the Polo Grounds in upper Manhattan. Hundreds of others scrambled to sights above the field on bluffs and elevated railway tracks. Downward upon the action they peered, praying, many trying to somehow will their Giants to victory. As a group, they were little more than a violent mob that had been momentarily sedated by optimism.

In the bottom of the ninth inning, the two enemy squadrons were tied at one run apiece. But the Giants were feeling more than a little confident and so were their fans. Even though there were two outs, New York had Moose McCormick on third, Fred Merkle on first, and standing at the dish wielding a most potent bat stood one Albert Henry Birdwell of Friendship, Ohio.

A strikeout would mean failure, but a base hit from Birdwell would most likely empty every beer keg in Manhattan, and a few whiskey bottles as well. The Giants' baserunners, McCormick and Merkle, stood at high alert, as did nearly every fan, some of whom, were hanging from the rafters.

What did Albert Henry Birdwell of Friendship, Ohio, do?

He socked the ball into the outfield and it dropped victoriously! Even before Moose touched home plate, dozens upon dozens of frenetic fans flowed onto the field to congratulate their underdogs.

Somewhere in the celebration, the nineteen-year-old Merkle was surrounded by well-wishers. He was so caught up in the happiness that he ran for the dugout without touching second base. This wasn't an unusual practice for the era; the move had never been penalized before by many of the game's senior umpires. To them, touching second base on a clean single to the outfield was as moot as it was to have a home team hit in the bottom of the ninth if they were already winning.

But *technically* touching second base was a rule in the books, and it was the Cubs second baseman, Johnny "The Crab" Evers, who saw the loophole. Amidst the celebratory frenzy, Evers set out to complete a force out before the naive Fred Merkle could realize the terror of his ways.

However, sharp-eyed Giants pitcher Joe McGinnity saw what the crabby Evers was up to and somehow found the baseball first. Heaving it far away, McGinnity seemed to secure the victory, but just to be sure, he tried to get word to Merkle to get back out onto the field to touch second base. But before the young first baseman could be reached, it happened.

Johnny Evers found himself a baseball, one that may not have been the actual game ball, and he bobbed and weaved his way through the crowd to second base. He then stepped on the bag in clear sight of umpire Hank O'Day, who hadn't departed the scene, and O'Day called Merkle out—per the rulebook. Moose McCormick's winning run was instantly nullified and so was the Giants' victory.

Giants players looked upon Johnny Evers as though he were the lowest sort of bottom feeder that had ever swum at the bottom of the ocean. The powerhouse Cubs had, in essence, got the Giants goat and escaped defeat through incredibly cheap means. To the thousands of Giants fans in attendance, the very essence of sportsmanship had been irreparably breached.

When the season ended two weeks later, the Giants and Cubs stood tied for first place. The "Merkle boner," as it came to be called, proved to be the difference in keeping the Giants from clinching the pennant, and a make-up game had to be scheduled. If the Giants could win, first baseman Fred Merkle would be redeemed, but if they failed, he would be a goat.

The Cubs once again took that long train ride into Manhattan and then bravely made their way into the Polo Grounds, knowing there were more than a few locals willing to put them into a hospital for their efforts. But despite the immense pressure, the Cubs came through by beating the Giants 4-2 in what was essentially the first-ever NLCS game.

In defeat, both the Giants and their fan base were spiritually demoralized. They had lost their chance for glory by a slim margin and by an even weaker circumstance. It is one thing to lose a game over a miscue, but to lose a pennant over one is another matter altogether. Merkle wore the nickname "Bonehead" and despite sixteen years in the majors, never lived up to his early promise. He died at the age of sixty-seven and was buried in an unmarked grave.

The Chicago Cubs went on to win the World Series that year, but strangely enough, they have yet to win a world championship since. More than one hundred seasons have now been played in which the Cubs have shown futility. A number of times the Cubbies seemed well on their way, but something has always occurred to trip them up.

One such example occurred in 1989. The Cubs seemed nothing short of unstoppable that season after posting more regular season wins than any other National League team. But that October they ran into one of Fred Merkle's franchise descendants in the form of Giants first baseman Will Clark, whose torrid 13 for 20 clutch hitting (and 24 total bases) destroyed the Cubs' hopes of playing for the championship.

If the Fred Merkle curse is indeed real, perhaps there is a way to reverse its power. Perhaps if the 1908 championship flag is lowered and burned, perhaps if the Cubs organization offers the Giants organization an official apology, and perhaps if reparations are made in the form of the Giants getting a free lifetime supply of Giordano's deep-dish pizza whenever they visit Wrigley, perhaps then *and only then* will the curse stand a chance to be lifted.

But then again, maybe not.

Even so, it probably wouldn't hurt the Cubs' chances if as many of their fans as possible begin wearing vintage Fred Merkle uniforms whenever the Giants come to play at Wrigley. It might not make a difference, but at this point, it makes a lot more sense than butchering a goat.

Follies Factoids

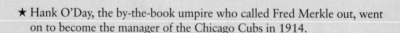

★ Hank O'Day, the by-the-book umpire who called Fred Merkle out, went on to become the manager of the Chicago Cubs in 1914.

★ The Chicago Cubs have been on the losing end of the World Series seven times since 1908. Additionally, since divisional play began in 1969, all six of the Cubs' postseason teams have failed to secure a pennant.

★ Since that painful 1908 season, the New York Giants went on to win four World Championships. However, ever since the franchise abandoned its loyal fans at the Polo Grounds in favor of moving to San Francisco, they have yet to win another.

23

The Longest Droughts

<<<<<<<<<<<<<<<<<<<<<<<<<<<<<<<<<<<<<<<<<<<<<<<<<<<<<<

Longest franchise droughts without a world championship

101 seasons*	Chicago Cubs (1909–2009)
87 seasons	Chicago White Sox (1918–2004)
85 seasons	Boston Red Sox (1919–2003)
77 seasons	Philadelphia Phillies (1903–1979)
63 seasons	St. Louis Browns / Baltimore Orioles (1903–1965)
62 seasons	Washington Senators / Minnesota Twins (1925–1986)
61 seasons*	Cleveland Indians (1949–2009)
55 seasons*	New York–San Francisco Giants (1955–2009)
52 seasons	Brooklyn Dodgers (1903–1954)
49 seasons*	Washington Senators / Texas Rangers (1961–2009)
48 seasons*	Houston Astros (1962–2009)
42 seasons	Boston-Milwaukee Braves (1915–1956)
41 seasons	Los Angeles-California-Anaheim Angels (1961–2001)
41 seasons*	Montreal Expos / Washington Nationals (1969–2009)
41 seasons*	San Diego Padres (1969–2009)
41 seasons*	Seattle Pilots / Milwaukee Brewers (1969–2009)
41 seasons	Philadelphia / KC / Oakland Athletics (1931–1971)
37 seasons	Milwaukee-Atlanta Braves (1958–1994)
34 seasons	Cincinnati Reds (1941–1974)
34 seasons	Pittsburgh Pirates (1926–1959)
33 seasons*	Seattle Mariners (1977–2009)
32 seasons	Detroit Tigers (1903–1934)
30 seasons*	Pittsburgh Pirates (1980–2009)

* Ongoing drought as of the end of the 2009 season

Follies Factoids

* There was no World Series to be won in either 1904 and 1994. Even so, the Cubs failed to finish in first place either season.

* From 1943 through 1944, the Philadelphia Phillies franchise played as the "Blue Jays."

* The Brooklyn Dodgers franchise intermittently played as the Superbas, Dodgers, and Robins up until 1932.

* The Houston Astros franchise was originally known as the Colt .45s during their initial three seasons.

* The Boston Braves franchise was known as the Boston Bees from 1936 through 1940.

* From 1954 through 1959, the Cincinnati Reds franchise played as the "Redlegs," lest no one associate them with communists.

24

Hammerin' Hank and the Say Hey Kid: Coincidences

◇◇

Both were born in Alabama during the 1930s.

Both briefly played in the Negro Leagues.

Both were scouted and signed by National League teams.

Both debuted in the majors at the age of twenty.

Both played in two World Series during the 1950s, winning one and losing the other.

Both were fleet outfielders.

Both possessed great home run power.

Both were Gold Glove winners.

Both won the NL MVP award.

Both won NL batting titles.

Both were teammates with Orlando Cepeda, Warren Spahn, and Hoyt Wilhelm.

Both led the National League in home runs four times.

Both players, during their prime, saw their ballclub
controversially relocate to a new city.

Both players, as their careers were winding down, were
traded back to their original major league city (where they played for
expansion teams).

Both played in a record twenty-four All-Star games.

Both retired during the 1970s after playing parts of two seasons with
their second ballclub.

Both retired at the age of forty-two.

Both are first-ballot Hall of Famers.

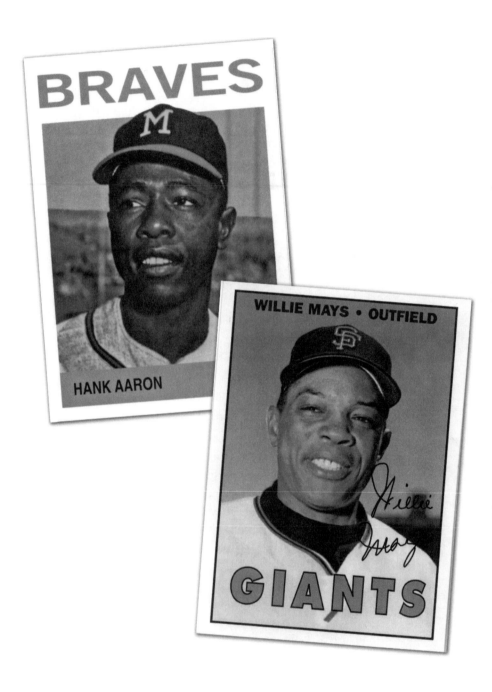

25

Thinking Outside the Box Score

Box scores are wonderful, but they don't always come close to telling you the *whole* story.

Take for instance a game played on April 7, 1971. If you were to dig back into the archives, you would see that Carlos May tagged me for a triple that day. However, that description doesn't come close to telling you what *really* happened.

Carlos May was a solid left-handed hitter for the Chicago White Sox. I knew better than most what Carlos was capable of doing at the plate because there were only a handful of hitters I had opposed on more occasions than Carlos.

During this particular at-bat, he came up with runners on first and third. My plan was to induce him to hit into an inning-ending double play. Carlos had a plan of his own. His plan worked better. He jacked my pitch over the left field wall for a home run. It was looking like it was going to be one of those days.

Carlos rounded the bases and was greeted near home plate by his teammates, who were jumping up and down, quite happy with the big lead he had created.

Just then, Gene Tenace, my catcher, got a strange look on his face—which for him was saying something. Like a hunter in the brush, his eyes began to trail Carlos as the slugger made his way back to the White Sox dugout. As the next Chicago hitter started to walk in from the on-deck circle, Jim Odom, the home plate umpire, fired a fresh baseball to me.

At that point, Geno breezily motioned for me to toss him the ball. I wasn't in the best of moods so I yelled, "What the hell do you need the ball for?" Geno once again made his request, with a bit more urgency, and was eyeing the White Sox dugout as he did so. Even though I had no idea what Geno was up to, I flipped him the ball.

As my exchange with Geno was going on, Jim Odom just stood near the plate, stoic and passive, in no hurry to get the game underway. With the ball in his hand, Geno turned and appealed to the umpire, who promptly called Carlos May OUT...for having missed home plate. Lost in the celebration, Carlos May forgot to *touch them all!!* Geno had not only noticed it, but knew to stay quiet about it long enough to keep Carlos from making a mad dash from the dugout.

A lot of catchers do a lot of great things to help their team, but this was the first time I had ever seen a catcher turn a home run into an out on the field (and to a triple in the box score).

I looked at Geno with a playful nod, and he looked back at me, smiling just a little. We were both thinking the same thing. I owed him an incredibly expensive steak dinner.

Follies Factoids

★ I, Rollie Fingers, came out of the A's starting rotation later that season.

★ Carlos May was a member of the famed 1977 New York Yankees, although he was traded in midseason prior to their winning the World Championship.

26

The Baltimore Setback

◇◇

In the autumn of 1996, the Baltimore Orioles were riding high. As the American League's wild card entrant, they had just knocked off the mighty Cleveland Indians by a margin of three games to one. The O's next mission would be to march into the House that Ruth Built to take out the New York Yankees in the ALCS.

The '96 Orioles were a team full with talented sluggers. Seven of their everyday players had banged out at least 20 homers and four had driven in at least 100 runs. No pitcher took them lightly. Eddie Murray and Cal Ripken were the leaders on the field, and Davey Johnson ran things from the dugout. This trio's previous World Series rings did nothing to placate their thirst for another.

In the opposite dugout stood Joe Torre. This baseball season was special for Torre as it marked the first time in his thirty-seven years of pro baseball that he was part of a postseason team. But despite his inexperience in the post, his Yankee team also possessed confidence, especially since they had solved Baltimore ten out of thirteen times during the regular season.

The umpire yelled "play ball" and the battle for the pennant broke out. The fierce rivals chipped away at each other in Game One until the score was tied at two at the end of three innings.

But in the top of the fourth, Baltimore slugger Rafael Palmiero hit a solo shot off Andy Pettitte to give his team a slight edge. In the sixth inning, they met again. This time, Palmiero worked Pettitte for a walk and eventually came around to score an insurance run.

The crowd at Yankee Stadium stayed loud and proud despite the losing score. However, their loyalty was rewarded in the seventh inning when pinch hitter Darryl Strawberry drew a bases-loaded walk off of reliever Armando Benitez. But the damage was quickly stemmed when Benitez struck out the next Yankee to end the inning.

A mere run separated the Bombers from the Birds.

In the bottom of the eighth, Benitez once again took the mound, and he immediately punched out the first Yankee hitter. All across Maryland, hopeful eyes stayed glued to their screens. Their O's had just five outs to go. It was Baltimore's first postseason in thirteen years, and every Yankee out was savored like a gourmet crab cake.

Then rookie Derek Jeter strode to the plate. It was his second time ever facing Benitez, who had struck him out looking the previous month during the regular season. The closer decided to challenge the young shortstop and gave him something to whack.

Yankee hearts were momentarily lifted when the wiry nine-hole hitter got ahold of the pitch and sailed it back toward the short right-field porch of Yankee Stadium.

This one was going to be close.

Oriole outfielder Tony Tarasco deftly sprinted back to the warning track. For both teams, the anticipation was maddening. But then Tarasco smoothly held up his glove in preparation to make the catch. Baltimore fans prepared to let out sighs of relief as the eyelids of Yankee fans crinkled a wee bit.

But oddly enough, the ball would not have a clear path to Tarasco's mitt. From the wrong side of the outfield fence came the outstretched hand of twelve-year-old Jeffrey Maier. Jeter's launch crashed down against the kid's bare hand, deflected sideways and careened like a pinball into the bleacher seats to Maier's right.

Incredulous, Tony Tarasco lowered his empty mitt and yelled for fan interference. However, the closest umpire didn't quite see things the same way. Tarasco was livid and so were his teammates. Skipper Davey Johnson was especially angry, perhaps in part because it was the first time in years he had to sprint all the way out to right field to argue a call.

As a Mardi Gras atmosphere broke out all over Yankee Stadium, Derek Jeter humbly rounded the bases, perhaps aware that a fan had given him a most precious gift.

Demoralized and feeling cheated, the Orioles failed to pull out a victory that night. Eventually, after seeing a replay, the umpire admitted that there had *indeed* been fan interference, but also noted that it wouldn't have mattered since he felt that the baseball was not catchable. Davey Johnson filed a protest, but the league backed the umpire.

Angrily, the Orioles rebounded the next night to win in the Bronx, but they then ended their season by dropping three straight in Camden Yards to Torre's poised Yankees. Seemingly, the Birds never got their mojo back after falling victim to this young fan's interference.

As for young Jeffrey Maier, he became a celebrity and went on to make appearances on a number of talk shows. He even received the key to New York City by the Yankee-loving mayor. It is one of the few instances in which a fan can actually take credit for putting a run on the board for his team.

By 2006, ten seasons after the incident, a lot had changed. Joe Torre's Yankees became a perennial playoff team, and the Orioles slipped into a hopeless pattern of haplessness. As for the young fan, he was hardly finished with his efforts to help the Yankees. After graduating from college in 2006, he had the gumption to knock on the hotel door of Yankees general manager Brian Cashman.

What did Jeffrey Maier want?

He asked for a job in baseball operations and came prepared to win Cashman over with an array of scouting reports he had personally compiled. Cashman took the meeting and although he didn't hire Maier, it did make for a nice story.

Some people think the Yankees should have hired this young good luck charm, if only for the fact that he already had a track record in helping the Yankees score without ever having set foot on the field. After all, what organization, including the Orioles, couldn't use a front office employee with powers such as those?

27

The All Dead-Ball Era Team
(1901–1920)

◇◇

All of the players on this twenty-five-man squad
had to meet two specific criteria:
1) They have to be inducted into the Hall of Fame
~ AND ~
2) The majority of their playing careers had to take place
between 1901 and 1920. (Sorry Babe).
Without further adieu...we now present...

PITCHING STAFF
**(CAREER STATISTICS FOR MANY OF THE DEAD-BALL ERA'S PREMIERE HURLERS,
ALONG WITH THE PRIMARILY BALLCLUB THEY PITCHED FOR)**

	Won-Loss	ERA	Strikeouts
CY YOUNG (Spiders)	511-316	2.63	2,803
CHRISTY MATHEWSON (Giants)	373-188	2.13	2,502
WALTER JOHNSON (Senators)	417-279	2.17	3,509
EDDIE PLANK (Athletics)	326-194	2.35	2,246
THREE FINGER BROWN (Cubs)	239-130	2.06	1,375
JOE McGINNITY (Giants)	246-142	2.66	1,068
ED WALSH (White Sox)	195-126	1.82	1,736
RUBE WADDELL (Athletics)	193-143	2.16	2,316
CHIEF BENDER (Athletics)	212-127	2.46	1,711
VIC WILLIS (Beaneaters)	249-205	2.63	1,651

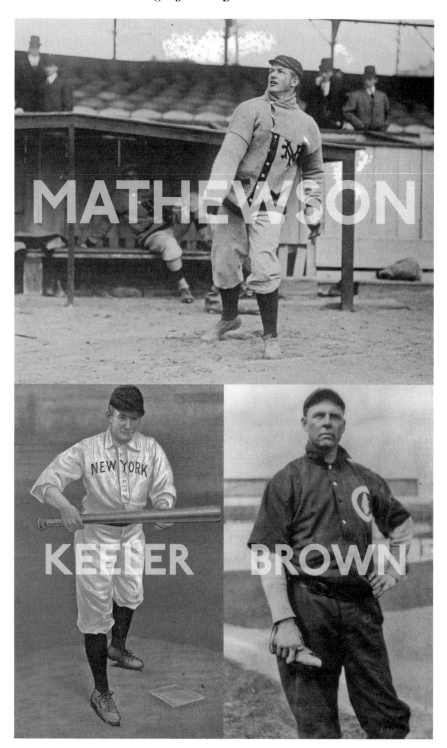

STARTING POSITION PLAYERS

(CAREER STATISTICS FOR MANY OF THE DEAD-BALL ERA'S PREMIER HITTERS, ALONG WITH THE PRIMARY BALLCLUB THEY PLAYED FOR)

		AVG	HR	RBI	SB
C	ROGER BRESNAHAN (Giants)	.279	26	530	212
1B-2B	NAP LAJOIE (Naps)	.338	83	1,599	380
2B	EDDIE COLLINS (White Sox)	.333	47	1,300	744
SS	HONUS WAGNER (Pirates)	.327	101	1,732	722
3B	HOME RUN BAKER (Athletics)	.307	96	987	235
LF	SAM CRAWFORD (Tigers)	.309	97	1,525	366
CF	TRIS SPEAKER (Indians)	.345	117	1,529	432
CF-RF	TY COBB (Tigers)	.366	117	1,937	892

RESERVES

		AVG	HR	RBI	SB
C-1B	FRANK CHANCE (Cubs)	.296	20	596	401
1B-SS	HUGHIE JENNINGS (Orioles)	.311	18	840	359
3B	BOBBY WALLACE (Browns)	.268	34	1,121	201
LF	ZACK WHEAT (Robins)	.317	132	1,248	205
LF	FRED CLARKE (Pirates)	.312	67	1,015	506
CF-RF	MAX CAREY (Pirates)	.285	70	800	738
RF	WILLIE KEELER (Highlanders)	.341	33	810	495

Players of this era often played more than one position:
Roger Bresnahan spent considerable time in center field.
Honus Wagner often defended at first base, third base, and in right field.
Sam Crawford was primarily a right fielder but also spent considerable time at first base and in center field.

THE OTHER EIGHT MAJOR LEAGUE PLAYERS PRIMARILY FROM THIS ERA WHO ARE ENSHRINED IN COOPERSTOWN

	Won-Loss	ERA	Strikeouts
JACK CHESBRO (Highlanders)	198-132	2.68	1,265
ADDIE JOSS (Naps)	160-97	1.89	920
RUBE MARQUARD (Giants)	201-177	3.08	1,593

		AVG	HR	RBI	SB
2B	JOHNNY EVERS (Cubs)	.270	12	538	324
RF	ELMER FLICK (Naps)	.313	48	756	330
RF	HARRY HOOPER (Red Sox)	.281	75	817	375
LF	JOE TINKER (Cubs)	.262	31	782	336

Loads of additional information on this era can be found on page 206.

28

Never Been Kissed

◇◇

Not every great player gets to play
for a world championship team.
Below are twenty-five of the game's best who
fit this unfortunate category.

Ty Cobb	Harry Heilmann
Ted Williams	Vladimir Guerrero
Barry Bonds	Ichiro Suzuki
Tony Gwynn	Gaylord Perry
Nap Lajoie	Rafael Palmiero
Paul Waner	Harmon Killebrew
Rod Carew	Ernie Banks
Ken Griffey Jr.	Craig Biggio
Carl Yastrzemski	Nellie Fox
Mike Piazza	Juan Marichal
Sammy Sosa	Willie McCovey
George Sisler	Gene Mauch
Chuck Klein	

Follies Factoid

★ In his nine years as a player and twenty-seven years as a manager, Gene Mauch was never part of pennant-winning team.

29

The Most Valuable Player
of the 1970s

◇◇

If you were to walk into any big league stadium
and start asking around who the most valuable baseball player
was during the 1970s, you likely would hear more than a few
different answers.

In our opinion, there is no obvious answer to this question,
especially since no player managed to win as many as three
league MVP awards during the decade.

But just for fun, we added up every single MVP vote point
that was cast from 1970 through 1979
just to see which fifty players ended up with the most.
Here are our findings:

(with the player's number of league MVP awards in parenthesis)
(and with pitchers noted by asterisk)

1.	WILLIE STARGELL (1)	1,060
2.	JOE MORGAN (2)	1,003
3.	JOHNNY BENCH (2)	898
4.	JIM RICE (1)	793
5.	REGGIE JACKSON (1)	702
6.	STEVE GARVEY (1)	693

7.	PETE ROSE (1)	666
8.	DAVE PARKER (1)	662
9.	GEORGE FOSTER (1)	650
10.	ROD CAREW (1)	613
11.	GEORGE BRETT	545
12.	KEN SINGLETON	539
13.	THURMAN MUNSON (1)	516
14.	GREG LUZINSKI	508
15.	FRED LYNN (1)	492
16.	SAL BANDO	442
17.	BILLY WILLIAMS	441
18.	MIKE SCHMIDT	411
19.	DON BAYLOR (1)	404
20.	JOE RUDI	363
21.	BOBBY BONDS	342
22.	LOU BROCK	340
	JIM PALMER *	340
24.	JOE TORRE (1)	333

25.	DICK ALLEN (I)	330
26.	AMOS OTIS	328
27.	REGGIE SMITH	315
28.	VIDA BLUE (I) *	314
29.	RON GUIDRY *	303
30.	BROOKS ROBINSON	271
31.	JEFF BURROUGHS (I)	264
32.	MIKE MARSHALL *	261
	JOHN MAYBERRY	261
34.	LARRY HISLE	255
35.	SPARKY LYLE *	252
36.	FRANK ROBINSON	251
37.	MICKEY RIVERS	244
38.	HENRY AARON	243
	CATFISH HUNTER *	243
40.	STEVE CARLTON *	240
	BOOG POWELL (I)	240
42.	CARLTON FISK	228
	CARL YASTRZEMSKI	228
44.	TONY PEREZ	226
45.	BOBBY MURCER	224
46.	TED SIMMONS	223
47.	AL COWENS	217
48.	KEITH HERNANDEZ (I)	216
	GRAIG NETTLES	216
50.	MICKEY LOLICH *	215

...and here are the twenty-five hurlers who
received the most Cy Young votes during the 1970s

(with their number of Cy Young awards in parenthesis)
(with relief pitchers noted by asterisk)

I.	JIM PALMER (3)	387
2.	TOM SEAVER (2)	259
3.	CATFISH HUNTER (I)	242
4.	GAYLORD PERRY (2)	240
5.	STEVE CARLTON (2)	235
6.	FERGIE JENKINS (I)	213
7.	RANDY JONES (I)	176
8.	RON GUIDRY (I)	171
9.	MIKE MARSHALL (I) *	166
10.	NOLAN RYAN	138
II.	MIKE FLANAGAN (I)	136
12.	VIDA BLUE (I)	126
13.	BOB GIBSON (I)	124
14.	MICKEY LOLICH	112
15.	TOMMY JOHN	106

16. WILBUR WOOD	84
17. BRUCE SUTTER (I) *	77
18. MIKE CALDWELL	76
19. JERRY KOOSMAN	74
20. ANDY MESSERSMITH	68
21. JOE NIEKRO	66
22. SPARKY LYLE (I) *	59
23. J.R. RICHARD	56
24. JIM PERRY (I)	55
DAVE MCNALLY	55

Follies Factoids

★ The trio of Ken Holtzman, Catfish Hunter, and Reggie Jackson were the only players to win five world championship rings during the 1970s (having done so with the '72, '73,'74 A's and the '77 and '78 Yankees).

★ Don Gullet won four consecutive championship rings with the '75 and '76 Reds and the '77 and '78 Yankees.

★ Reggie "Mr. October" Jackson was the only player during the 1970s to win the World Series MVP Award twice.

★ Willie Stargell never won the NL MVP award outright but did finish in a tie for the 1979 award with Keith Hernandez.

★ Vida Blue was the only pitcher during the 1970s to win a league MVP award.

★ 15 percent of the Cy Young awards during the 1970s went to relief pitchers

★ During the 2000s, Albert Pujols received more MVP votes than any other player, besting Barry Bonds and Alex Rodriguez. As for cumulative Cy Young votes, Randy Johnson topped them all.

★ Though baseball writers tend to strongly favor everyday players when voting for the league MVP awards, (and starting pitchers for Cy Young awards), that same level of disparity is nowhere to be found when it comes to player salaries—indicating that owners and GMs must feel quite differently on the subject. After all, in 1989, six of the ten highest paid baseball players were pitchers, despite the fact that only one pitcher cracked the top five in either league's MVP voting the previous year.

30

Kenny Rogers: A Life in Retrospect

◇◇

ew people can claim to have led *half* as interesting a life as that of dual superstar Kenny Rogers.

Details of his birth are sketchy, as they so often are for legends. One account has Kenny being born in Houston as early as 1938, but other accounts list his mama as having calved in Georgia as late as 1964. In either event (perhaps in part to plastic surgery) the Kenny of today seems much younger than his years.

Greatness found Kenny early, or perhaps he found it (as is so often the case with genius). As a youth, while spending time developing his vocals in a doo-wop band, he simultaneously crafted together the extraordinary pitching arsenal that would become the meat and potatoes to his bread and butter.

In his twenties, this Renaissance man was on the road living out of a suitcase. The world of this young wanderer was a seemingly endless array of bus rides, bright lights, and late-night diners. Charlotte, Tulsa, and Nashville were but some of the important hubs during these seminal years. Few in those early crowds could have realized that they were bearing witness to a man who would go on to earn five Gold Gloves and eighteen Gold Records.

Kenny's singing prowess was recognized first, but even though millions of dollars found their way into his pockets, he never gave up on baseball. Selling out Giants Stadium is one thing, but playing in front of a packed audience at Yankee Stadium is another thrill altogether—and Kenny would not let his appetite for dual-destiny be denied. The great ones never do.

Cowboy tales from the great American West were long a fascination for Kenny, and a number of his classic hits hearkened back to those dusty decades past. Therefore, it became quite appropriate when, in 1989, Kenny made his major league debut, for of all teams, the Texas Rangers.

Though he didn't start out with them as a featured attraction, he worked his way into the regular rotation, just as his records had done at hundreds of radio stations. Kenny's singing career continued to bring him most of his fame and fortune, but in 1994, he hurled a perfect game, and with it, this bristly voiced balladeer became a household name to baseball fans as well.

But pitching wasn't his only talent on the diamond. With greater frequency, he began picking off baserunners like frayed guitar strings.

Dual superstardom had finally found Kenny. High-profile collaborations with top stars like Dolly Parton, Ivan Rodriguez, Joe Torre, and Dottie West played important roles in propelling Kenny's career even further up the ladder of greatness. Critics couldn't help but notice what scouts had known all along. Though his delivery was a bit rough and scruffy, it somehow clicked on a melodic level. Indeed, Kenny always had a knack for knowing which pitch to select.

The hits kept coming for the double superstar—enough to keep him on the airwaves, but never so many that he lost his position on the Rangers' staff. Such a hefty load of achievements would be more than enough for any average man, but this non-average megastar was still starving for more, which is why in 1991 he branched out to form "Kenny Rogers' Chicken Roasters."

At the time, it seemed incredibly risky to foist the notion of an affordable wood-fired rotisserie chicken combo platter onto the taste buds of the American public, but no one had any luck trying to tell *that* to the man known worldwide as "The Gambler."

Well, his amazing gamble worked, and 1995 proved to be a crowning year for the crooner/hurler/chicken purveyor. His moist and flavorful poultry was everywhere, his classic country songs were being broadcast on mainstream stations, and for the very first time, he found himself invited to baseball's All-Star game. Not since the "We Are the World" taping ten years prior had Kenny had so much goodness heaped onto his plate.

After the '95 season, he signed a lucrative free agent contract with the New York Yankees. The world was Kenny's oyster, and he was more than prepared to shuck it.

But even mega-legends have their setbacks. In the Big Apple, while toiling so far away from his country roots, Kenny's productivity declined, though even an off year from Kenny Rogers had significant value. He managed to be part of the winning equation that brought the Yankees their first world championship in eighteen years. The great ones always rub their greatness off onto others. It's what they do.

But as hard as the climb to the top of the mountain can be, it can be an even more difficult fall. During the tail end of his Yankee run, Kenny's chicken sales plummeted, fewer gravelly voiced singers took over the airwaves, and New York City proved to be a worse cultural fit for him than it had been for Joe Buck in *Midnight Cowboy*.

But hope beckoned to the country superstar—for in 1997, a young general manager by the name of Billy Beane made his very first trade, bringing Kenny Rogers to the Oakland A's.

The change of scenery did the Gambler a world of good. He posted a 16-win season and shaved nearly two runs off his ERA. Folks began counting Beane as a genius. One could say that Kenny Rogers had been the first to put the money into moneyball.

Emboldened by Kenny's rise up the depth charts, Beane turned around and swapped him to the Mets in the middle of the 1999 campaign for less expensive players. The Gambler found himself back in the Big Apple, but this time he was at Shea Stadium—the only major league park situated on an island in the streams. With Kenny aboard, the Mets made the postseason for the first time in eleven seasons. Thank you, Kenny Rogers.

But 1999 was also special for it saw the release of the hit song "The Greatest," a folksy tune about a boy's interpretation of life as seen through his love of baseball. Never before had the heralded hurler/crooner so brilliantly blended his two professions.

On the dawn of the new millennium, the relatively aged Kenny Rogers was still far from retirement. The year 2000 not only brought him yet another number one record but a second run with the Texas Rangers. Indeed, the old dog was still teaching others his new tricks. Throughout the decade, high-profile appearances continued to dot Kenny's calendar, whether it involved appearances at the Country Music Awards or during his run-free postseason pitching streaks for both the Minnesota Twins in 2003 and the Detroit Tigers in 2006.

Nowadays, Kenny is largely out of the limelight. However, one can never count out for long a man of his supreme caliber. It wouldn't surprise anyone if he were to still go on to somehow master a fourth profession. After all, it's what we always expect of the great ones.

Follies Factoids

★ Kenny Rogers retired as the Texas Rangers' all-time leader in games pitched.

★ In 2008, though he was the oldest pitcher in the American League, Kenny Rogers pitched 23 consecutive scoreless postseason innings for the Detroit Tigers. However, controversy arose when television cameras picked up a noticeable smudge on Kenny's hand during this streak. Although never proven, Yellowstone Ritter has suggested that the foreign substance could have easily been grease from a rotisserie chicken.

★ Though very few Kenny Rogers' chicken roaster restaurants remain open in the USA, numerous franchises continue to prosper in the Phillipines and in Malaysia.

31

Willie Mays and Me

ou might be surprised to know that baseball wasn't a huge part of my early childhood. Though my family lived only about forty-five miles from Pittsburgh, attending games at Forbes Field was never that much of a priority.

In 1955, the Fingers family left Ohio and moved out to Southern California. I guess you could say my parents had the same idea Walter O'Malley had—only three years earlier.

When his Los Angeles Dodgers debuted in 1958, my dad took me out to ballgames at the LA Coliseum. In short order, the men in blue became my heroes. We were even there for some of the original moon shots (courtesy of Wally Moon) over that forty-foot screen in left field.

For some reason, the most exciting Dodger games were always against the San Francisco Giants. I hated that team with an orange-hot passion. However, the Giants had one player who I couldn't boo no matter how hard I tried, and that was Willie Mays.

Whether he was in center field, at home plate, or on the bases, he was the most riveting player I had ever seen. Watching Willie take a pitch was more exciting than watching anyone else swing. Of course, I always hated to see my favorite team lose, but when it was Willie Mays who did the damage, at least it seemed fair.

In 1962, the Dodgers moved into their new stadium in Chavez Ravine. It was a vast improvement over the old place, and I'm not just saying that because the left field fence was *more* than 250 feet away from the plate.

After one game, I was in the parking lot with a bunch of other teenagers shagging autographs when off in the distance something electric caught my eye. Could it be? Yes! It was Willie Mays, in street clothes, getting ready to leave.

Before my brain could react, my legs broke into a sprint that would have made Maury Wills proud. Zigzagging in between a number of cars (some of which were parked), I caught up to the legend, instantly composed myself, and breathlessly asked for his signature.

The Dodger cap on my head didn't seem to bother him because he scribbled an autograph for me. Willie couldn't have known at the time that he was signing for a kid who would become the last person in history to ever strike him out.

Eleven years later, I was handed the ball in Game One of the 1973 World Series. The A's had a slim one-run lead over the visiting New York Mets, and it was my job to protect it. I did okay and managed to work my way through the first eight hitters without giving up a run.

But at that point, Willie Mays came to the plate. It was an incredibly surreal sight. I found myself shaking my head a little even though Ray Fosse, my catcher, had yet to throw down any fingers. Willie looked a lot older than he'd been in that Dodger parking lot, but my respect for him had only increased with age. I took a deep breath, stared beyond the legend into Fosse's mitt, and began serving up my best.

Eventually, I had two strikes on him. It was crunch time. I took another deep breath, dropped one in, and struck him out looking. Watching Willie take that pitch was more exciting than watching anyone else swing and miss.

The next day he got another crack at me. Baseball is filled with such chances for redemption.

We were all tied up in the top of the twelfth inning, and the Mets were threatening with runners on first and third. With two outs, Willie came to the plate.

The nearly fifty thousand fans at the Oakland Coliseum were on the edge of their seats. More than anything, they wanted another strikeout. However, some in the crowd, especially the ones with Giants caps, wanted to see Willie get one last hurrah...so sentimental were they for the Bay Area legend. Not me. I wanted the strikeout!

Yet again, I stared past the legend into Ray Fosse's mitt and threw my best. But this time, Willie masterfully roped my out pitch into centerfield, knocking in what ended up being the winning run of Game Two.

After I gave up another single to the next batter, Dick Williams had seen enough and called for the pen. The forty-two-year old "Say Hey Kid" had not only beaten me, he had helped knock me out of a World Series game.

Even though I was disappointed as hell, the respect and admiration I felt for this giant only increased with the event. It sure wasn't any fun getting beaten by Willie Mays, but at least it seemed fair.

Right after that World Series, Willie hung up his cleats for good. As it turned out, I became the final pitcher that he reached base against, had an RBI against, and struck out against.

Who knows? Had he not signed that autograph for me back in '62, maybe he would have gotten his last HBP off of me as well.

Just kidding. No way would I ever hit Willie.

Follies Factoids

★ Initially, Dodger Stadium hosted *both* American and National League games since the Angels played there from 1962 to 1965 while the "Big A" in Anaheim was being constructed.

★ Willie Mays' final All-Star Game (in 1973) also happened to be Rollie Fingers' first.

★ The Oakland A's came back from a 3-2 game deficit in that 1973 World Series to defeat the Mets.

32

The Top AAA Cities

◇◇◇

In 1946, baseball's minor league farm system took a forward leap with a simple reclassification. Instantly, twenty-four teams calibrated up to the designation of Triple-A, the "new" highest level of minor league baseball. But Triple-A baseball back then was a bit different than it is today.

Stockpiling was common. Talented players could spend years languishing behind an established star in the bigs with little hope of being moved to another team. It wasn't uncommon for the average age of a Triple-A player to be in the vicinity of twenty-nine or thirty years old.

Also, minor leagues were still a relatively new concept and not every ballclub placed great emphasis on them. Back in '46, neither the Phillies nor Senators even had a Triple-A team. By contrast, powerhouses such as the Cardinals, Dodgers, Giants, and Yankees each had two.

But not every Triple-A team back in those days was even affiliated with a major league parent. A few ballclubs, such as those in Oakland and Seattle, developed players independently until they were ripe enough to open up a bidding market. Yet, they were always careful to keep a few key players for themselves to keep their gate revenues alive.

Among the twenty-four original host cities at the AAA level, eleven would field major league baseball before the end of the century (through expansion or relocation). Four of the other cities (Hollywood, Jersey City, Newark and St. Paul) currently have major league baseball within easy driving distance.

As for all the other originals, they remain in Triple-A to this day. These bulkheads have played a critical role in upgrading the quality of baseball.

However, among these nine anchors, only Indianapolis and Rochester hold the distinction of having fielded a Triple-A team each and every year since 1946.

The Hoosier State is proud of the Indianapolis Indians. It's a popular misconception that these Indians have only had a hand in developing players for Cleveland (because of their shared nickname). In reality, this storied Triple-A ballclub has been linked with eight major league organizations, with the Cincinnati Reds (twenty-four seasons) having been their most frequent affiliation.

The legacy of the Indianapolis Indians dates back to 1902. Those who once wore Indian red and black include Grover Cleveland Alexander, Nap Lajoie, Roger Maris, Harmon Killebrew, Randy Johnson, both Bret and Aaron Boone, Bob Uecker, and a great number of the cogs that went into Cincinnati's Big Red Machine during the 1970s.

The Indians now play their home games at Victory Field, a facility that many consider to be the finest Triple-A stadium ever built. It's no wonder that the club has had numerous years in which they were able to draw in excess of 600,000 fans.

Baseball's roots run deep in Indiana, but the one minor league city with even deeper roots is located in Rochester, New York. The Red Wings franchise dates back to 1899, and no other team at their level has posted as many league championships.

Perhaps the most popular man in Rochester's history is Joe Altobelli, who is best known nationally for being the manager of the 1983 World Champion Baltimore Orioles. Altobelli spent years managing the Red Wings prior to being called up to the big leagues as a skipper. He even chose to return to Rochester to broadcast games after his big league managerial career wound down.

But Altobelli was but one of Rochester's heroes. Stan Musial, Bob Gibson, Frank Robinson, Cal Ripken Jr., Curt Schilling, and Joe Mauer have all been wildly cheered at one time or another by the rabid rooters of Rochester.

Today, Triple-A baseball has thirty teams, all of whom have a distinct relationship with just one major league club, and the sport at this high level continues to thrive. Teams in Sacramento, Round Rock, Louisville, Pawtucket, and Buffalo all regularly draw crowds in excess of 9,000. The popularity of Triple-A ball is such that there is now a team just thirty-five miles away from Atlanta's Turner Field that has managed to become an attraction unto itself.

Indeed, since 1946, the Triple-A leagues have been places of incubation for the bulk of major league talent. We salute all the cities, especially the ones that carried the bulk of the load.

THE TOP 40 TRIPLE-A STRONGHOLDS FROM 1946 TO 2010
(WITH ACTIVE CITIES IN CAPITAL LETTERS)

INDIANAPOLIS, IN	65 seasons
ROCHESTER, NY	65
SYRACUSE, NY	60
COLUMBUS, OH	58
TOLEDO, OH	55
Richmond, VA	54
BUFFALO, NY	51
LOUISVILLE, KY	51
TACOMA, WA	51
OMAHA, NE	49
PORTLAND, OR	47
OKLAHOMA CITY, OK	43
DES MOINES, IA	42
Tucson, AZ	40
SALT LAKE CITY, UT	40
Denver, CO	38
PAWTUCKET, RI	38
ALBUQUERQUE, NM	37
Phoenix, AZ	34
Vancouver, BC	32
LAS VEGAS, NV	28
NASHVILLE, TN	26
Edmonton, ALB	24
Honolulu, HI	24
Spokane, WA	24
Tidewater, VA	24
Charleston, SC	23
COL. SPRINGS, CO	23
SACRAMENTO, CA	23
Toronto, ONT	22
SCRANTON, PA	22
NEW ORLEANS, LA	19
Ottawa, ONT	19
Calgary, ALB	18
CHARLOTTE, NC	18
NORFOLK, VA	18
Wichita, KS	18
San Diego, CA	17
Seattle, WA	17
MEMPHIS, TN	16

Follies Factoids

★ Aside from the thirty Triple-A teams in America, there are sixteen independent ballclubs in the Mexican League that are considered part of Triple-A baseball.

★ Similar to the NFL's Green Bay Packers, both the Rochester Red Wings and Indianapolis Indians are publicly held teams owned by their fans.

★ Despite a rich legacy of hosting Triple-A teams, the nation of Canada no longer hosts a single one.

★ The Triple-A markets of Portland, Sacramento, Las Vegas, Columbus, Indianapolis, Charlotte, Norfolk, Round Rock, Pawtucket, and Nashville all have greater population bases than the major league city of Milwaukee.

★ Triple-A teams that managed to reach the hundred-win mark include the 1946 Montreal Royals (w/ Jackie Robinson), the 1952 Milwaukee Brewers (w/ Gene Mauch), and the 1960 Toronto Maple Leafs (w/ Sparky Anderson and Chuck Tanner).

★ The newest Triple-A cities include Reno, NV, Round Rock, TX, (near Austin) and Allentown, PA.

★ The three most populated areas in the United States that are more than one hundred miles away from either major league or Triple-A baseball are Orlando, San Antonio, and Jacksonville.

★ Many historians consider the 1981 Albuquerque Dukes to be the best Triple-A team of all time. Their players included top Dodger farmhands Candy Maldonado, Mike Marshall, and Alejandro Pena.

33

La Russa and Leyland

◇◇◇

When most baseball fans hear the names of Jim Leyland and Tony La Russa, they rarely think of them in tandem. However, history shows that these two legendary skippers have had a knack for crossing paths.

Even though they were both born in 1944, they started out separately enough. Tony's debut occurred in Tampa, Florida, whereas the first dugout Jimmy emerged from was in a suburb of Toledo, Ohio.

As high school athletes, they both displayed skills far beyond their peers. However, it was Tony's ticket that got punched first. On the day he graduated from high school in 1962, he was drafted by the Kansas City Athletics as a middle infielder.

The next year proved to be memorable for both young men. The Detroit Tigers drafted Jimmy (as a catcher) while Tony made it all the way to the major leagues by season's end. The world was Tony's rose, but with the offseason came a terrible misfortune. During a softball game, he suffered a shoulder injury so severe that it permanently affected his play. When spring training concluded before following season, the diminished athlete found himself back in the minor leagues.

From 1964 to 1967, both Tony and Jim toiled exclusively in the minors. It was in '67 that they first crossed paths, as opposing players in the Southern League.

Jimmy's team, the Montgomery Rebels, was a good one and included a number of future major leaguers, such as Dick Drago. However, Tony's team, the Birmingham A's were even better. Their roster boasted Dave Duncan,

Reggie Jackson, Joe Rudi, and a young clean-shaven starter by the name of
Rollie Fingers. When all was said and done, these swingin' A's finished in first
place, three and a half games ahead of Jimmy's Rebels.

By 1968, Tony earned himself a second break and was called back up to
the parent club—who by that point had relocated to that other city by the
bay. Although he was limited to three at-bats with Oakland that season, it
was still great for Tony to be back at the top level, if only for the proverbial
cup of coffee.

Jimmy spent '68 playing yet another year of Class AA ball in Montgomery. He saw more playing time behind the plate, but his batting average,
never impressive, dipped below .200. The following year, he was demoted
and spent the majority of the season in Florida at Class A Lakeland.

In 1969 Tony managed eight more at-bats with Oakland, but he failed
to reach first base. Even so, it was apparent that this utility infielder was of
major league caliber, and in 1970 Tony stayed on Oakland's roster for the

entire season. Backing up second baseman Dick Green, he played in fifty-two games and hit .188 (a batting average 62 points lower than what he had posted before suffering his shoulder injury). But for Jimmy, 1970 was the end of a road. He was given his release. All told, across his seven seasons in the minors, he had only compiled a .222 batting average.

But there was a silver lining for Jimmy Leyland, as the organization gave him the chance to stay with the Rebels as a coach. This opportunity proved to be Leyland's second calling. He impressed the brass so much that in 1971, he was named to his first post as manager. The lucky team was the Bristol Tigers in the Appalachian Rookie League, and it marked the first of eleven consecutive seasons as a skipper for the Tiger organization.

For Tony La Russa, 1971 was also a year of transition. The A's had become formidable, and the chances of making the playoffs (for the first time in decades) were good. But in August, owner Charles Finley, looking for cash, sold Tony's contract to the Atlanta Braves.

It was a fresh start. Once again, he was in a clubhouse surrounded by future Hall of Famers (Henry Aaron, Phil Niekro, and Orlando Cepeda). But despite this team's relative mediocrity, Tony only managed to get seven at-bats during the final two months of the season. He could only watch on television as his former teammates clashed with Baltimore in October's ALCS.

In '72, Tony failed to make the Braves out of spring training and had to spend yet another year in the minors. Then, after the season's conclusion, the Braves swapped him to the Cubs organization.

It was yet another fresh start. With his trademark tenacity, he made the Cubs team—but his achievement was short-lived. After a solitary stint as a pinch runner, they sent him back to the minors. Tony didn't realize at the time that he had played his final major league game.

Few ever do.

Conversely, 1973 was a pretty good year for Leyland. After guiding his Class A team to a .589 winning percentage, he was promoted to manage in his old stomping grounds in Montgomery, Alabama. The student had become the teacher.

From 1973 to 1977, Tony bounced around AAA, playing for four clubs in five cities. There was simply no quit in him. Scrappy and inquisitive, he kept playing with the hope that he would one day be back in the Show.

As for Leyland, his managerial reputation caught fire when his Lakeland ballclub won the league championship in '76. The following year, his new squad won the championship as well, and their skipper was singled out as the league's "manager of the year." It would be the first of many such awards for the young prodigy.

In 1977 at the ripe old age of thirty-two, Tony La Russa was cut loose by the Cardinal organization. As a player, he was officially finished. All told, in the fifteen years since he'd been drafted, he had started forty major league games, was a replacement in ninety-two others, and had compiled a lifetime major league batting average of .199.

But though his glove had been hung up, La Russa's future was bright. He was not only spending part of his offseasons attaining a juris doctor degree, but there were those high up in baseball who thought he had managerial potential.

In 1978 Leyland and La Russa each filled out lineup cards. Leyland continued to mentor at Class A Lakeland while La Russa made his managerial debut a full level higher for the Knoxville Sox. By the end of that season, Leyland crowded his mantle by taking home yet another managerial award.

La Russa also did quite well as his team posted the best record in the Southern League. However, he was only around for the beginning of Knoxville's success because his organization promoted him to Chicago in midseason to become a major league coach—though he was only thirty-three years old.

Leyland and La Russa hadn't crossed paths since their playing days in '67, but their time apart ended during the '79 season.

Jim Leyland had received a huge promotion as the Tigers jumped him two levels to manage their Class AAA team in Evansville, Indiana. As for Tony La Russa, he became an odd man out when the White Sox fired his boss, manager Larry Doby. However, La Russa landed on his feet when the organization reassigned him to manage their Class AAA club in Des Moines.

Who could have guessed at the time, that these two thirty-four-year-old Class AAA managers would oppose one another twenty-seven years later in a World Series? No one. But in 1979, they were pitted against each other at ballpark chess whenever the Evansville Triplets battled the Iowa Oaks.

Leyland's arsenal of Hoosiers included Jack Morris, future manager Jerry Manuel, and a college football player with a bum knee by the name of Kirk Gibson. La Russa's troop of Hawkeyes included aces LaMarr Hoyt, Britt Burns, and a young hitter by the name of Harold Baines.

Both ballclubs posted winning records, but it was Leyland's team that took the trophy, and the skipper received his third consecutive manager-of-the-year award. But despite Leyland's success, Tony La Russa may have actually had the better year.

First of all, he passed the Florida state bar exam—quite an achievement. Then, for the second season in a row, he was promoted in midseason to work at Comiskey Field. This time, however, the White Sox didn't hire him as a coach—they hired him as their manager. La Russa finished the final fifty-four games of the '79 season, and though the White Sox weren't very good when he arrived, they played .500 ball for him the rest of the way. Then, over the next couple seasons, La Russa helped mold them into contenders.

Leyland, however, remained in Class AAA, log-jammed behind manager Sparky Anderson at the major league level. But in 1982, the dam broke when Leyland was passed over by Captain Hook for an opening as a major league coach. Tony La Russa, however, didn't blink when presented with that same opportunity and promptly hired Leyland away to become one of his coaches.

After eighteen seasons in the Tiger's minor league system as a player, coach, and manager, Leyland had finally reached the major league level. The tandem of La Russa and Leyland would spend the next four seasons together in the same dugout.

By 1983, the Chisox were dominating the American League. Under La Russa (and, to an extent, Leyland) the ballclub won ninety-nine games. Their players included Carlton Fisk, Ron Kittle, Greg Luzinski, and speedy Rudy Law. LaMarr Hoyt and Richard Dotson both won over 20 and even Jerry Koosman from the 1969 Mets made significant contributions. Though the Baltimore Orioles defeated them in the ALCS, it still had to be sweet for La Russa and Leyland to finally taste a major league postseason.

In 1985 Jim Leyland debuted as a big league manager when his boss was forced to serve a two-game suspension. This short stint did nothing to slow the rumors that the forty-year-old Leyland would make a great big league skipper in another city. The White Sox finished the year a respectable six games out of first place, but few knew at the time that their time as a front-line team was nearly over.

During the off-season, Jim Leyland became the manager of the Pittsburgh Pirates, a woeful team coming off a year in which they lost 104 games. Leyland was expected to repeat the same managerial magic that had warranted his stellar reputation.

As for the suddenly Leyland-less White Sox, they got off to a terrible 26-38 start, and Tony La Russa, quite improbably, found himself out of a job. But he wasn't unemployed for long. Within three weeks, the Oakland A's removed their manager and snapped up La Russa instead.

At the end of the '86 season, La Russa's A's finished in third place, two slots ahead of the White Sox. As for Leyland, the Pirates he inherited remained terrible, but under his watch, they improved by seven games. In his second year, they improved by another sixteen games and managed a second-place finish.

Both La Russa's A's and Leyland's Pirates steadily improved until, in 1988, La Russa guided his team to the first of what would be three consecutive pennants. In 1989, Oakland won its first World Series since the glory days of the '72-'74 dynasty. He reached the same pinnacle that so many of his former teammates back in Birmingham had gone on to experience.

But 1989 was not as sweet for Leyland. The Pirates had endured a set-back season, but success was just around the corner.

In 1990, both the A's and the Pirates took division titles (this feat was all the more remarkable at the time since there were only four playoff spots). That postseason, it became conceivable that Leyland and La Russa could collide in the World Series. However, the Cincinnati Reds played the part of spoiler by downing Leyland's Pirates in the NLCS (before going on to sweep La Russa's squad in the World Series).

The Pirates made it back to the postseason in 1991, but that year the A's finally fell from their perch.

In 1992, both La Russa and Leyland guided their teams to first-place finishes and both were chosen Manager of the Year in their leagues. But neither man could get his team out of the first round of the playoffs.

From 1993 to 1995, the Pirates and A's continued to mirror each other as they both slipped further and further from prominence. Finally, at the end of the '95 season, La Russa cleaned out his office at the Oakland Coliseum.

After nearly ten full seasons as their manager (and parts of four as a player), he was finished with the A's. But once again, he couldn't stay a free agent for long as the St. Louis Cardinals quickly snapped him up. Once again, he was managing for an organization that he had played for in the minors, and once again, he was managing head-to-head against Jimmy Leyland.

During his initial season managing in the National League, La Russa and his revitalized Cardinal team made it all the way to the NLCS. As for Leyland's Pirates, they skidded to a last-place finish. After eleven seasons in Pittsburgh, Leyland left and began looking for a franchise that was interested in fielding a contender. In short order, he found himself as the new skipper of the free-spending Florida Marlins.

In 1997 La Russa's Cardinals devolved into a fourth-place team, whereas Leyland guided his new franchise to their first playoff berth. It was an especially sweet achievement for Leyland, but on the eve of the postseason, he knew his real work was cut out for him. To win a world championship, he had to manage his Marlins past three strong teams. And that's what he did. He became a World Champion.

From 1998 to 2005, La Russa and Leyland took diverse paths.

La Russa stayed on as the Cardinals manager and guided them to six post-season appearances in eight seasons. Leyland walked away from managing after the '99 season to smell the roses. But he didn't really walk completely away, for in his adopted hometown of Pittsburgh he attended nearly every Pirate home game where he created scouting reports for La Russa's Cardinals.

Semi-retirement suited Leyland. He had made a lot of money managing the Marlins in '97 and '98 and the Colorado Rockies in 1999. But even so, after six seasons as a scout, he once again got the itch to manage. Of course, more than a few suitors lined up to attract his services.

In 2006, the Detroit Tigers, his original organization, hired him as their commander-in-chief—a mere forty-three years after they had drafted him as a player. At the time of his hiring, the Tigers had posted thirteen consecutive losing seasons.

Leyland quickly set about to turn the tide just as he had for so many prior teams, and once again his magic worked. The Detroit Tigers became a playoff team in his first season back.

In the senior league, Tony La Russa also tasted postseason success that year. As the playoffs began, both Tony and Jim found themselves wanting a second world championship more than anything.

Leyland's Tigers had little trouble handling the Yankees in the first round, defeating them in four consecutive games. La Russa's Redbirds took apart the San Diego Padres with similar ease. Only one more round of play-off action separated the former Montgomery Rebel / Evanston Triplet from the former Birmingham A / Iowa Oak. Old rivalries die hard.

In the American League Championship Series, the Tigers made short work of the Oakland A's, sweeping them in four games. The Tigers looked unstoppable.

As for the Cardinals, they fought the New York Mets for seven games and emerged victorious.

The stage was set for a modern showdown between Ty Cobb's old team and Stan Musial's, as well as a repeat of the 1968 Series.

Leyland's Tigers came into that Series with six days of rest/rust while the Cardinals entered the arena freshly banged up from their grueling series with the Mets.

Leyland and La Russa were once again playing ballpark chess—only this time, it was for ultimate stakes.

After two games, each team had a victory.

Everyone's focus sharpened up a wee bit more. Game Three saw the tide turn with St. Louis engineering a 5-0, three-hit shutout...and the Redbirds never lost again that year.

If it had to be someone else winning it all, Jimmy Leyland was glad it was his old friend and even older rival, Tony La Russa.

Follies Factoids

★ Tony La Russa's most frequent All-Star players over the years have been Albert Pujols, Mark McGwire, Jose Canseco, Dennis Eckersley, Scott Rolen, Carlton Fisk, Edgar Renteria, and Terry Steinbach.

★ Mark McGwire spent fifteen of his sixteen major league seasons playing for Tony La Russa.

★ La Russa's longtime pitching coach, Dave Duncan, has been part of five All-Star games, four as a coach and one as a catcher.

★ Jim Leyland's most frequent All-Star players over the years have been Bobby Bonilla, Andy Van Slyke, Barry Bonds, Carlos Guillen, Magglio Ordonez, Ivan Rodriguez, and Justin Verlander.

★ During Leyland's stint as an advance scout for the St. Louis Cardinals, he often attended games with former A's and Pirates manager Chuck Tanner.

★ Early in his career, Tony La Russa asked Chuck Tanner's advice on managing, to which Tanner succinctly replied "Always rent."

★ Tanner's advice turned out to be not entirely appropriate. La Russa's run as White Sox manager exceeded seven years, his Oakland stint exceeded nine years, and he is in his fifteenth year in St. Louis.

34

A Most Unusual Interview With Rollie Fingers

As conducted by Yellowstone Ritter

◇◇◇

Whenever Hall of Famer Rollie Fingers is interviewed,
he is almost always asked about, quite predictably,
the following FIVE subjects:

1) his famous handlebar moustache

2) his run with the Oakland A's in which they won three consecutive world championships

3) the stormy relationship he and his teammates had with spend-
thrift owner Charlie Finley.

4) his run with the
pennant-winning Milwaukee Brewers

AND

5) how the workhorse closers of his era were different from the
ninth-inning closers of today.

Since Rollie has been asked about these topics a few hundred times apiece, I've given myself the brutal challenge of conducting an interview with the legendary hurler without **EVEN ONCE** bringing up any of these FIVE easy subjects.

Instead, I've created a list of original questions that I've never heard anyone else ask him. An interview with Rollie Fingers in which the journalist never mentions relief pitching, the Brewers, the A's, Charlie O or the world-famous moustache???
Yep, you bet!

.....without further adieu.....

YR: Rollie, you were born in Steubenville, Ohio. As a kid, what were your favorite things to do there?

ROLLIE: As far as Steubenville goes, I actually grew up about eight miles north in a small town called Toronto. I enjoyed going to school, riding my bike, throwing snowballs, and waiting for baseball season to start. When you're a kid in a small town in the Ohio Valley everything is fun.

YR: So your childhood was a fairly athletic one?

ROLLIE: I was always throwing a baseball around either with my dad or my brother, who was two years younger than me. I played two years of Little League there before we moved to Southern California.

YR: Your hometown in Ohio was only about forty-five miles from Pittsburgh. Did you ever attend any games at Forbes Field?

ROLLIE: We went once or twice, but I never got into being a Pirate fan. I did collect baseball cards in the early 1950s but lost them all since I stuck them to the wheels of my bike to make it sound like a motorcycle. I probably had a '51 Mantle in the mix without even knowing it. That's a pretty expensive bike right now. Maybe that's why I hate motorcycles to this day.

YR: (laughs) Did you get to see any other major league ballparks before you signed professionally?

ROLLIE: I saw a lot of Dodger games as a teenager, first at the Coliseum and then at Dodger Stadium when it opened in '62. I also went to a couple Angel games. Other than Municipal Stadium in KC, I never saw any other big league parks until I got to the majors in '68. Walking onto the fields in Fenway and Yankee Stadium was something special, and pitching my first games there was even better!

YR: What brought you to Municipal Stadium in Kansas City?

ROLLIE: I was heading back home to California after pitching my first season of minor league ball in Florida. KC was the parent club for the A's at the time, and they invited me to join the ballclub for the last two weeks of the season. I wasn't on the roster, but I was in uniform for batting practice and infield practice, and then I sat in the stands during the games. It was just nice being in a big league park and in the clubhouse. Coming from Leesburg, Florida, it didn't get any better than that.

YR: Do you remember any game in particular?

ROLLIE: It just so happened that I was there when Charlie Finley activated Satchel Paige to start a game. I met Satchel in the dugout and then watched him pitch three shutout innings against the Red Sox that day. Unbelievable.

YR: He was fifty-nine years old at the time.

ROLLIE: That made him forty-one years older than me. He did pretty well though.

YR: Going back to your high school days, at what point did you realize that you had a shot to play in the majors?

ROLLIE: I never thought I was good enough until my junior year. A scout came up to me after seeing me pitch an American Legion game and asked me if I ever thought about playing ball professionally. I told him I hadn't up until that very moment.

YR: Did your focus narrow at that point?

ROLLIE: Sure, when a scout thinks you're good, then you try that much harder to improve, and that's what I did. My senior year, I started doing really well. I played for the Dodger rookies that summer and Tommy Lasorda wanted to sign me. But even though they were my favorite team and all, I went elsewhere.

YR: Were the Dodger pitchers big role models for you?

ROLLIE: Sandy Koufax and Don Drysdale could do no wrong in my eyes. I listened to Vin Scully and Jerry Doggett every night with my radio under my pillow. It didn't get any better than that.

YR: What kept you from signing with the Dodger organization?

ROLLIE: They actually offered the best signing bonus, but I thought my chances of getting to the majors would be better with an organization that didn't have their depth. All the way through at every level, the Dodgers were stockpiling players.

YR: You were also scouted as an outfielder, weren't you?

ROLLIE: Yeah, I played in the outfield whenever I wasn't pitching. A lot of scouts were after me—they just didn't know whether it was for my arm or for my bat. I had just led the nation in hitting for Legion Ball, and then I also pitched and won the final game of the 1964 American Legion World Series in Little Rock, Arkansas.

YR: So, did the A's sign you as a double threat?

ROLLIE: Sort of. They didn't know what to do with me when I got to training camp. I hit over .300 there, but I also pitched several shutout innings. Someone high up decided that I would be better as a pitcher, and it wasn't my choice. Looking back, I think I went the right way.

YR: I'll say. What part did your dad have in your success?

ROLLIE: My dad was a huge influence. I learned my body mechanics from him at a very young age, and he definitely knew what he was talking about. When he was young, he had been signed by the Cardinals organization and one of his roommates in the minors was Stan Musial. This was back when Stan was a pitcher. There are so many young pitchers that lack the proper mechanics, and it leads to their arms breaking down.

YR: Did your father also impart life lessons he learned from his time as a ballplayer?

ROLLIE: Sure. My dad actually had to quit baseball because he broke his back playing football in the offseason. So, when my high school football coach wanted me to join the team my dad said no.

YR: Was the football coach mostly interested in your arm?

ROLLIE: He tried to recruit me to either play quarterback or tight end.

YR: At 6'4", the basketball coach at Upland High must have wanted you on his team as well, right?

ROLLIE: Well, I did play varsity basketball there for two years. I even played later at the local junior college but had to quit when the A's signed me.

YR: You spent 1965 playing for the Leesburg ballclub just outside of Orlando. You were their workhorse and averaged seven innings per game.

ROLLIE: It built up my arm strength. If I had come along nowadays, they would probably have placed me under "Rollie Rules" and limited my pitch counts. I might have never seen the majors.

YR: Tell me about 1966 when you were promoted to Modesto in the California League.

ROLLIE: We had a pretty good ballclub there. Dave Duncan socked forty-six homers for us, and Joe Rudi and Reggie Jackson were there as well. Tony La Russa was our second baseman. We finished in first place.

YR: I bet. That team was the nucleus for your future championship teams.

ROLLIE: That was also the year that Duncan, Rudi, and myself all joined the Army Reserves.

YR: How did that come about?

ROLLIE: The war in Vietnam was escalating, and guys our age were getting drafted left and right. Charlie Finley found three open spots with the Army Reserves in Mobile, Alabama, and flew us down there to enlist.

YR: What was your experience in the military like?

ROLLIE: I served off and on for six years. It took up a lot of my time when I wasn't playing baseball. We had to do two weeks summer duty each year and make meetings once a month. I did my basic training at Fort Dix in New Jersey with snow up to my knees (laughs).

YR: What activities took up most of your time in the military?

ROLLIE: There was a lot of running, marching, KP duty, pushups, obstacle courses, and the like. I was working in gas chambers from time to time. They were always giving us special training of one kind or another.

YR: They were training you for life-and-death situations?

ROLLIE: Right.

YR: What ended up becoming your specialty in the Army? In their eyes, how did they ultimately see you?

ROLLIE: Well, they made me a typist.

YR: But a great typist, right?

ROLLIE: Oh, absolutely. I could bang out a hundred words a minute, in triplicate, on those old manual typewriters. I had taken some typing courses in high school, and it all carried over. Once again, it all comes down to good body mechanics.

YR: (laughs) Did your time in the Army Reserves have a big influence on you?

ROLLIE: Well, it made me more organized. Everyone in my outfit lived to get weekend passes, but those didn't happen unless everything was as clean as a whistle. You had to make your bed so tight that a quarter could bounce off of it. Were you ever in the military?

YR: No, but I did see *Stripes* about six times. In 1967, the A's promoted you to Double-A Birmingham. I believe you were even chosen as their Opening Night starter. But something horrible happened. Tell me about it.

ROLLIE: Yeah, Duncan was actually behind the plate when it all went down. The batter rocketed the pitch back up the middle and it hit me square in the face. That ball had to be going a hundred miles an hour. I lost my vision for five hours, my cheekbone was shattered, my jaw was broken, and I had to have my teeth wired together for two months. It wasn't a whole lot of fun. It ended up being about ten weeks before I could play baseball again. Even to this day, I have permanent wiring in my face from that incident.

YR: Rollie, is baseball a contact sport?

ROLLIE: (laughs) No, of course not. That's ridiculous. Football is the only contact sport. Seriously though, I was just glad that my vision returned to normal, as that would have been the end of my career. I was also thankful that the ball knocked me in the head and missed hitting a vital part of my body, you know...like my right arm.

YR: Yes, thank goodness. What was it like not being able to eat solid food for ten weeks with your jaw wired shut?

ROLLIE: I got a blender and was drinking everything through a straw for a while. My weight went from 204 all the way down to 168.

YR: Wow, someone should knock me in the face with a baseball, especially around the holidays. Seriously though, you must have had incredible cravings for solid food.

ROLLIE: Oh, yeah. Once in a while, I'd get food from McDonalds and kind of shove it through the slot in my mouth and push it back underneath my teeth. For me, that constituted a "Happy Meal."

YR: (laughs) Did this accident affect your pitching?

ROLLIE: Well, I learned to better protect myself after every pitch. My follow-through improved, and my reflexes may have even sharpened up a bit because of it.

YR: You finished that season with a 2.21 ERA, so it seems that despite the injury, your stock stayed high with the organization. When did you know that you were going to get called up to the majors?

ROLLIE: I never knew for sure I would get there. Promotions are always a surprise. What happened was that I pitched a second season in Double-A with Birmingham and did well enough to get a late September callup in '68. Then, I got an invitation to spring training camp in '69. They started me in a game against the Angels in Palm Springs and I threw seven scoreless innings. Afterward they came up to me and said "You made the ballclub."

YR: What a great feeling that must have been.

ROLLIE: You could say that. What ended up helping me is that this was the year that the Seattle Pilots and Kansas City Royals came to be. The A's didn't protect a couple players, and they got taken away in the expansion draft and it created an opening for me.

YR: That's interesting. What were your thoughts when you heard the parent club had moved from Kansas City out to Oakland?

ROLLIE: It wasn't a big deal. I would have been thrilled to play in either place. To me, it was just about getting to the majors. If anything, the more important concern was how the stadium would be there in Oakland.

YR: It sure was a friendly place for pitchers.

ROLLIE: Right. I found out the ball didn't travel far at night, and there was lots of foul territory.

YR: What are your best memories of the Bay Area outside of the games at the Oakland Coliseum.

ROLLIE: You don't really experience how nice the Bay Area is during the season. You're too focused on baseball. But in the offseason I played a lot of golf and went fishing on the Bay for striper once in a while. Crossing the bridge and going to Fisherman's Wharf for dinner was always a lot of fun.

YR: Along with Bender, Guidry, Smoltz, Johnson, you're known as having one of the best sliders in history.

ROLLIE: It comes back to mechanics. Take Randy Johnson. He's always been one of those guys with great mechanics. He proves there's no need for a lot of muscle, and there's that easy fluid motion he has. I never bulked up either. About the heaviest thing I ever lifted was a beer after a game.

YR: (laughs) Instead of hitting the weight room, did you do a lot of track work?

ROLLIE: We all would do the line-to-liners fifteen or twenty times a day, you know, running back and forth between the foul lines. I think the best activity for a pitcher is swimming. It stretches the muscles out and is great for your throwing shoulder.

YR: What was a typical day at spring training like for you?

ROLLIE: I would wake up around 8:30 AM get to the park by 9 and on the field by 9:30. We would do our drills—covering first base, throwing to the bases, and ground balls up the middle and pick-off plays—that sort of stuff. Then we would be the base runners for outfield drills. After drills we would do our running and get ready for the game to start, but we were usually done by 12:30. If you got your work done and weren't pitching that day, you got the rest of the day off. Usually, it was just the pitchers who got that luxury. When that was the case, we would go play golf that afternoon or sit in the stands and watch the game.

YR: What was a typical pre-game routine for a regular season game?

ROLLIE: I'd get to the park maybe three hours before game time, run back and forth between the foul lines fifteen to twenty times, get in some light throwing, shag outfield flies. On the road, I'd probably get to the park four hours early.

YR: What did you hydrate with? Did you prefer sports drinks, water, soda, coffee?

ROLLIE: Mostly water, maybe an occasional soda.

YR: What was the typical diet like for you and your teammates?

ROLLIE: We ate a lot, but we always burned it off. We went through a lot of pizza, pasta, and hamburgers.

YR: Besides eating, what took up most of your time in the clubhouse?

ROLLIE: I played a lot of bridge when I was with the A's. My roommate, Ken Holtzman, and I learned the game and played all the time. We would land in cities and pick up the newspaper and see where there was a bridge tournament going on and then go play with all the old folks. We usually did real well. We were always playing in the clubhouse too. When I went to the Brewers my partner was Ted Simmons, and we taught a few guys to play. We mostly played against Paul Molitor and Bob McClure. That's all we did on the planes and in the clubhouse was play cards.

YR: I interviewed Jim Gantner for the preceding book. Have you ever had a teammate with a better sense of humor than Gantner?

ROLLIE: Gumby was always a trip. He was always coming up with strange sayings, or he would get the meaning of words wrong. We called those Gumbyisms.

YR: Molitor tells the story about how Gumby once got caught in a run-down and how he thought he'd best avoid making an out by steamrolling over the infielder. Right after the collision, Gumby started yelling to the umpire "Construction! Construction!! Construction!!"

ROLLIE: (laughs) Yup, that's Gumby all right. They don't make them any better than Gumby.

YR: Did you play a lot of golf during the season?

ROLLIE: Hardly ever. That was mostly an offseason activity. I never once brought my clubs on the road.

YR: How did your slider come about?

ROLLIE: Well, I didn't have a great curveball and needed a better breaking pitch. After trial and error, the slider came to be. It was like throwing a cut fastball, only I was snapping it off in a way that didn't hurt my arm. It would break four or five inches down and four or five inches away.

YR: So, was it like a slightly faster breaking ball?

ROLLIE: Right, it's thrown with the same arm speed as a fastball but comes in about ten miles per hour slower. A curveball, by contrast, comes in around twenty miles per hour slower.

YR: You very nearly played for Boston, St. Louis, and Cincinnati. Seemingly, you were just never destined to wear red. What happened with the Red Sox?

ROLLIE: Joe Rudi and I were in the Oakland clubhouse one night right before gametime when we received word we had been sold to the Boston Red Sox, who were actually in town playing us. It was shocking. We'd been in Oakland together for over seven years. So Joe and I just cleaned out our lockers and walked across the hall to enemy territory. I found myself at the locker right next to Carl Yastrzemski. But Rudi was nursing an injury and couldn't play in that series. As for me, the Red Sox had me warm up twice, but never brought me in. Then after three days, Bowie Kuhn, the commissioner, stepped in and voided the transaction. So we were forced to return to the A's. Finley was so angry that he didn't play either of us for the longest time out of spite for Kuhn until our A's teammates threatened a mutiny.

YR: It seems that if either Joe Rudi or you had gotten into just one play for the Sox the transaction wouldn't have been reversed.

ROLLIE: Right, I think that's true. Fenway Park would have been my home, and combined with the lineup the Red Sox had in place there at the time, it would have been just fine with me.

YR: Over the course of your career, was there a particular prank you played that stands out?

ROLLIE: Just one?

YR: Well, of the ones that you can talk about in mixed company.

ROLLIE: (laughs) Okay, well, before one game, Ken Holtzman and I were shagging flies during batting practice. We saw that Charlie Finley had come down from his office and was sitting by himself in the A's dugout. That gave us an idea. Instead of throwing our fly balls back in, Holtzy and I started hoarding them in our pockets. After we each had four or five, we put our plan into action. From right field, we skied each baseball rapid fire toward the A's dugout with the intent of giving them as much hang time as possible.

YR: Ray Guy would have been proud.

ROLLIE: Exactly. Right after we chucked the last of them, we broke into a dead sprint over to centerfield, hit the deck and began doing sit-ups. The balls were on target and bombarded down right near Finley, one after the other. He immediately looked out to right field to see who had thrown them, but no one was there for him to blame.

YR: That's brilliant. So, you guys had poker faces during all of this?

ROLLIE: Yep, he never did figure out where those baseballs came from.

YR: (laughs) You went from making about 67K your final year in Oakland to making 250K a year with San Diego not to mention the 500K signing bonus the Padres gave you. Did coming into that kind of money change your life overnight?

ROLLIE: No, the biggest difference was that it gave me peace of mind. I didn't go hog wild and start buying sports cars or anything. I did spend about 190K on a house in the San Diego area that I lived in from '77 to '85 and the rest just sort of got invested.

YR: In the earliest days of free agency, you were one of the biggest. What went down when you hit the market after the '76 season?

ROLLIE: The Pirates and Padres made strong plays for me and some other teams put feelers out. I was surprised the Red Sox didn't chase me, since they had shown interest earlier that year by buying my contract from Oakland.

YR: Why did you go with San Diego?

ROLLIE: The Padres deal came about because the owner, Ray Krok, personally called me with an invitation to come to San Diego for an informal meeting. So my agent and I went down there, and without any small talk whatsoever, Krok opened by saying he wanted to give me 250K per year for five years plus a 500K signing bonus. I said, "Hand me a pen." That was the entire negotiating process.

YR: What are your favorite memories of playing for the Padres?

ROLLIE: The fans were great, the ballpark was beautiful, and there's probably no team that gets better weather than the Padres do. I also liked how it was close enough for my parents to come in and see a lot of the games. Oakland was sort of out of driving range for them.

YR: It's too close to fly to and too far drive to.

ROLLIE: Right.

YR: From '72 through '76, you averaged 21 saves a year for the A's. But with the Padres, you had years where you saved 35 and 37. Why was that?

ROLLIE: It was how the managers used me. Dick Williams and Alvin Dark in Oakland both used a number of guys to close out ballgames. Knowles, Lindblad, Todd, and Locker all got a bunch, but in San Diego, that wasn't the case.

YR: Right around this time, you developed a forkball that became yet another formidable weapon in your arsenal.

ROLLIE: Yeah, well, I needed a changeup since I was becoming less of a hard thrower. The forkball worked great for me because I could locate it well. As you get older, you throw a lot less and pitch a lot more.

YR: During your seasons in San Diego, the Padres never finished higher than third. What could have been done differently?

ROLLIE: It was a good team. We had Dave Winfield and Ozzie Smith and we scored some runs, but not a whole lot of runs. It seemed every season we were out of the running early, and the only thing we had to look forward to was to play spoiler. It was frustrating. I wanted to see the team do better. I thought we needed more starting pitching, but Ballard Smith and Jack McKeon didn't see eye to eye with me on that.

YR: How did you feel when the Padres traded you to the St. Louis Cardinals?

ROLLIE: I would have been sad to leave the Padres if they were contenders. But I was happy to hear the Cardinals wanted me because they were going places.

YR: Shortly after Whitey Herzog acquired you, he turned around almost immediately and swapped you to the Brewers.

ROLLIE: Yes, it was a little surprising. I had dropped everything and gone to the winter meetings and met with Whitey. We talked about the upcoming season and everything. Then, I went home to San Diego and opened up the paper one morning and read that I had been traded to Milwaukee. But that was good news to me as well. Each of those trades made me happier than I was the day before.

YR: Some would say that this trade essentially made pennant winners out of both teams.

ROLLIE: Right. Playing for the Brewers was great. We always had a chance to win, the stadium was packed, my teammates were all a lot of fun, and the fans in Milwaukee have always been very smart and really know the game.

YR: Is there one memory that sticks out?

ROLLIE: Yeah, in 1981, when I struck out Lou Whitaker to clinch the playoff spot. Milwaukee went insane. We were all overjoyed and laughing hysterically. Adrenaline was flowing. Ted Simmons ran out to the mound, and he jumped up and I caught him and practically carried him halfway across the field. He's no lightweight, but I was so happy, I could have lifted a car over my shoulders.

YR: You were one of the rare pitchers whose ERA actually went down after going from the National League to the American League.

ROLLIE: All the pitchers on those Brewers teams loved knowing that the offense was capable of getting us back into any ballgame. That showed in the way we pitched. The defense behind us was solid as well. We pitched looser, took more risks on the mound, and they often paid off. We were never on pins and needles. I also liked the ballpark. It was short down the lines and had deep gaps, but it wasn't too bad.

YR: After you parted company with the Brewers, you got a call from Pete Rose to come to Reds' spring training camp in 1986.

ROLLIE: Rose was the manager by that point, and he told me he needed a closer. I told him I'd come to spring training camp no problem. The next day, the Reds' GM called me to make arrangements but also mentioned that the owner, Marge Schott, insisted that I report clean-shaven. After all my years in the majors, that request didn't sit well with me. I told the GM to relay a message to Marge. "Tell her that I'll shave my moustache if she shaves her St. Bernard." I never heard back from them.

YR: (laughs) So that's when you hung up your cleats for good?

ROLLIE: I thought to myself if that's the way it has to be, then I'm done. I never understood why Marge was so worried about my moustache. She had more facial hair than I did.

YR: For someone who didn't know a lot about baseball, she knew even less than that.

ROLLIE: Yes. Well, that was the end of the line for me. I knew I had gas left in the tank, but that's how it goes sometimes. I left the game with no fanfare.

YR: To many fans, it's like you never really left, especially since you ended up in Cooperstown. Who are the three guys who should be in the Hall of Fame who aren't?

ROLLIE: Let's see. Bert Blyleven should have been a lock. He has 60 shutouts and only four guys in history have more strikeouts. I was always surprised Mickey Lolich didn't have better luck. Al Oliver is another one.

YR: All things being equal, if you could have played for another ballclub besides the A's, Padres and Brewers, who would it have been?

ROLLIE: I guess I would have liked to play for the Red Sox. I actually have a picture of me in a Sox uniform in my office as a conversation piece.

YR: Do you miss all the airports and all the flying?

ROLLIE: I still go through a lot of airports. I play in celebrity golf tournaments and am available for fantasy baseball camps and for spring training appearances and that sort of thing. I was even in Oakland last year in April at a game, and it was great seeing the fans there again.

YR: Does it get to be tiresome to be recognized in public so often?

ROLLIE: Not really. It can be dangerous though.

YR: How's that?

ROLLIE: One time around 1991, I was at an airport in Chicago. There was a couple in front of me in line to board the plane and their little girl, probably five years old, kept turning around to stare at me. All of a sudden, she kicks me hard in the shins. Her parents were shocked! They asked her what she was doing but she just ignored them and looked up at me and sneered, "Why were you SO MEAN to Peter Pan?"

YR: (laughs) That's hilarious. So she thought you were Captain Hook from the movie that had just come out?

ROLLIE: Right, I just started busting out laughing. I was just glad she didn't have pointed shoes.

YR: Of all the cities you've traveled to, were there some you dreaded having to visit over and over again?

ROLLIE: No—all the major league cities are fine. Well actually, what happens is that they are all great for two or three years, and then you just end up wanting to do nothing else but hang out in your hotel room or in the clubhouse playing cards.

YR: Was Candlestick Park the worst place you ever pitched?

ROLLIE: I think Cleveland Municipal was worse. Sometimes, they'd only have fifteen or sixteen hundred fans a game, and it would be freezing so bad we'd burn bats to keep warm. Candlestick at least had a lot of foul territory. The joke about the Stick was that there wasn't a good seat in the house. It was very windy so they had a very dusty infield. One time, I walked four guys on sixteen pitches because the wind was shifting so much. One pitch landed four feet outside. It was crazy. But my least favorite place to pitch was probably the Met in Minnesota. I got knocked around pretty good there.

YR: What ballparks today wouldn't you want to pitch in?

ROLLIE: (laughs) Well, the game is different now and it starts with the ballparks. They've moved the alleys and fences in ten to fifteen feet. Ever notice all the home runs nowadays that land in the first three rows of the bleachers? Those were all flyouts back when I was pitching. Even the older ballparks like Dodger Stadium reduced their foul territory so they could sell more seats. Bats nowadays are denser and lighter. Balls travel farther than they used to.

YR: It's a different game but still a very exciting one.

ROLLIE: Absolutely. It's always changing. It always has. It even changed during the course of my career. In 1971, I notched 17 saves and they gave me a raise. In 1985, I notched 17 again and that got me released (laughs).

YR: Tom Seaver once said that the top players from every era would have no problem playing in today's major leagues, but that the average player from earlier times wouldn't stack up to the average player of today. Is that your impression as well?

ROLLIE: Maybe so. The guys today are stronger and better conditioned. They report to spring training in shape. Another advantage they have is they can watch replays and analyze everything so much better. Whenever we made a mistake, there was no replay to watch, no slow motion, no freeze frame. If you made a mistake, you had to make sure to remember it.

YR: You've intimidated a lot of hitters over the course of your career. Who were the most intimidating hitters you squared off against?

ROLLIE: I was never really intimidated by anyone. Frank Howard was a bit scary though. Willie Stargell, Richie Allen, John Mayberry too. With those guys, you had to be very careful not to make a mistake. If you pitched them away, there was always the possibility that they would hit a line drive up the middle.

YR: Did you have any close calls in the majors?

ROLLIE: One day, Richie Allen hit a line drive back at me in Comiskey Park, and I actually started to jump for it. The ball ended up hitting the speakers in dead center 440 feet away for a homer. That ball never got over ten feet off the ground the whole way. That's how hard he hit it. Scary!

YR: I guess it was no picnic to face the batting champion type players either.

ROLLIE: Guys like Rose, Brett, and Carew were a pain in the butt to face. They were all contact hitters and would wear you down fouling off pitch after pitch until you made a mistake. These were guys you didn't want to face with the game on the line.

YR: What was it like to grab a bat and face Nolan Ryan?

ROLLIE: I loved to go up there to hit against the top pitchers. I always swung a bat well. But whenever I was asked to bunt off of a guy like Nolan, then that's a different story altogether. That was never fun.

YR: Was he the most intimidating pitcher to bunt off of?

ROLLIE: I think maybe J.R. Richard was.

YR: You jacked a couple home runs during your career. In recent years, you've also gone long a few times during the legends games that they play during All-Star week. Do you credit your power surge to your days swinging the lumber in the American Legion or does it come from your golf game?

ROLLIE: (laughs) I just always enjoyed hitting.

YR: If you had been a lefthander, would you still be in the majors today?

ROLLIE: (laughs) Well, I'm sixty-three now, so probably not.

YR: You put up impressive lifetime stats against the likes of Mike Schmidt (.167), Tony Perez (.067), Willie Stargell (.182), and Brooks Robinson (.167). Why do you think this is?

ROLLIE: With great hitters, you tend to bear down more. You get very careful, there's no laziness, and then you can get good luck. Other greats like Frank Robinson (.348) and Harmon Killebrew (.345) hit me well. Sometimes, it's just in the matchup.

YR: Were there ever any instances when you were called into a game where you were unhappy to pitch?

ROLLIE: No, but you would get upset with managers who would wait too long to bring you in. Sometimes I would start throwing before the call would come down just to make sure I was ready. After a while I would know exactly when I was coming in and which hitters I would be facing. The biggest thing in relief pitching is knowing how to warm up and save as many pitches as you can. You can burn yourself out if you don't.

YR: Who was great at managing a pitching staff?

ROLLIE: Dick Williams was masterful. He and I were always on the same page (laughs).

YR: Did you ever try to talk a manager out of having you issue an intentional walk?

ROLLIE: I'd try sometimes, but they have their minds made up, so you go with it.

YR: You must get asked for advice from young pitchers a lot. What do you generally tell them?

ROLLIE: You throw from the neck down, but you pitch from the neck up.

YR: That's great. Do you work during spring training with some of the prospects?

ROLLIE: I'm generally available for that. Arizona isn't that far from my home in Las Vegas. A lot of it has to do with getting a youngster to become his own pitching coach. It's an art form to teach pitching, but it only works if you can get the student to become the co-teacher. They have to find out what works best for them because no two pitchers are going to throw a slider or a curve the exact same way. You have to encourage them to change speeds, throw the least obvious pitches at the least expected time, and really set up a process of trial and error for them to maximize their learning.

YR: Did you learn a lot from Mudcat Grant?

ROLLIE: I sure did. I learned from watching Mudcat and Catfish and Holtzy as well. It's not about being overpowering once you're in the majors. It's about pinpoint control, moving the ball around, reducing mistakes, and learning from every experience.

YR: When you watch baseball on television today, what aspect of the game do you concentrate on?

ROLLIE: I'll catch a couple games, especially in the postseason. But I don't watch many. It's hard for me to see all the mistakes the pitchers makes. Throwing right down the middle with two strikes? I can't stand to watch when that happens. When Greg Maddux was pitching, he was a pleasure to watch. He would hit his spots perfectly. I don't think I ever saw a catcher have to chase one of his pitches.

YR: How is it that your former catcher Dave Duncan went on to become an exceptional pitching coach? After all, he never pitched an inning.

ROLLIE: Duncan has all the mechanics down. He can see a pitcher and notice everything at once—the arm position, the push-off, the stride, everything. He can see the tiniest of flaws, sometimes before they even become a problem. If anything, I'm surprised more catchers haven't become pitching coaches. After all, they spend their playing careers handling a pitching staff so it's a logical progression.

YR: That makes sense. You're recognized often in public, sometimes even as yourself instead of as Captain Hook. Do you have any strange autograph stories?

ROLLIE: Once, I was signing autographs at an event and shooting the breeze with everyone. Well, this beautiful woman makes her way to the front of the line, and I'm looking around for the baseball or for the playing card she wants me to sign, but she isn't holding anything. Then, out of the blue, she asks me if I will sign her breasts. Before I can answer, she flips her shirt up. I just sort of looked around for a couple seconds but then I thought, hey, no problem. I grabbed the pen and started signing. The best part was I didn't even have to dot the "i" s.

YR: That's hilarious. You were saving ink and paper. That's very environmentally sound of you.

ROLLIE: Well, you do what you can to help.

YR: (laughs) Thanks so much for this interview. How do people get in touch with you for public appearances and autograph requests and all that good stuff?

ROLLIE: They can go to www.rfingers34.com for info or just write me at rfingers34@gmail.com.

YR: I have one last question. If you hadn't gone into baseball, what would you have done with your life?

ROLLIE: I never thought about that. The thought never even entered my mind. I might have become a better golfer. (laughs)

35

The Prolific Stealers
Decade by Decade

◇◇

(American Association, Federal League, and Players League stats not included)

1886–1889
Jim Fogarty, PHILLIES – 289
King Kelly, WHITE SOX/BEANEATERS – 261
John Montgomery Ward, GIANTS – 247
Ned Hanlon, WOLVERINES/ALLEGHENYS – 210
Pebbly Jack Glasscock, MAROONS/HOOSIERS – 205

1890–1899
Sliding Billy Hamilton, PHILLIES/BRAVES – 730
Tom Brown, (four teams) – 493
Dummy Hoy, (five teams) – 439
Bill Lange, COLTS/ORPHANS – 399
Herman Long, BEANEATERS – 361

1900–1910
Honus Wagner, PIRATES – 487
Frank Chance, ORPHANS/CUBS – 357
Sam Mertes, (four teams) – 305
Jimmy Sheckard, SUPERBAS/ORIOLES/CUBS – 295
Elmer Flick, PHILLIES/NAPS – 275

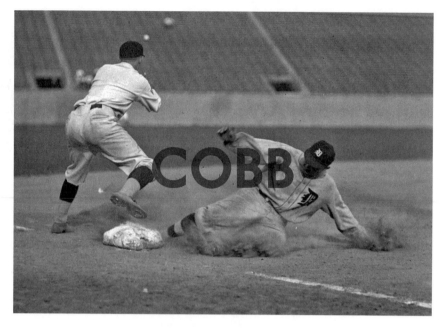

1910–1920
Ty Cobb, TIGERS – 576
Eddie Collins, ATHLETICS/WHITE SOX – 489
Clyde Milan, SENATORS – 434
Max Carey, PIRATES – 392
Bob Bescher, (four teams) – 364

1920–1929
Max Carey, PIRATES/ROBINS – 336
Frankie Frisch, GIANTS/CARDINALS – 310
Sam Rice, SENATORS – 254
George Sisler, (three teams) – 214
Kiki Cuyler, PIRATES/CUBS – 210

1930–1939
Ben Chapman, (three teams) – 269
Billy Werber, (three teams) – 191
Lyn Lary, (seven teams) – 158
Gee Walker, TIGERS/WHITE SOX – 158
Pepper Martin, CARDINALS – 136

1940–1949
George Washington Case, SENATORS/INDIANS – 285
Snuffy Stirnweiss, YANKEES – 130
Wally Moses, (three teams) – 124

Johnny Hopp (four teams) – 117
Pee Wee Reese, DODGERS – 108
Mickey Vernon, SENATORS/INDIANS – 108

1950–1959
Willie Mays, GIANTS – 179
Minnie Minoso, INDIANS/WHITE SOX – 167
Richie Ashburn, PHILLIES – 158
Jim Rivera, BROWNS/WHITE SOX – 150
Luis Aparicio, WHITE SOX – 134
Jackie Jensen, (three teams) – 134

1960–1969
Maury Wills, (three teams) – 535
Lou Brock, CUBS/CARDINALS – 387
Luis Aparicio, WHITE SOX/ORIOLES – 342
Bert Campaneris, ATHLETICS – 292
Willie Davis, DODGERS – 240

1970–1979
Lou Brock, CARDINALS – 551
Joe Morgan, ASTROS/REDS – 488
Cesar Cedeno, ASTROS – 427
Bobby Bonds, (six teams) – 380
Davey Lopes, DODGERS – 375

1980–1989
Rickey Henderson, A'S/YANKEES – 838
Tim Raines, EXPOS – 583
Vince Coleman, CARDINALS – 472
Willie Wilson, ROYALS – 451
Ozzie Smith, PADRES/CARDINALS – 362

1990–1999
Otis Nixon, (7 teams) – 478
Rickey Henderson, (6 teams) – 463
Kenny Lofton, (3 teams) – 433
Delino Deshields, (4 teams) – 393
Marquis Grissom, (4 teams) – 381

2000–2009
Juan Pierre, (four teams) – 459
Carl Crawford, DEVIL RAYS/RAYS – 362
Ichiro Suzuki, MARINERS – 341
Jimmy Rollins, PHILLIES – 326
Jose Reyes, METS – 301

36

The Forrest Gump Award

◇◇

ew of you will have ever heard of Rusty Torres before this chapter. That's understandable. Though this journeyman played nearly nine full years in the bigs, not once did he participate in a postseason, nor was he ever invited into the national spotlight of an All-Star Game.

And yet this longtime outfielder can still lay claim to something unique, because he possessed a knack, better than any other ballplayer, for being in the right place at the wrong time. Rusty Torres is, if nothing else, the Forrest Gump of the baseball world.

In the past hundred years, forfeits have become rarities. We are long past the era when managers would pull their teams off the field to protest a blown call. Similarly, long gone are the times when umpires would assess forfeits upon those ballclubs (behind in runs) that conspired to drag out a game so that it could be called due to darkness.

Since 1910, on average, there has been less than one forfeit every five years. Most modern players have gone their entire careers without having seen one. But don't tell that to Rusty Torres, who during the 1970s somehow happened to be part of three forfeits—all of which were the result of fans storming the field.

The first of these dangerous donnybrooks occurred late in 1971. With just a handful of games left in the season, the Washington Senators *quietly* announced they were relocating to another city. The news shocked the beltway's longtime (and long-suffering) fans. It would have broken their hearts, but those organs had long been smashed to pieces by decades of Senatorial gridlock.

Over fourteen thousand souls showed up for that final night to watch the fadeout to seventy-nine years of Washington Senators baseball. Those in attendance solemnly stared at their team like a hospital patient who looks at a beloved big toe that's about to get amputated.

The opponents were the New York Yankees, an also-ran squad that had been using the final weeks of '71 to give their September callups playing time. One such rookie was Rusty Torres, a stickball legend from the Bronx, who entered the game with an impressive .364 average. To cherry the top, Rusty was celebrating his twenty-third birthday, and he did so in style with a single and home run.

However, entering the ninth inning, his Yankees were losing, as the Senators stood poised to take a final, bittersweet victory. But as the end neared, the natives turned restless.

After the Yankees made their second out, a rogue wave of fans pounced over the rails and stormed the field, where they swirled about with molotovic vengeance. Some looted the bases and others filled their pockets with infield dirt as though it were gold dust from Sutter's Mill.

In the stands, other fans were ripping out seats with the urgency that only an adrenalized souvenir hunter can muster. Like jilted locusts, the Washingtonians ravaged the terrain. Congress had nothing on this group.

Rusty, who had been swinging a bat in the on-deck circle, couldn't believe the scene. His time spent growing up in the Bronx hadn't acclimated him to such chaos. He made a quick departure before he and his Yankee teammates could get taken apart as well. Welcome to the show, meat!

Three seasons later, a more seasoned Rusty Torres had moved on to play for the Cleveland Indians. His career since the debacle in D.C. had gone relatively smoothly. All was well.

But one night, the very team that the Senators had morphed into—the Texas Rangers, came to town. Although there had been friction between the two ballclubs from an earlier series, Rusty and the others had no reason to think things could ever get out of hand like they had in Washington. But fate conspired against them by way of the Indians' front office.

To help bring additional fans into the monstrously large East European soccer stadium that the Indians called home, the Tribe's braintrust opted to offer their fans a limitless supply of ten-cent cups of beer. It sounded like a plan. Thousands of thrifty alcoholics and underage thrillseekers came to Municipal Stadium—a few of whom liked a little baseball with their beer.

Of course, trouble brewed throughout this game. Rowdy fans got into scrums with everyone from groundskeepers to concession vendors to each other. Ranger players were even used for target practice.

But the suds kept pouring. In fact, when the initial supply ran dry, they simply started serving customers directly off of Stroh's trucks that had been driven onto the property. Yet the game chugged along and stayed a tight contest.

Approaching last call, (the bottom of the ninth), Rusty Torres was called upon and delivered a pinch-hit single. He eventually wound up on second base as the potential winning run. But he never got the chance to score. A situation broke out in left field between Texas player Jeff Burroughs and a trespassing Cleveland fan.

Both combatants quickly received reinforcements, but the Rangers were quickly outnumbered. The home plate umpire had no choice but to call the game—and the hunting knife he later found sticking behind home plate did nothing to make him regret the decision.

Sensing imminent peril, the Rangers began to circle their wagons. But rather quickly, the Tribe's manager, Ken Aspromonte, summoned Rusty and all his teammates to left field to assist Texas to safety. Shortly thereafter, both the Rangers and Indians found themselves behind locked doors as they listened to a riot escalate on the other side.

It was a bit like the mob scene in Washington, except that this Cleveland crowd was far more intoxicated and the seats they ripped out were intended as weapons instead of as souvenirs.

The years then rolled by somewhat peacefully for Rusty Torres. After a couple of forfeit-free seasons in Anaheim, he went back to the Midwest, roaming the outfield for the White Sox. It appeared that he had already seen the most bizarre sights that baseball had to offer. Yet, little did he know that fate had a hat trick in store for him.

The marketing blueprint at Comiskey Park in 1979 was similar to how it had been in Cleveland. The front office was looking for clever ways to bring thousands of fans into their nearly empty stadium.

Their newest idea was novel. Trying to capitalize on the growing hatred for "disco music," the White Sox allowed anyone into the park for only ninety-eight cents if they would also donate one of their old disco records to the team. In between games of the doubleheader, a most unusual show had been planned. The White Sox would take all the records they collected, and blow them to smithereens with powerful explosives.

Fan attendance exceeded all expectations—seventy-five thousand people packed the park, including some who paid. But many of these folks were not all that much into baseball. If anything, they were in the mood for a rock concert and, unfortunately, the national anthem and the sparse organ music did nothing to take their edge off.

When the first game ended, the big event they were waiting for finally arrived. With hungry eyes and wet lips, they longed for the big explosion. A box containing twenty thousand records was carted onto the field and detonated. Boom. The air filled with smoke, vinyl chips, brimstone, and outfield grass. The fans got their wish. Disco had symbolically been demolished.

But Rusty Torres and all the other players soon learned that *these* fans were not content to just sit back down and to watch another nine innings of baseball. They had other ideas. They took to the field and started to batter the place apart as though Comiskey Park was one huge Bee Gees album.

There was no second game that evening…and with that, Rusty Torres witnessed the decade's third and final instance of fan rioting. As his many teammates can attest, there was never any quit in Rusty, but in retrospect, it sure does seem like there was at least a little forfeit.

For more details on Ten Cent Beer Night, check out Chapter 5.

For more details on Disco Demolition Night, check out our companion book, Rollie's Follies.

Follies Factoids

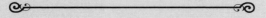

★ The opposing managers during the final ill-fated Washington Senator game were Ralph Houk (for the Bombers) and Ted Williams (for the Politicians).

★ Rusty "Trade Bait" Torres was on the opposite end of three high-profile swaps. Respectively, they brought Graig Nettles to the Yankees, Frank Robinson to the Cleveland Indians, and Bobby Bonds to the Texas Rangers.

★ Rusty played 103 career games at the Big A in Anaheim, none of which were forfeited.

★ Rusty Torres now runs youth clinics and counsels ballplayers on Long Island through his organization winningbeyondwinning.org

★ From 1970 through 2009, there were only five major league games that were forfeited. Hometown fans caused four, and Earl Weaver caused the other.

For a list of some of the other unusual forfeits in history, you can check out page 274.

37

The Secret Strategy of Casey Stengel

◇◇◇

Casey Stengel remains the only manager in history to have guided his team to five consecutive World Championships. Let that fact sink in for a moment, especially after trying to remember how few teams can even manage to win *two* rings in a row.

But with success comes criticism. Some of Casey's detractors have argued, given the tremendous firepower of his Yankee ballclubs, that even a drunk monkey could have gotten similar results. Of course this notion is ricockulous! *At best*, a drunk monkey would have only managed a three-peat.

Perhaps the Old Perfesser's brilliance is so often overlooked because of his nearly constant clowning. He was always making funny faces or tossing off amusingly convoluted statements. But alas, Casey was not anonymous for no reason! His ability to turn a phrase made him a worldwide favorite of the New York media. But even so, seldom has less fuss been made about a Hall of Fame manager who didn't have fewer triumphs to show for it.

But underneath all of the wordsmithery, Casey was known as a shrewd and innovative chessmaster. Some even believe that he used his persona mostly to take pressure off of Joe DiMaggio, Mickey Mantle, or whoever else needed a break from the press after a game.

But many think Casey really made his bones as a manager's manager by how well he platooned his players.

When Casey was handed the keys to Yankee Stadium in 1949, the popular mindset was in having your eight best position players out there as often as possible. There were exceptions, but players of the era were expected to play through almost every tough injury, to gut their way through fatigue, and to adjust to every pitching matchup that didn't automatically favor them.

Although the concept of platooning existed well before Casey's historic run, he became one of its most innovative practitioners. Besides employing the standard strategy of rotating righty and lefty hitters in the lineup based on their offhandedness to the opposing pitcher, he also subbed in defensive players in later innings to better protect his leads. In addition, Casey had no problem pinch-hitting for his pitcher in early innings if he felt the hitter could break the game wide open.

But Casey's ideas about platooning went even further. He even made adjustments based on whatever road ballpark he found himself in. Sometimes he would use a more home-run oriented player if the fences were short, and at other times he would favor a speedy run-manufacturer to take advantage of power alleys and/or the throwing arms of the opposing catchers and right fielders.

Because Casey was so far ahead of his time (and ahead of so many of his peers), it's no wonder that he captured ten pennants in twelve years. Of course, it didn't hurt having the great Mickey Mantle on his roster. After all, Mantle was a platoon manager's dream, in that he was essentially five ballplayers rolled into one. Not only was Mick a switch-hitter, with awesome power and incredible speed, he was gifted defensively as well.

Casey's advocacy of the platoon system came from his playing days. In 1914, future Hall of Fame manager Wilbert Robinson took over as Brooklyn's skipper. Sharing that dugout was a young and wrinkle-free Casey who soaked up the vast knowledge surrounding him. Under Robby, Casey got up to the plate fewer times than he had in '13, but his batting average improved 44 points. The best team in the National League that season was the Boston Braves, and their manager, George Stallings, was also a strong advocate of the platoon. In fact, sixteen position players on that team had more than one hundred at-bats.

During the 1914 World Series, these Bravos faced Connie Mack and his heavily favored Philadelphia Athletics, a team that featured only two bench players who regularly got their uniforms dirty. Stallings' "Miracle Braves" went through the Athletics like a buzzsaw in four straight games.

More than a few teams noticed how platooning helped dismantle the powerful Philadelphia machine. The following season, even Connie Mack started spreading the playing time around more liberally.

The Boston Red Sox began using a platoon at first base with good results, proving that a first baseman could be used primarily as an offensive force rather than a defensive specialist, a concept we take for granted today.

The idea of platooning catchers was popular because it not only preserved knees, it extended careers. But perhaps no manager had greater success with the concept than Ty Cobb from 1921 to 1925. During this span, each of his two backstops topped .300 every season.

Another platoon that greatly impressed Casey Stengel occurred in 1922. That season, the lefty Casey was one of two centerfielders manager John McGraw used. Casey hit .368 in eighty-four games while the righthanded Bill Cunningham hit .328 in eighty-five. The following season, Casey hit .339 in seventy-five games. Since Casey's career batting average was .284, it's no wonder he became a disciple.

But once the effects of the Great Depression reached baseball, the use of platoons went into steep decline. It had to. Cost cutting by owners led to roster reductions, and this attrition hampered the manager's ability to improvise. In addition, baseball fans of the era began to see specialization as effete and lazy. Less patience was granted to anyone who couldn't handle showing up for work in every inning of every day.

Yankee first sacker Lou Gehrig was but one of many ironmen during the 1930s. In fact, not a single member of the 1936 championship Yankees (outside of the primary eight) managed to tally as many as 162 at-bats. This was not their Daddy's baseball.

With the start of World War II, the level of talent at the major league level dropped significantly. However, when the war ended in 1945, dozens of qualified ballplayers came home to find that some of their replacements had grown to be fairly qualified. In essence, some soldiers found themselves leaving one platoon overseas to join another one back home.

During that time, Casey was managing in the minor leagues. He had washed out as a big league manager after the '43 season and took work where he could find it. But after five seasons in the minors, his reputation for brilliance and for winning had grown to where the Yankees offered him the job that would make him a legend.

Under Casey's supervision in 1949, the Yankees hit fewer home runs than the year before, but their run total actually improved—a feat made more impressive by the fact that superstar Joe DiMaggio missed half of the games (mostly due to a heel injury).

If you had told oddsmakers in spring training that DiMaggio would miss half the season and mentioned that Yogi Berra, Bobby Brown, Tommy Henrich, and Johnny Lindell (all .300 hitters on the third-place 1948 Yankees) would see reduced playing time, few would have picked the Yanks to get above fourth place.

But with the secret strategy of Casey Stengel, the Yankees not only improved, they became champions of the world.

Follies Factoids

★ The 1930 NL champion St. Louis Cardinals had four outfielders rack up impressive credentials.
  • Taylor Douhit (the only non-platooner) played every game and hit .303 with 201 hits and 60 walks.
  • Hall of Famer Chick Hafey hit .336, slugged .652, and drove in 107runs in 120 games.
  • In his 119 games, lefty George Watkins hit .373 and slugged .621.
  • Lefty Showboat Fisher hit .374 and slugged .587 during his 92 games.

★ The well-traveled Casey Stengel spent thirty-nine seasons in the major leagues, twenty-five of them as a manager. Here's a list of the franchises for which he played or managed the most games:
  New York Yankees—1,851
  Brooklyn Dodgers/Superbas/Robins—1,139
  Boston Braves—1,103
  New York Mets—582
  New York Giants—177
  Philadelphia Phillies—153
  Pittsburgh Pirates—128

38

Crabs and Croixs

 or forty seasons, the San Francisco Giants played in a chilly, windy stadium so ill suited for baseball that they were once successfully sued by a ticketholder for discomfort.

Candlestick Park had a lot going against it from the beginning. It was built on the cheapest plot of land the owner could find, in a remote area far from both neighborhoods and public transit, right on a point of the Bay that was monumentally breezy. Even having a prominent politician (vice-president Richard Nixon) throw out the stadium's first pitch did nothing to reverse the misfortune.

In its favor, the park did have a lovely view of the bay, but this panorama came at a hefty price. Prior to one game, a violent wind lifted the entire batting cage up into the air before dumping it some sixty feet away.

The wind was such a constant issue that a study was commissioned to see what could be done about it. The investigation concluded that the situation could have been averted had the park been built just a couple hundred yards away. Ooops.

In addition, this concrete cookie cutter had been built between the bay and a steep mountain—a formation that redirected the stiff winds blowing in from the bay by funneling them right down into the park. Had even ten more feet of distance been placed between the stadium and Mount Sirocco, Willie Mays might have hit anywhere from fifty to seventy-five more homers.

The great breaking winds of Candlestick led to high levels of disgust.

With regularity, the ballcaps of infielders flew off and cartwheeled all the way to the warning track before so much as a curse word could be uttered. Pitchers lost degrees of accuracy. Right-handed hitters saw what would have been home runs in other ballparks turn into infield flyouts. Outfielders had it tough as well. They had to learn not to get too early a jump on a fly ball, because the wind would so often shift the ball's trajectory.

But in early 1972, mankind valiantly struck back against Mother Nature. The owners enclosed the park and, momentarily, there was a grand hurrah. Although the fans lost their lovely view of the bay, it seemed a small price to pay to avert hypothermia.

The new sugar bowl shape reduced the wind's velocity, but this "improvement" unwittingly backfired. The circular chutes that had been created kept most of these winds that were still ricocheting down off the mountain from ever leaving. In essence, the engineers had made Candlestick even swirlier than its toilets.

To be fair, the ballplayers were hardly in a no-win situation. After all, their opponents had to put up with the same terrible conditions and hadn't adapted to them. The Giants posted winning records at home for each of their first twelve seasons at the Stick.

The true victim of the situation was the poor soul whose job was to attract paying customers to the frigid juggernaut of windswept hell that was Candlestick Park. His name was Pat Gallagher, and no one envied his task. He had come to the Giants after working for a number of those watery zoo parks where killer whales thunderously splash fecal-scented saltwater into the joyous faces of children. Since Pat had successfully marketed that sort of experience, the team figured he might be the right man for this job.

Most ad executives would have just ignored the many downsides of the Candlestick and thrown together some slick and overly positive marketing campaign. But after a few years on the job, Pat had an epiphany. He decided to embrace the fact that the park frequently suffered gale-force winds and freezing temperatures.

Television commercials began running in 1983 that featured Giants fans bundled up in blizzard wear as though they were watching the game from the South Pole. For comic effect, some of these shivering stalwarts even had icicles stalactiting off of their faces. But despite the hardship, they rooted for their boys with valor.

The message was clear.

Fans shouldn't see themselves as idiots for coming out to Candlestick for night games. Instead, they should see themselves as tough and loyal, with a sense of humor about the situation.

The commercials were a big hit. But Pat Gallagher had another idea that may have even been better.

To the fanatics who managed to stay to the bitter end of any extra-inning night game, they were given an honor in the form of badges. These plasticons featured the team logo (semi-covered in snow) and proudly displayed the words "Veni, Vidi, Vixi," which is Latin for "I came, I saw, I survived."

These orange-and-black pins became baseball's version of a purple heart, and they became cherished possessions. What made them truly special is that you couldn't buy them—you had to earn them. Also, since no one can ever predict when a game will go into extra-innings, few posers ever came into possession of one of these highly coveted "Croix de Candlesticks."

After a while, some of the more frosted regulars ended up with a great number of Croixs pinned to their caps. The amount of free beers these folks received (and still do) as tributes to their loyal endurance is noteworthy.

Indeed, Pat Gallagher and the Giants had somehow found a way to make delicious snow cones out of bitter ice, but they weren't finished yet.

They surveyed fans to find out what kind of mascot the team should have. Mascots were becoming all the rage across baseball, and the front office didn't want the fans in San Francisco feeling left out. The survey results, however, showed that 63 percent of the faithful hated the idea of bringing in any mascot whatsoever. To these weather-beaten fans, the idea was seen as cheesy, rah-rah, and unoriginal.

Of course, fans at the Stick had a right to be crabby, simply because it was such an inconvenient place to get to and an even more uncomfortable place to stay. After all, it's hard to be cheery when at any second, a gust of wind can knock your expensive beer out of your hands into the faces of your three closest neighbors.

Pat Gallagher accurately sensed that any mascot would get booed out of the stadium—and possible drilled by flying objects of all kinds (and not just from the wind). Candlestick was simply not a place that an adorably sly foam-rubber caricature would have worked.

But Gallagher's imagination kept whirling away. Eventually, he had the idea to introduce an anti-mascot, something so mocking of the genre that fans might actually enjoy booing it. With that concept in mind, the Giants introduced the Crazy Crab.

Pandering, spastic, and obsequious, the crustacean creation succeeded in garnering both legitimate boos and play-along boos from the fans. It was a pathetic excuse for a mascot, just as Gallagher had intended. If anything, it sort of looked like a sunburned Mayor McCheese suffering through the final throes of cholera.

Players regularly drilled the unsuspecting crab with rosin bags, and more than a few drinks were poured on him as well. Even children didn't like the mascot, perhaps in part because its oversized claw pinchers were at their neck level.

Though the Crazy Crab and the Croix de Candlestick were both eventually discontinued (save when they are brought back from time to time for nostalgia), they were both major feathers in the cap of Pat Gallagher, the ingenious man who was to ballpark promotions what ice-chilled crab legs have become to Las Vegas buffets.

Candlestickoids

★ The 1945–1955 New York Giants drew more home fans than did the 1965–1975 San Francisco Giants.

★ Candlestick Park was the first baseball stadium to be built from reinforced concrete. Upon its completion in 1960, Richard Nixon called it "the finest ballpark in America." Among those in attendance for the park's inauguration was seventy-three-year-old Ty Cobb.

★ Astroturf carpeted its playing surface for nine seasons.

★ The "Stick" hosted Oakland Raider home games in 1961 and the Beatles' final full concert in 1966.

★ During one game in 1967, the Giants used all twenty-five players to defeat the Houston Astros (in fifteen innings).

★ Candlestick is the only current home field in the NFL that was not originally designed for football (the 49ers didn't become tenants until 1971).

★ The Giants' average attendance for its 3,185 games at Candlestick (including twelve postseason games) from 1960 to 1999 was 17,187. By contrast, the team's average attendance at the downtown ballpark in the decade of the 2000s (including twelve postseason games) was 39,044.

★ Even after figuring in inflation, Candlestick Park only cost about 25 percent as much to construct as did the current ballpark. ($15 million as compared to $357 million).

39

Another "Odd but Modest Proposal"

By Yellowstone Ritter

◇◇

Those of you who've read the first book in the Rollie's Follies series already know what's coming. Yours truly will be getting drunk and then screed about what can be done to make the grand old game *even better.*

However, for the record, I'd like to state that when I type sober (such as I am at the moment), I think baseball is great as it is and should be left alone.

But since that wouldn't make for a very good chapter, I'm going to go off now and tilt back five or six bourbon bombs. By the time you get to the very next paragraph, rest assured, that I will, at that point, possess a genius level of baseball expertise normally reserved for the likes of an Alexander Cartwright, Branch Rickey, or maybe Bill Veeck.

Baseball parks need more colored bunting hanging from the rafters!! Fans should get free cinnamon rolls whenever a fat first baseman hits a triple! Also, men should be allowed to use the ladies' restrooms every odd inning. It would reduce the incredibly long lines at the men's rooms and also greatly encourage every casual fan who is a female to be sure to pay attention to what's going on in the game.

I have yet another idea, and this brainstorm is so thunderiffic that it will not only would make the game more fun for kids and for casual fans alike, but it would also give the serious fans more to sink our teeth into.

Here is that idea ┅⟩ Ready? I can't hear you!! I said, "Are you ready!?!?!"

All of the World Series games should be played at times when children can better appreciate them. Few kids sleep during the Super Bowl, and we need to make it the same for baseball. Adults will just have to be mature enough to adjust around this extremely positive change.

It will be great, though. No longer will baseball's young fans in Baltimore or Miami or Dayton or Nova Scotia or Cuba have to battle crusty eye and bobblehead whenever the game moves past ten o'clock on a school-night. Even if the networks get fewer dollars in advertising revenue, so be it, because they will be able to sell ad time *for so much more* when these kids grow up to actually become baseball fans.

However, we should let one World Series game start later than usual (at eight o'clock on the East Coast) so these little kiddies have a chance at one cool rite of passage. It would be a huge event for them, like riding a bike unassisted or falling out of a tall tree right onto their elbows.

Their parents could help them stay alert into these late hours by keeping sugary snacks and caffeinated beverages at the ready. This would be great! After all, what better way for parents to bond with their kids than by bombarding them with stimulants while pressuring them to stay awake well past their physical threshold? If only Norman Rockwell were still with us, this picturesque scene would make for one of his classics.

Secondly, from this point forward, games have to start right at the top of the hour. Baseball is a game of precision and all the pomp and circumstance should step aside for that fact. I don't think ANY of us needs the numbing foreplay of a dim-witted baseball player *sorta reading* his team's batting order off of a prompter while interjecting lame nicknames for each teammate. Yes, I *am* talking to you, Dustin Pedroia!

Before the game starts, I also don't want to see extravagant graphics and plugs for whatever non-baseball show the Fox Network is trying to ram down our throats. I really don't mind curt shilling, but lengthy shilling is beyond obnoxious. Do you know what I want to hear right at the top of the hour? An umpire yelling "play ball" and the immediate sound of a baseball smashing into wood or leather.

As for the unquestioned beauty of our national anthem, that needs to be featured as the climax of the 7:30 preview show. This is also the half-hour slot where all the analysis and endless teasers for the next Jack Bauer terrorist hunt adventure need to happen. Baseball teaches children so much about life, and it is time it teaches them punctuality and organization as well.

Top of the hour ⋯⟩ first pitch, nuff said!!!

Thirdly, and owners have got to like this idea to the point that they send me generous checks in the mail for infinity…the Fall Classic should once again become a best-of-nine series.

No, no, no! Don't get off the toilet and quit reading just yet. You'll come to like this idea and here's the first reason why: the chances of the better team winning will increase. Also, the uneven effects of one team coming into the series depleted from a seven-game LCS while the opponent breezed through their own LCS in four games would be greatly diminished (this disparity happened during the 2006 World Series).

I will swig down yet another bourbon bomb before I get to my biggest big idea. Mmm...who knew cookie dough ice cream went so well with Kentucky's best? Okay it's time for me to unveil my best idea yet, excluding the one about free cinnamon rolls whenever a fat guy hits a triple.

Game Five of this nine-game World Series needs to be played at a neutral site—sort of like the Super Bowl. Numerous cities would bid for this opportunity like crazy. Conceivably Game Five could be played in precipitation-proof parks such as the ones in Houston, Milwaukee, Phoenix, Seattle, or Toronto.

With some alterations to existing venues, this Game Five could also take place in such highly interesting cities as Miami, Montreal, or New Orleans. It could even take place in a completely non-interesting city like Indianapolis.

(I'm so sorry about that preceding rude comment—I'm still quite wasted. Indy is a lovely city with lovely people, but it is a boring place to visit.) (Now, I feel I should apologize for that *second* rude comment. You see, it's just that the hotel I once stayed at in Indianapolis felt the need to adopt a New Orleans theme just to liven things up. I found this attempt desperate and somewhat of an admission that the city was dull. After all, I guarantee you that there are no hotels in the Big Easy that went with an Indianapolis theme.)

Yes indeed, my extraordinarily brilliant notion of having Game Five in a neutral site accomplishes a number of wonderful goals.

One) it is a far more equitable way to parcel out the number of home games that each team gets and

Two) in case we have a World Series with a cold weather team, this neutral weatherproof venue is "at the ready" and can be used as a last resort to prevent the World Series from being postponed. As is, it's a small miracle that Boston and Colorado managed to play through the 2007 Classic without a blizzard rolling through either town.

Just for the nerds, I've created the following section to let you know how this would all perfectly play out.

For the non-nerds, just skip ahead to the section where it says "the possibilities for excretement" and, once again, I apologize for any previous misspellings or slights toward the fine people of Indianapolis, the town where people drive faster than anywhere else in the world (probably because they are so bored with the surroundings). But through all these slurs and mistakes, please remember that I am drunker than a cruller in a toboggan and cannot be held responsible for my metaphors.

GAME ONE of the WORLD SERIES would take place on a Saturday at the home field of the team that had the most wins during the season. (It's time to scrap that ludicrous All-Star game "prize" of home-field advantage for the winning league. It's not fair to the elite teams, and I can't remember the last time an All-Star manager cared more about winning than he did about keeping everyone's pitch count low). This initial World Series game would start at noon PST and three EST sharp.

GAME TWO is the next day, in the same venue, but would instead start at four PST and seven EST. (This gives players a little more rest and also gives some fans a little breathing room in case they wanted to watch football earlier in the day to whet their appetites for this superior sport).

Monday is a travel day. (It is also a day for all the children to get ahead on their homework so that they can catch the following day's action without anyone yelling at them to finish a book report right at the moment when their hero strides up to the plate with the bases loaded).

GAME THREE takes place on Tuesday at the home of the team with the inferior regular season record. This game starts sharply (remember...for the kids) at four PST and seven EST. (However, a replay would be broadcast at seven PST for people in the Western states in case they had a commute, homework, housework, afterschool sports, or some other extracurricular activity to do).

Wednesday is a day of rest and great anticipation.

GAME FOUR takes place on Thursday, once again at the home of the team with the inferior regular season record. This game also starts at four PST and seven EST.

Friday is a day of travel to the neutral site (and a day for players to deal with the countless friends who come out of the woodwork and use high-pressure tactics to finagle World Series tickets).

GAME FIVE takes place on a Saturday in the neutral domed stadium with the team with the best regular season record pretending to be the home team. This game starts at two PST and at five EST. This event will become known as SUPER SATURDAY...or in Latin America as **SUSTANTIVO SABADO**... or in Japan as SUPER SATURDAY.

GAME SIX, if necessary, takes place Sunday back at the sight of Games One and Two with the game starting at four PST and seven EST.

Monday is a day of travel and quiet reflection.

GAME SEVEN, if necessary, takes place Tuesday at the sight of Games Three and Four with the game starting at four PST and seven EST.

Wednesday is a day of rest and rehabilitation.

GAME EIGHT, if necessary, takes place Thursday at the same sight as Tuesday's game with this contest starting at the four/seven timeslots fans have come to expect.

Friday is a day of travel and high anticipation.

GAME NINE, if necessary, takes place Saturday night at the site of Games One, Two, and Six with the game starting at four/seven. The ratings for such a game, on the years that they do occur, would be monumental.

· · · · · · · · ·

The possibilities for excitement in the scenario are incredible.

Of course, some will complain that baseball is being played too far into November, but this would be taken care of by beginning the regular season seven to ten days earlier and by having veterans report to spring training a week later, unless they want to come in and practice with those competing for their jobs. As is, players take such good care of themselves in the offseason as compared with eras past that this only makes sense.

Yet, aside from the best-of-nine World Series, there is yet another wrinkle I have divined, and this is one that will raise millions of dollars for charity and entrepreneurs alike:

At the neutral site where Game Five takes place, there shall also be an extraordinary slate of activities and events during the five days prior that lead up to the game. Among them, there will be live screenings of Games Three and Four inside that neutral domed stadium for all the fans and tourists in the area to watch.

In addition to these two simulcasts, over the course of the week, the domed venue will also host three live baseball games of high interest with respectable stakes—ones that get scheduled on the days of rest between World Series games.

Here's how the entire five-day schedule for "BaseballMania" would play out.

DAY ONE AT THE PARK—MONDAY

A regulation baseball game is played that pits sixteen left-handed major league players against sixteen right-handed major league players with each winning player (and their manager) receiving 100K to give to their favorite charity. These players would come from the teams that didn't advance to the World Series. As for the losing team, they would only receive $25K apiece to pass along. As for the talent themselves, since this is designed as a selfless endeavor, they receive nothing—except for travel, hotel, and meal expenses. Of course, their participation is completely voluntary.

DAY TWO AT THE PARK—TUESDAY

Fan-fest exhibitions and a screening of Game Three of the World Series at the dome.

DAY THREE AT THE PARK—WEDNESDAY

A regulation game that pits sixteen major league players less than twenty-five years of age against sixteen major league players over thirty-seven years of age. Once again, each winning participant gets 100K for their charity and each loser receives only 25K for theirs.

By the way, the reason for the teams only having sixteen players is because a four- or five-man pitching staff along with a bench of three or four reserves should be sufficient for a one-game matchup, and if it isn't, then that's just more drama for your mama.

DAY FOUR AT THE PARK—THURSDAY

Meet-and-greet events with Cooperstown legends and a screening of Game Four at the dome.

DAY FIVE AT THE PARK—FRIDAY

A regulation game that pits sixteen players from the USA against sixteen players who were born elsewhere with each winning player getting 100K for their charity and with each loser getting only 25K for theirs. Do you think the television rating for this game might be good globally? I do! And unlike the World Baseball Classic, fewer players would be holding back.

DAY SIX AT THE PARK—SATURDAY

This is when Game Five of the actual World Series would be played live at this neutral stadium.

Okay, it's nine hours later and I finally sobered up. You know what? These crazy ideas will never work. Not in this buttoned-down world. I'm so sorry I brought them up. Now, if you'll excuse me, I have to call up my incredibly wonderful mother-in-law (who I e-mailed this chapter to at the height of my intoxication) as I don't think that she's going to be too pleased with what I wrote about her former hometown of Indianapolis—which is a smart and lovely town with smart and lovely people (although not quite as lovely and smart as when she lived there).

40

Baseball from 1901 to 1920

(a series of mini-features about the Dead-Ball Era)

◇◇◇

THE FIVE MOST DOMINANT TEAMS

1

The Boston Americans/Red Sox

5 world championships
6 pennants
1,641 total wins
ICONS: Cy Young, Jimmy Collins, Tris Speaker, Harry Hooper, Babe Ruth

2

The Philadelphia Athletics

3 world championships
6 pennants
1,505 total wins
ICONS: Connie Mack, Eddie Collins, Nap Lajoie, Eddie Plank

3

The Chicago Orphans/Cubs

2 world championships
5 pennants
1,728 total wins
ICONS: Mordecai "Three Finger" Brown, Joe Tinker,
Johnny Evers, Frank Chance

4

The Chicago White Stockings/White Sox

2 world championships
3 pennants
1,649 total wins
ICONS: Ed Walsh, George Davis, Red Faber, Ray Schalk,
"Shoeless" Joe Jackson

5

The New York Giants

1 world championship
6 pennants
1,750 total wins (tops for the era)
ICONS: Christy Mathewson, John McGraw, Rube Marquard,
Roger Bresnahan

A TIMELINE OF THE ERA

1901 The American League debuts, doubling the number of professional major league teams from eight to sixteen. Rosters are set at fourteen players. The schedule is a mere 140 games. Baseballs are often dirty, tattered, and moistened (legally) with various substances. Wooden grandstands are standard. Spectators often overflow onto the field during games, sometimes to argue with players or umpires. Connie Mack begins his fifty-year run as manager of the Philadelphia Athletics. Nap Lajoie and Cy Young win Triple Crowns for hitting and pitching respectively. The owner of the New York Giants refuses to allow a particular umpire into the Polo Grounds—on allegations of incompetence.

1902 John McGraw begins his first of thirty-one years managing the Giants. Baseball legend Pud Galvin passes away at forty-five. The Orioles forfeit a game because they only have five available players. Dachshund sausages (hot dogs) become a ballpark staple, replacing such standard fare as hard-boiled eggs and ham sandwiches. Players routinely stay at boarding houses. Dummy Hoy bats against Dummy Taylor, marking the first time that two deaf mutes play against each other in the majors. Connie Mack sends two Pinkerton agents to the West Coast to sneak away the mentally erratic Rube Waddell from the minor league team (the Los Angeles Loo Loos) that Rube thought it would be a gas to play for.

1903 The Chicago "Cubs" officially begin play. The first motion picture of a baseball game is recorded. Ed Delahanty of the Washington Senators perishes and goes over Niagara Falls, not necessarily in that order. Boston beats Pittsburgh in the first modern World Series. Boston is helped by their "Royal Rooters," fans so fervent that they venture to Pittsburgh in droves to distract Honus Wagner and the other Pirates with taunting sing-alongs.

1904 Baseball adopts a 154-game schedule. The pitching mound is officially recognized. Cy Young hurls the first perfect game of the modern era. Jack Chesbro wins 41 games, a single-season record that stands to this day. However, his Highlanders lose the pennant to Boston on a wild pitch from Chesbro—marking the first of many times that the Yankees and Red Sox franchises will battle down to the wire. The World Series is cancelled when John McGraw's Giants refuse to participate— citing, in part, the overall superiority of the National League. McGraw's longtime enemy, American League President Ban Johnson, fumes in disgust.

1905 Ty Cobb and batting helmets both debut. Baseball draws five million fans for the first time. Archibald "Moonlight" Graham makes his lone major league appearance. Charles Ebbets heroically prevents his Brooklyn team from moving to Baltimore by purchasing additional shares of the franchise. Christy Mathewson and Rube Waddell both pitch their way to Triple Crowns.

1906 Frank Owen pitches two complete games on the same day. Baseball legend Buck Ewing passes away at forty-seven. The Cubs win 116 games and post a .763 winning percentage—two records that stand to this day. However, the White Sox upset the mighty Cubs in history's only all-Windy City World Series.

1907 The Dominican Republic's first professional team is organized. Walter "Big Train" Johnson debuts. Female hurler Alta Weiss causes a sensation by achieving success against men in a semi-pro league. A World Series game is called in extra-innings due to darkness and officially recorded as a tie.

1908 The world is introduced to the Boston "Red Sox." Shinguards debut, as does the song "Take Me Out to the Ballgame." Offensive production sinks to an all-time low. Baseball sets a new attendance record. The Cubs meet the Giants for a tiebreaker to decide the pennant. Fans literally pack the rafters at the Polo Grounds in Manhattan to watch. The Cubs win—but do so under less than noble circumstances. Fearing for their lives, they flee the grounds with a police escort but one player is knifed. (see chapter 22) The Cubs go on to win what will become their final world championship for over one hundred years.

1909 Rosters expand to twenty-five, but many clubs stay beneath this limit to save money. Legendary manager Frank Selee (.607 lifetime winning percentage) passes away at forty-nine. The first two ballparks made primarily from concrete and steel open for business (Shibe Park in Philadelphia and Forbes Field in Pittsburgh). An umpire spits on a hometown player, causing the crowd to riot. For his offense, the umpire is banished for life. Ty Cobb wins the hitting Triple Crown, and his Tigers win their third consecutive pennant. However, they also lose their third straight "World's Series."

1910 The saloon atmosphere at ballparks continues to evolve into something more civil. William Howard Taft becomes the first President to throw out a first pitch. Cy Young wins his 500th game. Ty Cobb sits out the last two games of the

regular season to protect his claim on the batting title (and on the fancy car being promised to the batting champ). Cobb's rival, Nap Lajoie, is allowed by his opposing team to reach base seven times on bunts to edge Cobb for the award. To avoid controversy (and to garner publicity), the manufacturer gives a car to both Cobb and Lajoie.

1911 Due to the introduction of cork-centered balls, hitters gain a much-needed advantage. Ty Cobb unanimously wins the league MVP award. Christy Mathewson and Cy Young duel for the only time in history, with Mathewson prevailing. The great hurler Addie Joss is struck down by illness at the age of thirty-one. To raise funds for Joss's family, the first version of an All-Star game is played despite objections from owners. Cy Young retires at the age of forty-four. The Giants and Athletics meet in the World Series but this Fall Classic is delayed by six consecutive days of rain—which sounds terrible, but at least it wasn't an earthquake that interrupted.

1912 Fenway Park in Boston officially opens for business, and their archrivals from New York are on hand to receive the first loss. It is commonplace for fans to gather in city squares beneath elaborate *Play-o-Gram* scoreboards where details of faraway games are transmitted play by play via telegram. Christy Mathewson records his 300th win. The first player's strike takes place when the Detroit Tigers take a powder to protest the suspension of Ty Cobb for going into the stands to beat up a heckler. They do so on principle, not out of affection. A replacement team made up of college boys, sandlot players (and two of the Tiger coaches) is promptly routed 24-2. Consequently, the strike ends after one day.

1913 The New York "Yankees" officially begin play. Brooklyn's jewel of a ballpark, Ebbets Field, opens for business on the former site of the Pigtown garbage dump. Walter Johnson pitches his way to a Triple Crown. Frank "Home Run" Baker leads the AL in homers with 12. Many pitchers learn that scuffing the ball is advantageous and gain yet another edge over hitters. Connie Mack's Philadelphia Athletics win their third world championship in four years.

1914 Babe Ruth debuts as does the Chicago ballyard that will later be known as Wrigley Field. The upstart "Federal League" raids eighty-one major league players and begins to compete with the American and National leagues. Salaries escalate across the board, particularly Tris Speaker's, who sees his salary double to $18,000. Honus Wagner and Nap Lajoie join retired legend Cap Anson as the only members of the 3,000 hit club. Approximately 100,000 people in Cleveland attend a championship game between two amateur ballclubs.

1915 During spring training, Wilbert Robinson attempts to catch a baseball dropped from an airplane 525 feet overhead. The pilot instead drops a grapefruit, which splatters on impact, leaving the confused Robertson to momentarily fear that the pulpy liquid is his own blood. The Cleveland "Indians" officially begin play. Albert Goodwill Spalding (pitcher, manager, promoter, executive, and sporting goods magnate) passes away at sixty-five. The Yankees debut their pinstripes. Eddie Plank records his 300th win. Both pennant winners decline the grandstand challenge of the Federal League's Chicago Whales and the rebel league disbands shortly thereafter.

1916 Grover Cleveland Alexander wins his second consecutive NL Triple Crown for pitching. Babe Ruth posts the lowest ERA in the American League. For the first time, "The Star-Spangled Banner" is sung before a game.

1917 Numerous games in April are cancelled due to the US's declaration of war on Germany. While 247 players would leave the major leagues to fight overseas, only 244 would return home. Fred Toney and Hippo Vaughn both pitch no-hitters through nine innings on the same day—against each other. The Chicago White Sox win their final World Championship of the century.

1918 World War I forces the regular season to conclude on September 2. During the war in Europe, Christy Mathewson is accidentally gassed and develops a life-shortening case of tuberculosis. The Boston Red Sox win their third world championship in four seasons...and their last of the century.

1919 The Boston Red Sox get seasick on their boat ride to spring training in Florida. New York City legalizes Sunday baseball. The St. Louis Browns have a game in which their outfielders do not record a single putout. New Cardinal manager Branch Rickey innovatively uses classroom instruction, batting cages, sliding pits, and a minor league farm system to help give St. Louis a competitive edge that will benefit them for years to come. Cleveland hurler Ray Caldwell is struck by lightning during a game but finishes the contest. Two weeks later, Caldwell no-hits the Yankees. For the first time, a league's home run leader (Babe Ruth) reaches a higher total than did the triples leader. Ty Cobb wins his twelfth and final batting title. Foul lines during the World Series are defined by spectator ropes, which are occasionally pushed or pulled to advantage the home team. Baseball is greatly harmed by a scandal in which players on the Chicago White Sox conspire to throw the World Series. During the offseason, in a move nearly as criminal, the Boston Red Sox sell Babe Ruth's contract to the New York Yankees.

1920 With the Great War ended, baseball plays out its first full season since 1916. New bylaws that outlaw tampering with the ball help spell an end to the Dead-Ball Era. Webbing is added to baseball gloves, creating a pocket between the thumb and index finger. The most prominent of the seven Negro Leagues begins play. Judge Kenesaw Mountain Landis begins his twenty-four-year run as commissioner. The Cincinnati Reds win two out of three in history's only tripleheader. Leon Cadore and Joe Oescheger pitch a twenty-six-inning, 1-1 tie. Walter Johnson records his 300th win. Tragically, Ray Chapman is killed by a pitched ball. In rapid response, baseballs are required to be clean and white at all times. Home run totals begin to skyrocket. Baseball attracts nine million fans, more than breaking the 1908 attendance record. A new era has been set in motion.

FOUR OF THE GREATEST PLAYERS FROM THIS ERA

Walter Johnson

- Nicknamed the "Big Train"
- Enjoyed a rural upbringing in both Kansas and California.
- A sidearmed slingshot pitcher
- Kind demeanor
- Pitched twenty-one seasons, all for the Washington Senators.
- Though a pitcher, he managed to hit .435 one season
- The greatest strikeout artist of his half-century

Christy Mathewson

- Nicknamed "The Christian Gentleman"
- Native Pennsylvanian
- Known for his "fadeaway" pitch
- Pitched seventeen seasons for the New York Giants
- Managed three seasons for the Cincinnati Reds
- Never pitched on Sundays
- Over a six-day period, Mathewson pitched three shutouts—during the World Series

Tris Speaker

- Native Texan and rodeo cowboy
- Perhaps the best defensive center fielder in history
- As a child, he broke his right arm falling off a horse, prompting him to permanently go southpaw
- Played twenty-two seasons, primarily for the Red Sox and Indians
- Managed eight seasons for the Tribe, totaling 617 wins
- Still the all-time leader in doubles and outfield assists
- Struck out fewer than once every forty-six at bats
- Turned six unassisted double plays in his life, a remarkable feat for a center fielder.
- Boston once considered his trade to the Cleveland Indians an even worse debacle than the selling of Babe Ruth to New York

Honus Wagner

- Nicknamed "The Flying Dutchman"
- Native Pennsylvanian
- A child laborer in coal mines who later trained as a barber
- Perhaps the greatest shortstop of all time
- Played twenty-one seasons, primarily for the Pittsburgh Pirates
- Eight-time hitting champion
- In retirement, ran a sporting goods store before being named deputy county sheriff of Allegheny County
- Late in life, he spent nineteen seasons as a coach for the Pittsburgh Pirates, retiring at age seventy-eight
- Tutored four future Hall of Famers, including Ralph Kiner

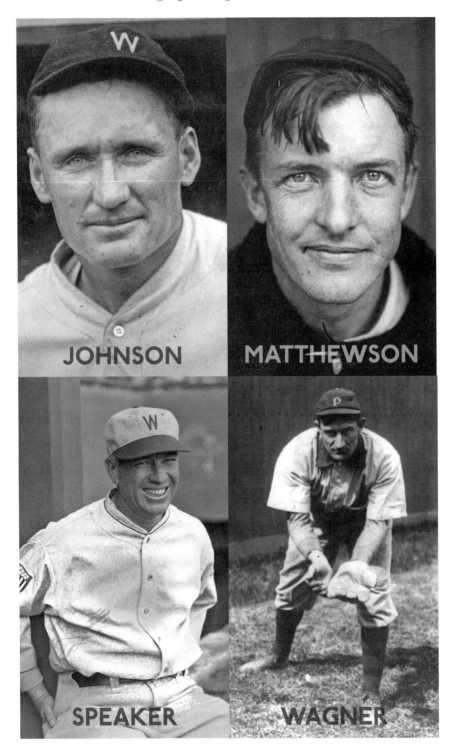

JOHNSON MATTHEWSON

SPEAKER WAGNER

THE TWO UMPIRES PRIMARILY FROM THIS ERA ENSHRINED IN COOPERSTOWN

Tom Connolly

- British-born umpire by way of Massachusetts, credited with establishing high ethical standards
- Among the first umpires to never back down from players
- Worked 4,768 games
- Regarded as the ultimate expert on baseball rules

Billy Evans

- Nicknamed the "Boy Umpire" because he was twenty-two upon entering the major leagues
- One of the first umps without big league playing experience
- Worked 3,319 career games while also working as a sportswriter
- Once single-handedly umpired fourteen games in eight days
- Once brawled with Ty Cobb underneath a grandstand

THE FIVE EXECUTIVES PRIMARILY FROM THIS ERA ENSHRINED IN COOPERSTOWN

Charles Comiskey

- Brought major league baseball to South Chicago
- Owned the White Sox for thirty years
- Built Comiskey Park (1910–1990)
- Stingy and frugal
- As a younger man, was a highly successful player-manager for twelve seasons

Barney Dreyfuss

- German-born owner of the Pirates for thirty-two seasons
- Credited as the creator of the World Series concept
- Possessed a knack for discovering talent
- Built Forbes Field in Pittsburgh

Clark Griffith

- One of the founding fathers of the American League
- Managed the Senators for nine years before mortgaging his Montana ranch to buy the team
- Operated the Senators on a shoestring for thirty-six seasons.
- Over his twenty-year pitching career, topped 20 wins seven times

Ban Johnson

- Founder of the American League, a cleaner variety of baseball designed to be suitable for women and children
- Helped his owners raid the National League for players
- Presided over this junior circuit for twenty-seven seasons
- Empowered umpires and fought player corruption

Sol White

- Highly important Negro League historian and pioneer
- Played twenty-three seasons, five in the integrated minor leagues
- Successful manager and sportswriter
- Extremely versatile, on and off the field

THE THREE MANAGERS PRIMARILY FROM THIS ERA ENSHRINED IN COOPERSTOWN

Rube Foster

- Leading Negro League manager
- Exceptional pitching tutor
- Great strategist
- His Chicago Leland Giants once won forty-eight consecutive games
- Was also a great hurler, an owner, and an influential executive

Connie Mack

- One of the few owner-managers
- Earned 3,731 wins, first on the all-time list
- Known as an exceptional tactician
- Employed an easy-going style but preached against alcohol
- Due to financial constraints, finished in last place numerous times and actually compiled a losing career record.
- Retired from managing at the age of eighty-seven
- Played as a catcher for eleven seasons

John McGraw

- Earned 2,763 victories as a manager, second on the all-time list behind Connie Mack
- Exceptional talent evaluator
- Employed a fiery, brawling, and risk-taking style
- Ejected by umpires on 131 occasions
- Finished under .500 only twice in thirty-three seasons
- Was also a great player and part-owner

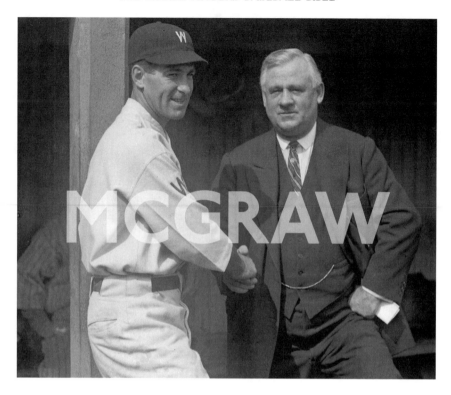

KNOW YOUR HALL OF FAME RUBES

RUBE WADDELL Eccentric southpaw pitcher from 1897 through 1910. Childlike mind. Pennsylvanian, huge drawing card, strikeout artist, alligator wrestler, bartender, binge drinker, melodrama actor, humanitarian, ended up in a sanitarium.

RUBE MARQUARD Streaky southpaw pitcher from 1908 through 1925. Received nickname because he resembled Rube Waddell. Intelligent mind. Ohioan, a New York Giant, performed schtick on the vaudeville circuit, ended up a ticket clerk at Maryland racetracks.

RUBE FOSTER Gifted righty pitcher from 1897 through 1917. Received nickname in 1902 when he defeated Rube Waddell in an interracial barnstorming game. Brilliant mind, Texan, friend and consultant to John McGraw, shrewd businessman, extraordinary coach, ended up in an asylum.

AFRICAN-AMERICAN PROFESSIONAL BASEBALL
FROM 1901 THROUGH 1920

At the turn of the century, the best all-black team was probably the Columbia Giants. They were an extraordinarily gifted squad out of Chicago that barnstormed (and steamrolled) throughout the Midwest. But in 1901, the team folded, in part because they had no home field. However, in their absence, numerous other teams began to dot the landscape.

In 1903, the Philadelphia Giants lost the "Colored Championship" to the newest best team, the Cuban X-Giants. They did so largely because of a twenty-five-year-old hurler named Rube Foster. Philadelphia promptly signed Foster away, essentially making him an ex-X-Giant. The following season, Foster proved to be the difference as Philadelphia beat the Cuban X-Giants in a rematch to take the 1904 championship.

In 1905, the famed Columbia Giants were resurrected in Chicago. After merging with another ballclub, they were rechristened the Leland Giants, named after their prominent owner (and former Negro League player) Frank Leland.

By 1907, Leland's Giants ripped a page out of the Philly playbook and raided away the phenomenal Rube Foster. But this time around, Foster had the leverage to demand that he not only manage the ballclub but also control the bookings.

Besides being an ace chucker, Foster was also a highly skilled manager and coach. He taught his hitters to take pitchers deep into the count and was also a staunch advocate of hit-and-run baseball. But his talents didn't stop there, for he was also an exceptional businessman. With Foster in charge of Leland's Giants, business boomed to the point that he was granted 40 percent of the gate receipts.

By 1909, Rube Foster demanded that Frank Leland step back and grant him full control. Of course, that idea was met with resistance. A court battle ensued that left Foster and Leland running different ballclubs. Ironically, Foster ended up with legal control of the Leland Giants name whereas Leland had to make due with the Chicago Giants moniker.

Foster's ballclub prospered while Leland's did not.

In 1911 Rube Foster renamed his team the Chicago American Giants to help broaden their appeal nationally. He also caught the lucky break of getting to use the ballpark the Chicago White Sox vacated when Comiskey Park opened for business. But Foster had even grander designs to consider; he was dreaming of starting an entire league.

With each passing year, Rube used his arm less and his brain more. By 1917, he began pitching ideas instead of baseballs.

By 1920, the timing was finally right for Rube's dream to manifest.

He was named president of this new eight-team "Negro National League." However, he also stayed on as the owner of the Chicago American Giants. He made additional money as the league's exclusive booking agent, a position that netted him 5 percent of every team's gate. He also had the sole right to sell equipment to each of the eight teams. Good work if you can get it.

After thirty-five years of loosely organized barnstorming, the Golden Age of the Negro Leagues was finally set to begin, and the man most responsible for this institution that would entertain millions was none other than Andrew Foster, a man who in essence, was anything but a Rube.

THE FIVE NEGRO LEAGUE PLAYERS PRIMARILY FROM THIS ERA ENSHRINED IN COOPERSTOWN WHO ARE NOT NAMED RUBE FOSTER OR SOL WHITE

Pete Hill

- Came out of Pittsburgh, PA
- Played 1899–1921 and 1923–1925
- Excellent center fielder with shotgun arm
- Considered by Rube Foster to be his field general
- His barnstorming team went 123-6 one year
- Once hit safely in 115 out of 116 games
- Could continuously foul off pitches at will
- Went into managing and also worked in the front office

John Henry "Pop" Lloyd

- Came out of a small town in Florida
- Played 1906–1925 and 1930–1931
- Extraordinary shortstop and highly skilled baserunner
- Gentlemanly demeanor
- Switched teams fourteen times in twenty-six years, not including his time playing Cuban winter ball
- Extraordinary shortstop
- Early nickname was "El Cuchara" (the shovel)
- Later nickname was "Pop," a nod to his mentoring skills
- Referred to as the black Honus Wagner, a comparison Wagner felt honored by
- Widely considered to be one of the top three Negro League players of all time along with Satchel Paige and Josh Gibson
- Went on to manage for ten seasons

José Mendez

- The first famous Cuban-born player
- Played 1908–1926
- Righty with a blazing fastball and a twelve-to-six curveball
- In 1908, during a three-game exhibition series, he held the Cincinnati Reds scoreless for twenty-five consecutive innings
- Pitched a perfect game in 1909
- Only 5' 9"
- A legend in his homeland
- Nicknamed "Black Diamond"
- Nearly managed a .700 winning percentage
- Managed the Kansas City Monarchs to three successive pennants

Louis Santop

- Texan
- Strong-armed catcher with tape-measure home run power
- Played 1909–1926
- Nicknamed "Top"
- Drawing card
- Cocky
- 6' 4"
- Hit .470 in 1911
- Credited with hitting a dead-ball era baseball in excess of five hundred feet.
- The first player to be called "The black Babe Ruth"
- World War One veteran
- Later became a bartender in Philadelphia

Ben Taylor

- Raised in South Carolina
- Played 1908–1929
- Slugging first baseman with a golden glove
- Nicknamed "Old Reliable"
- Soft-spoken personality
- Originally a pitcher
- Natural leader
- Consistent .300 hitter
- Mentored Buck Leonard
- Later owned a game program concession in Baltimore

THE TEMPORARY MAJOR LEAGUE BALLCLUBS, 1901–1920

Baltimore Terrapins
Brooklyn Tip-Tops
Chicago Whales
Indianapolis Hoosiers
Kansas City Packers
Newark Pepper
Pittsburgh Rebels
St. Louis Terriers

THE SIXTEEN BALLCLUBS THAT PLAYED BALL EVERY YEAR 1901–1920

Baltimore Orioles/New York Highlanders/New York Yankees
Boston Americans/Red Sox
Boston Beaneaters/Doves/Rustlers/Braves
Brooklyn Superbas/Dodgers/Robins
Chicago Orphans/Cubs
Chicago White Stockings/White Sox
Cincinnati Reds
Cleveland Blues/Bronchos/Naps/Indians
Detroit Tigers
Milwaukee Brewers/St. Louis Browns
New York Giants
Philadelphia Athletics
Philadelphia Phillies
Pittsburgh Pirates
St. Louis Cardinals
Washington Senators/Nationals

NOTABLE DIFFERENCES BETWEEN THE 1908 CLEVELAND NAPS AND THE 2008 CLEVELAND INDIANS

- One team played 154 games, the other played 162.
- One team was one of eight competing for the pennant, the other was one of fourteen.
- One played at League Park, the other played at Jacobs Field.
- One played in a ballpark that seated 9,000 fans; the other's home field could accommodate 43,000
- One team attracted 422,000 fans; the other drew 2,169,000.
- One had outfield dimensions of 375–420–290;
  the others had dimensions of 325–405–325
- One team used thirty-two players over the course of the year; the other used forty-nine

- One team didn't have any starters hit .300; neither did the other
- One team had an average age of 28.2; the other's was 28.0.
- One team hit three times as many triples as home runs; the other team hit seven times as many home runs as triples.
- One team scored an average of 3.7 runs per game; the other scored 4.9 per game.
- One team surrendered 3.0 runs per game; the other gave up 4.7 per game
- One team had an ERA of 2.02; the other had an ERA of 4.46.
- One team committed 257 fielding errors; the other only made 106.
- One team knocked out 18 homers and walked 364 times; the other team hit 170 homers and walked 444 times.
- One team had a fella (Bill Hinchman) lead the team with 6 homers; the other had a guy (Grady Sizemore) top his squad with 33 dings.
- One team swiped 177 bases; the other stole only 77.
- One team had three pitchers reach 262 innings; the other had only one reach as many as 162.
- One team had a pitching staff that combined for 5 saves; the other staff saved 31.
- One team's pitching staff hit .171 with 78 hits; the other staff hit .105 with 2 hits.
- One team had a 24-game winner (Addie Joss); the other had a 22-game winner (Cliff Lee)

To review our 25-man dream team comprised of the era's best players, check out Chapter 27.

Follies Factoids

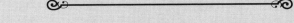

★ Christy Mathewson and Mordecai "Three Finger" Brown dueled twenty-five times over the course of their careers and retired on the same day after facing each other.

★ Ty Cobb faced Walter Johnson more times than any other hitter-pitcher combination in history.

★ Only two teams in history managed to win 116 games during the regular season (the 1906 Chicago Cubs and the 2001 Seattle Mariners). However, neither became world champions.

41

The
Tom Seaver
Dossier

SEAVER, Tom

DOSSIER - 41

BIRTHPLACE: Fresno, California
177 miles from the future site of the Oakland
Coliseum and 217 miles from the future site of
Dodger Stadium

NICKNAME: Tom Terrific

TRAITS: Righthanded, studious, intensely
scrutinized himself, great control, strong legs,
used a drop-and-drive overhand delivery

HIGH SCHOOL: Fresno High

HIGH SCHOOL ACCOMPLISHMENTS: All-city in
basketball.

OTHER ALUMNI FROM SAME HIGH SCHOOL INCLUDE:
Frank Chance, Pat Corrales, Bobby Jones

MILITARY: Spent over a year as a Marine Corps
reservist in California.

ALUMNI OF: Fresno City College

1964: Seaver pitches a no-hitter for the
independent Alaska Goldpanners

SEAVER, Tom

1965: Seaver joins the team at the University of Southern California and becomes a top prospect. The Dodgers draft him but refuse to meet his $70,000 price tag.

OTHER ALUMNI FROM USC INCLUDE: Jim Barr, Bret Boone, Ron Fairly, Dave Kingman, Randy Johnson, Bill "Spaceman" Lee, Fred Lynn, Mark McGwire, Barry Zito

THE GREAT CONTROVERSY OF 1966: Seaver is drafted number one by the Atlanta Braves and signs a contract with them. However, baseball's commissioner voids the deal when he discovers that USC had played some unsanctioned baseball games, even though Seaver had not participated, essentially compromising Seaver's status as an amateur. However, by signing a professional contract, he cannot return to the USC roster. He is left without a playing option. Eventually, the commissioner rules that any team willing to match the Braves' original offer can have a crack at Seaver in a lottery. Three teams take the chance (the Cleveland Indians, New York Mets, and Philadelphia Phillies). The Mets win this lottery.

MINOR LEAGUE GAMES BEFORE HIS MLB DEBUT: 34

SEAVER, Tom

DOSSIER - 41

CAREER MINOR LEAGUE TOTALS: 1 full season
1 organization - 1 city (Jacksonville) - 34 games
12-12   3.13 ERA   188K

MLB DEBUT: 1967

AGE AT DEBUT: 22

OTHER PLAYERS WHO DEBUTED IN 1967 INCLUDED:
Johnny Bench, Rod Carew, Reggie Jackson, Jerry
Koosman, Sparky Lyle, Mike Marshall, Joe Niekro,
Graig Nettles

PLAYERS WHO RETIRED IN 1967 INCLUDED:
Lew Burdette, Whitey Ford, Dick Groat,
Johnny Klippstein, Curt Simmons, Bill Skowran

SEAVER'S EARLIEST METS TEAMMATES INCLUDED:
Tommy Davis, Don Shaw, Ron Swoboda

SEAVER'S ROOKIE YEAR:
16-13 with a 2.76 ERA and 170 K
(won the NL Rookie of the Year Award)

ROOKIE TRIVIA: Was named to the All-Star team
and recorded the save by pitching a scoreless
fifteenth inning.

SEAVER, Tom   DOSSIER - 41

IN 1969: As part of the Miracle Mets, Seaver won a
world championship

IN 1973: Seaver's Mets won the pennant but lost
to the Oakland A's in the Fall Classic.

IN 1977: Traded to the front-running Cincinnati Reds

IN 1978: Pitched a no-hitter

IN 1979: His Reds won the NL West before falling in
the NLCS to the Pittsburgh Pirates

In 1983: Returned to the Mets

IN 1984: Surprisingly claimed by the White Sox
in a compensation draft. The Mets had left him
unprotected figuring no one would want to pay
a pitcher Seaver's age his high salary. Seaver's
only choices were to report to Chicago or retire.
The vacated roster spot on the Mets went to
Dwight Gooden.

FINAL YEAR: 1986

AGE AT FINALE: 41

SEAVER, Tom   DOSSIER - 41

FINAL TEAMMATES INCLUDED: Don Baylor, Wade Boggs,
Oil Can Boyd, Bill Buckner, Roger Clemens,
Dwight Evans, Jim Rice

MAJOR LEAGUE CAREER TOTALS:
20 seasons - 656 games
5 stints with 4 different ballclubs
311-205   2.86 ERA   3,640K

IN 1992: Seaver was inducted into the Baseball
Hall of Fame on the first ballot with the highest
voting percentage in history (98.8%).

NUMBER OF SEASONS ON WINNING TEAMS: 13

MAJOR LEAGUE AFFILIATIONS:
New York Mets (61%)
Cincinnati Reds (24%)
Chicago White Sox (12%)
Boston Red Sox (2%)

TOTAL MANAGERS PLAYED FOR: 15

MOST FREQUENT MANAGER: Gil Hodges

MOST FREQUENT CATCHER: Jerry Grote

PITCHING ROLE: Starter - 99% / Reliever - 1%

SEAVER, Tom

STATS AS A FIREMAN:
0-1   7.71   3K
Converted 1 out of 3 save opportunities

BEST SEASON: (1969)
25-7   2.21 ERA   208K

CY YOUNG AWARDS: 3

LEAGUE ERA CROWNS: 3

LEAGUE WINS LEADER: 3

LEAGUE STRIKEOUT LEADER: 5

TRIVIA: Reached the 200 strikeout plateau nine
consecutive seasons

HIS FREQUENT OPPOSING PITCHERS: Steve Carlton,
Bob Forsch, Bob Gibson, Ferguson Jenkins,
Randy Jones, Phil Niekro, Gaylord Perry,
Rick Reuschel, Steve Rogers, Don Sutton

CAREER FIELDING RECORD: .960

CAREER HITTING STATS: .154 BA, 12 HR, 86 RBI, 4 SB

INJURY AND REST RATE: 3%

SEAVER, Tom

PLAYOFF RECORD: 3 postseasons - 8 games
3-3   2.77 ERA   4 K
3 divisional titles
2 pennants
1 world championship

ALL-STAR TEAMS: 12

ALL-STAR STATS: 0-0 / 4.85 ERA / 16K

THREE MOST FREQUENT FOES: Lou Brock
157 plate appearances (.250 BA, 1 HR, 9 RBI, 4 BB, 21K)

Pete Rose
149 plate appearances (.281 BA, 3 HR, 9 RBI, 12 BB, 20K)

Willie Stargell
140 plate appearances (.242 BA, 8 HR, 20 RBI, 10 BB, 38K)

A HITTER HE OWNED: Dal Maxville
.087 (4 for 46) with 0 HR, 2 RBIs, 3 BB, 20K

A HITTER WHO OWNED HIM: Rick Monday
.349 (30 for 86) with 11 HRs, 17 RBIs, 17 BB, 29K
(no other hitter smacked as many as 9 HRs
against Seaver)

SEAVER, Tom   DOSSIER - 41

HIS RECORD AGAINST HALL OF FAMERS: 1,676 AT-BATS
.230 BA, 53 HR,183 RBIs,161 BB, 369K

MOST FREQUENT STRIKEOUT VICTIM: Tony Perez (41)

TRIVIA: Issued 6 intentional walks to Willie
McCovey, more than any other player

MOST FREQUENT TEAMMATES: Jerry Grote,
Bud Harrelson, Ed Kranepool

HOME AWAY FROM HOME:
San Diego (Jack Murphy / Qualcomm Stadium)
18-5   1.58 ERA   159K

MOST FREQUENT OPPONENT: Atlanta Braves

CLOSEST STATISTICAL TWIN: Tom Glavine

PERSONAL INTERESTS IN RETIREMENT:
Broadcasting, winemaking

HALL OF FAME CALIBRE RATING: 188%

42

Shoulders Jackie Robinson Stood Upon

◇◇

Every major league ballpark proudly displays the retired number 42 to honor Jack Roosevelt Robinson, who not only endured an extraordinary burden but remained excellent in spite of it.

In the late 1940s, Jackie Robinson reversed a great deal of prejudice that existed within the culture, and in doing so, paved the way for countless other ballplayers to advance. Like any good infielder, he was always on the lookout to eradicate the rocks and other imperfections from his environment. In a sense, Jackie engaged in this process away from infields as well.

But just as Jackie is the man who felled the sport's mighty tree of segregation, additional credit should go to the many before him who took chunks out of that same tree with ax swings of their own.

If you were to ask one hundred Americans the identity of the first African-American to play major league baseball, a resounding majority would answer Jackie Robinson. However, this is not true. There were at least three people of African-American descent who played in the big leagues well before the color barrier was enacted.

A man with the ironic name of William White may have been the pioneer. His background was somewhat unique because his mother was a slave, and his father was a plantation owner. Because of the superior advantages offered to Caucasians, their son chose to pass himself off as white. Eventually, the half-black White ended up attending Brown University in Rhode Island—where he became a fixture on the baseball field.

One day in the summer of 1879, the first baseman for the National League's Providence Grays broke his finger. Because rosters were so spartan in those days, major injuries necessitated the hiring of outside players.

The Grays dispatched a search party to the local university diamond, and that's where they found William White. He did very well for the Grays (with his glove, bat, *and* legs), but after just one game, he was never used again. Was it because they had discovered his genetic secret? The answer is unclear.

Five years later, the majors had a brief re-infusion of color when the Toledo Blue Stockings signed Moses "Fleetwood" Walker and his brother Welday. But the duo didn't last long with the team because most of their teammates refused to accept them as equals. The situation was so bad that whenever Fleetwood was behind the dish as the catcher, his batterymate would often refuse to tip him what pitch was coming.

When the Walker Brothers left the Blue Sox, it marked the beginning of the sixty-three-year color barrier that Jackie Robinson was destined to break. But even so, like White, the Walkers had proved that they could run with the best.

Another man who made a significant impact is a largely forgotten college player. His name was Charles Thomas and in 1901, a young coach named Branch Rickey befriended him on the Ohio Wesleyan University campus. Thomas eventually found himself penciled in as the university's first baseman. Rickey's experiences with Thomas were very positive and only cemented his belief that blacks and whites blended together as well as chocolate and milk.

But it wasn't all peaches and cream as Branch saw how unfairly his friend was treated. Bearing witness to such prejudice encouraged the young coach to fight segregation whenever he could, a mission that much later in life, he succeeded in.

Even though the major leagues had more than a few racists in key positions, many others despised the color barrier. One such man was legendary manager John McGraw. While visiting Arkansas in 1901, McGraw saw a great talent by the name of Charlie Grant, a bellhop who played for his hotel's semi-pro team.

McGraw badly wanted to bring this jewel to the major league level but had little opportunity to do so. Since Charlie had relatively light skin and straight black hair, McGraw decided that he might be able to pass himself off as a Cherokee Indian. Soon enough, McGraw began talking up his newest player, "Chief Tokohoma," while fabricating a story as to how he had met the chief on a reservation in Arkansas.

To the unfamiliar eye, Grant was able to pull off the ruse. But it was not to be, for during his first preseason game, he knocked a mighty home run that caused all of his longtime African-American fans to pour onto the playing field to wildly congratulate their hero—a celebration that essentially blew his cover.

Ban Johnson, the chief of the American League, went on to ban "Chief To-kohoma" on grounds of his ethnicity. John McGraw fought for the cause long and hard but to no avail, and McGraw and Johnson remained thorns in each other's sides for years afterward. It can even be argued that the 1904 World Series didn't take place because of McGraw's hatred for Ban Johnson.

McGraw remained a friend to the Negro Leagues, though he wasn't able to directly employ any of their players. He was often spotted at their games and talking shop afterward. He even arranged numerous exhibitions between them and his Giants, many of which ended with his team on the losing end. In essence, through these exhibitions, McGraw helped to both legitimize their talent and give them some of the prestige (and payoffs) they deserved.

One of the players who McGraw wanted to sign was ace pitcher Rube Foster. Like McGraw, Foster started out as a talented player but turned into an even better manager and teacher. Though the color barrier kept them from working together in an official capacity, both went on to achieve a level of greatness worthy of Cooperstown.

Another Negro League superstar who helped blaze the trail was Satchel Paige. Thirteen years older then Jackie, the mercurial one did a great deal to get people to ask why these great ballplayers weren't allowed to compete in the majors. Because of his personality and talent, he became a major drawing card, so much so that Negro League teams featuring Satchel were finally allowed entry into the first-class venues of the era like Wrigley Field and Cleveland Stadium.

To many white superstars, Satchel was a measuring stick. Bob Feller, Stan Musial, and numerous others relished the chance to play exhibition games against Satchel. In fact, just prior to joining the Yankees, Joe DiMaggio clashed with Satchel Paige in a Northern California exhibition game in which Joe managed to go 1 for 4. The Yankee scout in attendance was ecstatic and wired the following message back to New York:

DIMAGGIO EVERYTHING WE'D HOPED HE'D BE:
HIT SATCH ONE FOR FOUR

By 1941, Satchel Paige had grown so popular that *Life* magazine even ran a pictorial on him.

During World War II, with DiMaggio, Feller, Ted Williams, and numerous other stars overseas, the barnstorming Satchel Paige actually became the sport's highest-paid attraction, despite the fact that he wasn't even allowed in the major leagues. Satch attracted fans of all colors and made more than a few major league owners wonder why they were missing out on hiring such an exceptional player.

Yet another trailblazer for the cause was Cool Papa Bell, a man so quick that many believed he could outrun Olympian Jesse Owens. After a lengthy and productive career in the Negro Leagues, Cool Papa Bell turned to coaching. Among the youngsters that he guided were Ernie Banks, Elston Howard, and a returning WW2 veteran on the verge of superstardom by the name of...Jack Roosevelt Robinson.

The road was surely a hard one for Jackie, but it was no doubt made possible by the many greats preceding him whose shoulders he was able to climb upon.

Jack Roosevelt Robinson Factoids

★ In the late 1930s, he was on a Pomona-based All-Star team with Ted Williams of San Diego and Bob Lemon of Long Beach.

★ In ten years with Brooklyn, he made the All-Star team six times and although he played in six World Series, his Dodgers only ended up with one ring.

★ He spent most of his rookie year playing first base before moving to second. He was moved away from second base at the age of thirty-three and spent his final four seasons as an outfielder and third baseman.

★ He averaged 12 errors a year and ended up with a .983 career fielding permillage.

★ He was almost court-martialed for refusing a direct order from a superior officer to move to the back of a segregated military bus. His defiance predated Rosa Parks by eleven years.

★ He won one league MVP award and hit .311 across his career. However, he only managed to hit .234 in the postseason.

★ In an average year, he had 487 at bats, 94 runs, 152 hits, 13 homers, 73 RBIs, and 20 stolen bases out of 23 attempts.

★ Since the 1910s, no one has stolen home as often as Jackie Robinson—who did it on 19 occasions.

★ In 1973, Jackie Robinson passed away in Connecticut at the age of fifty-three. He was diabetic and virtually blind at the time.

43

The Best Bet Middlers

WHO ARE THE BEST MIDDLE RELIEF PITCHERS OF ALL TIME? It's a long overdue question...for middlers rarely get the respect they deserve. These stopgappers have never been inducted into Cooperstown, and only on rare occasions have any made it onto an All-Star team.

Yet, since around 1990, these unsung bridgebuilders have been the ones, more often than not, who strand baserunners (since this era's "firemen" usually only enter with a clean slate at the top of the ninth inning). Indeed, it's extremely rare for a championship club nowadays to not have at least two top middle relief specialists on their roster.

Even on the three Oakland championship teams I played for, I'd hate to think how many fewer games we would have won if we didn't have Darold Knowles, Paul Lindblad, and others doing such a great job in the middle. Not only were they adept at holding onto leads, but they also kept us close in games where we were only down a few runs.

But despite the respect that middlers garner from the sport's insiders, they're still a highly underrated group to the public. I suppose many folks are still locked into the ancient assessment that middle relievers are little more than second-rate pitchers not durable enough to start or exceptional enough to close—a myth that dissipates more and more each year.

However, during baseball's earliest decades, this "myth" actually had *some* merit. But back then if you had great stuff, you automatically got thrown into the rotation. There's little doubt that if a Bruce Sutter or a Billy Wagner had somehow come along in 1908, they would have been expected to go nine innings every four days.

But in 1918, the perception of relief pitching shifted a bit when George

Mogridge of the upstart Yankees led all pitchers with 45 appearances. What made this notable was that 23 of his 45 games had been in relief (more than 50 percent). Since this was the first time anyone other than a starter had led the league in games pitched, Mogridge was as a window into baseball's future.

Just four years later, yet another innovative ballclub on the verge of winning championships (the St. Louis Cardinals) used a talented pitcher in the same fashion. This veteran's name was Lou North, and although he both started and closed, he was primarily used as a middler. Like Mogridge before him, he led baseball in games pitched one season, but what made North's feat unprecedented was that he was technically the first middler to do so.

Across the next couple of decades, it was always a crapshoot as to whether a starter or a reliever would lead the leagues in games pitched. But even when the starters managed to do so, hybrid pitchers who primarily relieved (such as Jack Russell, Russ Van Atta, and Clyde Shoun) helped bring new respect to the role of the relief specialist. Finally in 1946, for the very last time, a starter led baseball in games pitched. That workhorse was the legendary Bob Feller. The times, they were about to be a changing.

The trend fully blossomed in 1952 when a twenty-nine-year old rookie named Hoyt Wilhelm arrived at the Polo Grounds. Long story short: Hoyt Wilhelm's impact on relief pitching is still felt today. Many people mistakenly think that I'm first relief pitcher to be inducted in Cooperstown. That honor belongs to Hoyt Wilhelm.

During Hoyt's rookie campaign for the Giants, he went 15-3, pitched 159 innings and posted a measly 2.43 earned run average.

Those are pretty impressive numbers for a starter, but perhaps you'll find them even more impressive if I tell you that Hoyt did all of this without so much as starting a single game.

There's no doubt that Leo Durocher's use of the righty began opening eyes, especially since the majority of Hoyt's relief appearances in '52 had been in middle relief. Hoyt ended up pitching until the ripe old age of forty-nine, at which point he retired with 143 wins, 227 saves and an ERA of 2.52. But because he spent a lot more time as a closer than he did as a middler, we must look deeper into the annals of baseball history to find out the identity of baseball's first premiere middle reliever.

It's a tough call, but I think this ball needs to be passed to Steve Hamilton, a 6' 7" former NBA player who pitched for the Yankees and five other teams from 1961 to 1972. Tossing out all of the numbers he accumulated either as a starter or in save situations, (he spent 1968 as the Yankee closer) Hamilton ended up with a highly impressive 34-16 record with a 2.62 ERA in 296 games.

But if not Ham, another candidate for the honor could be Bob Miller, who played for the Dodgers and nine other teams from 1957-1974. Solely in the middle, Bob pitched in 487 games and posted a 44-33 record to go along with a 2.80 ERA. In a sense, these two paved a middling path for hundreds to follow.

One such pitcher, Paul Lindblad, debuted during the 1965 season. He finished his middler career with a 51-33 record and a 3.22 ERA across 450 games.

Any list of top middlers from the 1970s would also have to include lefthander Steve Mingori—who middled 280 games while posting 18 wins and a 3.02 ERA for the Indians and Royals. There's no doubt that Mingori played a key role in Kansas City's three consecutive divisional titles from 1976 to 1978. During the '76 season, Mingori was sometimes in the bullpen with another pitcher who warrants mention—Bob McClure, who was no stranger to starting and closing, but primarily spent his nineteen seasons in the bigs as a middle reliever.

In the 1980s, closers received far more attention than middle relievers, but some standouts emerged all the same. In 1983, Craig Lefferts made the scene. His twelve-year run, primarily for the Padres and Giants, saw him middle for all but three of them. This lefthander was an instrumental part of two pennant-winning ballclubs, and as a reliever in non-save situations, totaled 40 victories and a 3.11 ERA in 427 games.

The American League had someone of similar caliber in the form of Mark Eichhorn, who became best known for his role as the set-up man in Toronto for Tom Henke. Solely as a middler, Eichhorn racked 43 wins and had a 2.98 ERA across 420 games. He even went on to pitch 4.1 scoreless postseason innings during Toronto's back-to-back championship period in 1992 and 1993.

The times, however, were a changing again.

The year 1989 marked the last time that a true closer (Mitch "Wild Thing" Williams of the Cubs) would lead a league in games pitched. The rise of the prominent middler was gaining momentum, especially since everyone had started to use their closers far more sparingly than they had before.

This became an era of Jesse Orosco, a former Mets closer who had been shifted to the middle upon the emergence of Roger McDowell. Orosco ended up spending twenty-two of his twenty-four seasons as a middle reliever and as a result, went on to become baseball's all-time leader in games pitched (with 1,071). Solely as a middler, Orosco won 72 games while managing an extremely low 3.02 ERA.

Two of the other all-time great middlers actually played high school baseball against each other in Midland, Texas, before becoming college teammates at Southwestern. They didn't often cross paths in the major leagues, but they both did enjoy immense success. They were part of six world championship teams, which is six more than Trevor Hoffman, the all-time saves leader. I'm talking about Mike Timlin and Mike Stanton.

Besides sharing a hometown, an alma mater, an era, and the same first name, these two middlers were also among the first to use entrance music, an additional sign that the importance of the middle reliever was escalating.

The lefthanded Stanton, primarily with the Braves and Yankees, pitched 750 games in non-save situations and racked a 60-45 record, a 3.96 ERA, and 592 strikeouts in the process. Righthander Timlin played primarily for Toronto, St. Louis, and Boston, hurling 650 games in non-save situations and posting a 63-34 record, a 3.55 ERA, and 537 whiffs.

What will the future hold for the role of the middler? Time will tell, but the way things are trending, it won't be long before they will be recognized in the All-Star games with far greater frequency.

FOURTEEN OF THE BEST MIDDLERS
2000-2009
(non-save situations only)

	W–L	ERA	Games	K/9
Rafael Betancourt	24-17	3.13	263	8.70
Brendan Donnelly	26-6	3.09	236	8.50
Octavio Dotel	22-10	2.82	280	11.56
Scott Downs	9-4	2.53	161	8.24
Pedro Feliciano	16-13	3.49	268	8.38
Mike Gonzalez	12-13	2.73	177	10.27
Matt Guerrier	13-12	3.24	232	5.84
Ray King	20-15	3.27	416	5.77
Scott Linebrink	29-18	3.29	300	8.30
Ryan Madson	25-13	2.60	224	7.57
Carlos Marmol	8-9	3.10	120	11.27
Peter Moylan	11-6	2.44	141	7.45
Takashi Saito	14-7	2.15	130	10.24
Scot Shields	34-23	2.98	293	8.08

Follies Factoids

★ Outside of his accomplishments as a middle reliever, Paul Lindblad also tallied 64 saves, notched a complete-game shutout, and even managed to go his entire fourteen-year career without committing a fielding error. In addition, on September 25, 1975, Lindblad, along with ace Vida Blue, Glenn Abbott, and closer Rollie Fingers combined for a no-hitter.

★ The highlight of middler Bob McClure's career occurred as a starter in 1982 when he notched 12 victories for the incredibly talented, extremely well-behaved and somewhat well-groomed AL champion Milwaukee Brewers.

★ Top middlers Graeme Lloyd and Peter Moylan are both Australian.

★ The list of other middle relievers who prospered during the Orosco era included Paul Assenmacher, Rheal Cormier, Alan Embree, Mike Jackson, Steve Kline, Graeme Lloyd, Kent Mercker, Mike Myers, Jeff Nelson, Dan Plesac, Eric Plunk, Paul Quantrill, Scott Radinsky, Steve Reed, Mike Remlinger, Arthur Rhodes, Felix Rodriguez, Ron Villone, and David Weathers. Although the trend is reversing, middle relievers often tend to be journeymen. Of the nineteen names mentioned above, the average middler played for more than six franchises.

44

Perspective

◇◇

At the age of twenty-six,
Mark Fidrych threw his last major league pitch.

At the age of twenty-seven,
the Metrodome in Minneapolis hosted its final Twins game.

At the age of twenty-eight,
Jackie Robinson debuted for the Brooklyn Dodgers.

At the age of twenty-nine,
Hideki "Godzilla" Matsui debuted for the New York Yankees.

At the age of thirty,
Joe DiMaggio was fighting World War Two.

At the age of thirty-one,
the California Angels changed their name.

At the age of thirty-two,
Alex Rodriguez hit his 500th home run.

At the age of thirty-three,
Robin Yount was playing in his sixteenth season.

At the age of thirty-four,
Eric Wedge was named the manager of the Cleveland Indians.

At the age of thirty-five,
"The Rookie" Jim Morris made his major league debut.

At the age of thirty-six,
Sandy Koufax was elected to the Hall of Fame.

45

Have Morgan Will Travel

In lieu of presenting another dossier on a Hall-of-Fame-caliber superstar, we are instead shedding light on the career of Mike Morgan, the sort of "under the radar" workhorse who forms the backbone of major league baseball.

BIRTHPLACE
172 miles from the future site of Dodger Stadium (in Tulare, CA)

CHILDHOOD ANECDOTE
While repeating the second grade, Mike told his teacher that he'd become a major league baseball player

NICKNAME
Mo-Man

TRAITS
Righthanded, rubber armed,
old-school work ethic, fast-talking, upbeat

STUFF
As a teenager, possessed a major league fastball
(but only a high school curve ball)

HIGH SCHOOL
Valley High, Las Vegas

HIGH SCHOOL ACCOMPLISHMENTS
Lettered in baseball and football

OTHER ALUMNI FROM SAME HIGH SCHOOL INCLUDE
Tyler Houston, Greg Maddux, Doug Mirabelli, D-I softball coach Josh Musselman

DRAFTED
Was the 4th overall pick in the 1978 draft.

PLAYERS DRAFTED AHEAD OF HIM IN THE '78 DRAFT
Bob Horner, Lloyd Moseby, and Hubie Brooks

MINOR LEAGUE GAMES BEFORE HIS MLB DEBUT
Zero.
Under the guidance of owner/GM Charlie Finley
and skipper Jack McKeon, Morgan debuted for the
A's organization in the majors.

DEBUT YEAR
1978

AGE AT DEBUT
18

OTHER MLB PLAYERS WHO DEBUTED IN 1978 INCLUDED
Danny Darwin, Pedro Guerrero, Bob Horner, Carney Lansford,
Paul Molitor, Ozzie Smith, Bob Welch

PLAYERS WHO RETIRED IN 1978 INCLUDED
Sandy Alomar, Bob Bailey, Clay Carroll, Ron Fairly,
Jim Fregosi, Davey Johnson, Wilbur Wood

MORGAN'S EARLIEST A's TEAMMATES INCLUDED
Matt Keough, Mitchell Page, Dave Revering

HIS ROOKIE YEAR
After going 0-3 with a 7.30 ERA, Morgan was sent to the minors.

HIS SOPHOMORE YEAR
After pitching thirteen games at AAA, Morgan was promoted back to
Oakland in June where he went 2-10 with a 5.94 ERA.

HIS JUNIOR YEAR
Spent entirely in the minors

IN 1980
After three years in the organization, Morgan was traded away for
thirty-three-year-old Fred "Chicken" Stanley (who hit .193 in successive seasons
for the A's before retiring)

MAJOR LEAGUE RE-EMERGENCE
1982
Morgan became the fourth starter in the Yankee rotation
after Ron Guidry, Tommy John, and Dave Righetti

EARLY SIGNS OF BOUNCING BALL SYNDROME?
Affirmative.
After the Yankees traded Morgan to the Blue Jays, the Mariners plucked him
away in a Rule 5 draft. Morgan would go on to play for twelve organizations.

MINOR LEAGUE RATIO
From 1983 to 1985, 69% of Morgan's games
were played in the minors.

CAREER MINOR LEAGUE TOTALS
(including eventual rehab stints)
3 full seasons, parts of 9 others
8 organizations, 10 cities, 127 games
39-48   4.61 ERA   244K

MOST FREQUENT MINOR LEAGUE STOP
Syracuse, NY

HIS NEXT MAJOR LEAGUE EMERGENCE
1986
Morgan became the third starter in the Mariner rotation
after Mike Moore and Mark Langston.

IN 1990
Dodger pitching coach Ron Perranoski altered Morgan's mechanics by shifting him from the right side of the rubber to the left. Orel Hershiser tutored him as well.

IN 1991
Morgan was selected to the All-Star team.

IN 2001
While playing for the Arizona Diamondbacks, Morgan became a World Champion.

FINAL YEAR
2002

AGE AT FINALE
42

FINAL TEAMMATES INCLUDED
Mark Grace, Luis Gonzalez, Randy Johnson, Curt Schilling, and Matt Williams

MAJOR LEAGUE CAREER TOTALS
22 seasons – 597 games
13 stints with 12 ballclubs
141-186   4.23 ERA   1,403K

MAJOR LEAGUE AFFILIATIONS
Arizona Diamondbacks (20%)
Los Angeles Dodgers (18%)
Chicago Cubs (15%)
Seattle Mariners (8%)
St. Louis Cardinals (6%)
Cincinnati Reds (6%)
Texas Rangers (6%)
New York Yankees (5%)
Baltimore Orioles (4%)
Oakland A's (3%)
Toronto Blue Jays (3%)
Minnesota Twins (3%)

NUMBER OF SEASONS ON WINNING TEAMS
10.5

CAREER EARNINGS
> $20 Million

TOTAL MANAGERS PLAYED FOR
21

MOST FREQUENT MANAGER
Tommy Lasorda

MOST FREQUENT CATCHER
Mike Scioscia

PITCHING ROLE
Starter (69%) | Middler (30%) | Closer (1%)

STATS AS A FIREMAN
0-1   3.79
Converted 8 out of 9 saves

BEST SEASON
(1992)   16-8   2.55 ERA

CAREER FIELDING RECORD
.965

CAREER HITTING STATS
.109 BA, 0 HR, 15 RBI

INJURY AND REST RATE
11%

PLAYOFF RECORD
2 postseasons, 10 games
0-0   4.00 ERA   4 K
2 divisional titles, 1 world championship

MOST FREQUENT FOE
Barry Bonds—72 plate appearances
(.311 BA, 2 HR, 11 RBI)

A HITTER HE OWNED
Ozzie Smith
.080 (2 for 25) with 0 HR and 0 RBIs

A HITTER WHO OWNED HIM
Tim Salmon
1.000 (3 for 3) with 2 HRs and 3 RBIs

HIS RECORD AGAINST HALL OF FAMERS
441 AT-BATS
.308 BA   16 HR   58 RBI   49 WALKS   46K

MOST FREQUENT TEAMMATE
Mark Grace (7 seasons)

HOME AWAY FROM HOME
Candlestick Park
4-4   2.58 ERA

MOST FREQUENT OPPONENT
San Diego Padres

CLOSEST STATISTICAL TWIN
Jim Clancy

ODD TRIVIA
Morgan is the only pitcher to have faced both
Thurman Munson and Albert Pujols

HALL OF FAME CALIBRE RATING
17%

IN 2002
Morgan was inducted into the Southern Nevada Sports Hall of Fame.

Follies Factoids

★ Morgan pitched against both high school opponents and the Baltimore Orioles within seven days.

★ Rickey Henderson, Mike Morgan, Jesse Orosco, and Tim Raines are the only four players who competed in the majors during the 1970s, '80s, '90s, and '00s.

46

The Kids Not in the Hall

◇◇◇

This is a somewhat interactive chapter...so wake up!

The challenge we now present to you, the erstwhile reader,
is to put together the

⌐ BEST 25-MAN TEAM OF ALL TIME ⌐

among those players **NOT ALREADY** in the Hall of Fame.
(Sorry Ty Cobb, Walter Johnson, Stan Musial, and Babe Ruth)

There is one additional criterion:
Each candidate must have **ALREADY** been on a
Hall of Fame ballot and been passed over,
so recently retired greats
(like Barry Bonds, Roger Clemens, and Greg Maddux)
and active players
(such as Derek Jeter, Albert Pujols and Alex Rodriguez)
aren't eligible to join this dream team.

Please make anywhere from one to twenty-five player selections
along with one managerial selection and send it along to
Yellowstone@baseballprism.com for tabulation.
Everyone who votes will receive a complimentary issue
of the *Baseball Prism* newsletter.
In the interest of fairness, please don't stuff the ballot box.
From time to time, we will post updated results on the
www.rolliesbaseballfollies.com Web site.

BASEBALL GREATS NOT ENSHRINED IN COOPERSTOWN
Position Players

Dick Allen	Mark Grace	Lance Parrish
Harold Baines	Dick Groat	Tony Pena
Albert Belle	Stan Hack	Vada Pinson
Bobby Bonds	Babe Herman	Tim Raines
Bob Boone	Keith Hernandez	Willie Randolph
Ken Boyer	Shoeless Joe Jackson Bob	Pete Rose
Pete Browning	Johnson	Jimmy Ryan
Brett Butler	Harvey Keunn	Ron Santo
Bert Campaneris	Herman Long	Ted Simmons
Jose Canseco	Denny Lyons	Reggie Smith
Joe Carter	Sherry Magee	Rusty Staub
Ben Chapman	Don Mattingly	Vern Stephens
Cupid Childs	Roger Maris	Harry Stovey
Jack Clark	Mark McGwire	Jim Sundberg
Will Clark	Ed McKean	Mike Tiernan
Dave Concepcion	Minnie Minoso	George Van Haltren
Cecil Cooper	Thurman Munson	Joe Torre
Lave Cross	Dale Murphy	Alan Trammell
Bill Dahlen	Buddy Myer	Mo Vaughn
Chili Davis	Lefty O'Doul	Bobby Veach
Darrell Evans	Al Oliver	Dixie Walker
Dwight Evans	Paul O'Neill	Lou Whitaker
George Foster	Tip O'Neill	Deacon White
Andres Galarraga	Tony Oliva	Ken Williams
Steve Garvey	Dave Parker	Maury Wills

Pitchers

Babe Adams	Jim Kaat	Deacon Phillippe
Rick Aguilera	Jimmy Key	Billy Pierce
Bert Blyleven	Silver King	Jack Powell
Vida Blue	Jerry Koosman	Jeff Reardon
Tommy Bond	Sam Leever	Allie Reynolds
George Bradley	Mickey Lolich	Ed Ruelbach
Charlie Buffinton	Sparky Lyle	Dan Quisenberry
John Candaleria	Nick Maddox	Bret Saberhagen
Bob Caruthers	Dennis Martinez	Lee Smith
Eddie Cicotte	Bobby Mathews	Urban Shocker
David Cone	Carl Mays	Jack Stivetts
Jack Coombs	Dick McBride	Frank Tanana
Mort Cooper	Jim McCormick	Jesse Tannehill
Wilbur Cooper	Sam McDowell	Luis Tiant
Larry Corcoran	Denny McLain	Hippo Vaughn
Mike Cuellar	Dave McNally	Fernando Valenzuela
Paul Derringer	Ed Morris	Bucky Walters
Bill Donovan	Jack Morris	Lou Warneke
Freddy Fitzsimmons	Tony Mullane	Bob Welch
Dave Foutz	George Mullin	John Wetteland
Mark Fidrych	Randy Myers	Gus Weyring
Dwight Gooden	Art Nehf	Doc White
Ron Guidry	Robb Nen	Will White
Guy Hecker	Don Newcombe	Jim Whitney
Orel Hershiser	Milt Pappas	Hooks Wiltse
Bill Hutchison	Jim Perry	Smoky Joe Wood
Tommy John	Jack Pfiester	

Managers

Felipe Alou	Phil Garner	Pat Moran
Joe Altobelli	Charlie Grimm	Jack McKeon
Frank Bancroft	Fred Haney	John McNamara
Hank Bauer	Mike Hargrove	DannyMurtaugh
Bob Brenly	Art Howe	Jim Mutrie
Bill Carrigan	Ralph Houk	Steve O'Neill
Fred Clarke	Dick Howser	Bill Rigney
Alvin Dark	Davey Johnson	Pants Rowland
Larry Dierker	Fielder Jones	Mayo Smith
Chuck Dressen	Tom Kelly	Gene Stallings
Eddie Dyer	Johnny Keen	Gabby Street
Jimmy Dykes	Billy Martin	Chuck Tanner
Jim Fregosi	Gene Mauch	Bobby Valentine

... and anyone who was passed over on the 2010 ballot

Follies Factoids

★ Joe DiMaggio was a **THIRD** ballot Hall-Of-Famer.

★ One of the most exclusive clubs at Cooperstown belongs to third basemen. Since 1939, only eleven have been inducted. By contrast, the Hall has sixty-three pitchers, twenty-three right fielders, twenty-two shortstops, twenty left fielders, eighteen first basemen, eighteen second basemen, seventeen centerfielders, and thirteen catchers.

47

The Cincinnati Reds
(1970-1979)

◇◇◇

THE OVERVIEW

If you happened to be a baseball fan living in Cincinnati in 1970, you might as well have won the lottery. Over the course of the next decade, no other team tallied as many victories as did the Cincinnati Reds, and arguably, no other team provided as many thrills.

Powerful, fast, colorful, and clutch, the Big Red Machine drew thousands of extra fans to ballparks all across the majors. So popular were the Reds with their hometown fans that attendance during the 1970s skyrocketed 139 percent, compared to the decade before.

Six times the Reds reached the postseason in the 1970s, a mark no team in either league surpassed (and only one, the Pittsburgh Pirates, matched). But the Pirates usually came up short against their bitter red rivals. On the four occasions that these two crews collided in the NLCS, Cincinnati downed Pittsburgh in three of them.

The Reds' leader for the first nine seasons was George "Sparky" Anderson, a man who would not only go on to the Hall of Fame but also become the winningest manager of the half-century. White-haired before his time, Sparky blended traits of enthusiasm, superstition, and impatience to great effect. Some even called him "Captain Hook," a nickname earned for his tendency to yank pitchers out of ballgames at the first whiff of trouble.

In these postseasons, his Big Red Machine sliced and diced the mighty Boston Red Sox and steamrolled both the New York Yankees and Philadelphia Phillies. During the regular seasons, divisional rivals such as the Houston

Astros and San Diego Padres never once finished ahead of Sparky's gang.

So consistently solid were the '70s Reds, that if the wild card playoff system had been in place, they would have made the postseason three more times. But even without that opening available to them, Cincy still managed to be the only 1970s ballclub to win as many as four pennants.

Interestingly, this was a team not carried on the back of any one player. Here, it was excellence by committee. In fact, four Reds players combined to win six of the NL's MVP awards that decade.

Leadoff hitter Pete Rose was the hometown favorite, a hustling workhorse who brought a number of different fielding gloves to the party. He was slightly older than the rest but a tenacious hit machine. Pete was especially well known for his headfirst slides (a style well ahead of its time) and for having bowl hair that looked like an homage to Moe Howard of the Three Stooges (a style well behind the times).

Joe Morgan was the sparkplug. A native of Oakland, he combined speed, sure fielding, and surprising power for a man of his size. Little Joe arrived in the Queen City from Houston in what became the most lopsided trade of its era.

Johnny Bench was the folksy valedictorian from Oklahoma. He possessed gorilla-sized hands and a bazooka for an arm. When he wasn't quarterbacking the team from behind the plate, he was an especially intimidating slugger with power to all fields. Early in his career, Ted Williams tabbed him as a future Hall of Famer, and the humble Bench never proved him wrong.

George Foster was the tall lanky kid out of Tuscaloosa with serious hitting potential. Willie Mays and Willie McCovey, his fellow Alabamans, quickly saw that ability when he arrived in the majors with San Francisco. However, Giants management didn't see it and swapped George to the Reds for a middle infielder who hit .179. Just after the middle of the decade, George had matured into a home-run-hitting phenom causing the Giants almost as much remorse as the Astros felt for losing Morgan.

But the depth of the Reds squad went well beyond the previous quartet of MVP winners. Other significant cogs in the Big Red Machine were Hall of Famer Tony Perez from Cuba, perennial All-Star shortstop Davey Concepcion from Venezuela, and Ken Griffey Sr. from the even more exotic locale of suburban Pittsburgh.

As a skipper, Sparky was the very definition of proactive. He moved his players around the field and up and down the lineup with the compulsive artistry of a feng shui master. Should you ask a Reds fan who the first baseman was during the 70s, settle in for an answer so complicated that it would have confused Bud Abbott. If you should ask for the name of the man on third base, bring camping equipment.

Many Reds players owned more than one mitt and most every hitter in the lineup could expect to be in a different hole from where he'd been slotted the game prior. Catcher Johnny Bench, for instance, not only spent ample time hitting third, fourth, fifth, and even sixth, but defensively he played all five of the chalk positions and even logged a little time in center field. Leadoff hitter Pete Rose was the only guy who had a set place in the batting order, but on the diamond, he fielded every position but shortstop, catcher, and pitcher. Pete even managed to play two different positions at an All-Star game.

The Midsummer Classics of the 1970s were dominated by the National League—and these NL rosters were dominated by Cincinnati Reds. All in all, fifteen pieces from the Big Red Machine combined to make fifty-two All-Star appearances. At one time or another, a Red played each of the nine positions.

Seven Reds pitchers made All-Star rosters during the 70s. Sparky was just as deft at restocking hurlers around his everyday players as Bobby Cox was at doing the opposite.

THESE UNSUNG RED PITCHERS

Historians rarely give these Reds credit for their pitching. Of all the Cincinnati hurlers that decade, only Tom Seaver made it to the Hall of Fame. However, it should be noted that Seaver and the Big Red Machine joined forces after they had already won their respective jewelry.

But despite being in the tall shadow of the hitting legends, a number of Reds hurlers did very well during the pivotal postseasons of 1975 and 1976. This was an especially mean feat considering they were facing the likes of Willie Stargell, Dave Parker, Carlton Fisk, Carl Yastrzemski, Fred Lynn, Mike Schmidt, Greg Luzinski, Thurman Munson, and Graig Nettles. But the Reds' pitching corps not only came through in the clutch, they excelled under the pressure. All in all, they posted a surprisingly low team ERA of 3.05 across these two postseasons.

Don Gullet pitched forty-one innings and went 4-1 with a 2.93 ERA. Jack Billingham gave up only one earned run in his 11.2 innings. Pedro Borbon surrendered just two in ten innings, and Will McEnaney only gave up three in 12.2 innings.

All four of these pitchers were significantly better in the post season than they had been during the regular season.

They stepped up when it mattered most.

IN THE CLUTCH (1975 AND 1976)

The Reds' hitters also had their work cut out for them during these pivotal postseason matchups. The aces they drew included Jerry Reuss, Luis Tiant, Spaceman Lee, Steve Carlton, and Catfish Hunter. In the pens, they faced Kent Tekulve, Tug McGraw, and Sparky Lyle.

Unlike their teammates on the mound, the Reds hitters didn't go to the next level during the playoffs, but they did manage to be very consistent. During the regular seasons of '75 and '76, the Big Red Machine manufactured an average of 5.238 runs per game. During the postseasons, against a higher caliber of competition, they managed to produce 5.235 runs, more than enough to cover the stingy amount of runs their pitching teammates surrendered.

Here's how nine of the main cogs did across these nineteen pivotal postseason games when the chips were down:

- Pete Rose hit .338 with 24 hits.
- Ken Griffey hit .250 with 11 RBIs and 8 steals.
- Joe Morgan hit .250 with 11 runs, 15 walks and 10 steals.
- Tony Perez hit .258 with 4 homers and 17 RBIs.
- Johnny Bench hit .275 with 4 homers, 13 runs and 11 RBIs.
- George Foster hit .303 with 10 RBIs.
- Cesar Geronimo hit .220 with 2 doubles, a triple and 2 homers.
- Dave Concepcion hit .270 with 10 runs and 6 steals.
- Dan Driessen hit .294 with 2 doubles and a homer.

THE NEAR SPOILERS

- Richie Zisk of the Pirates went 5 for 10 with 2 walks in the 1975 NLCS.
- Luis Tiant of the Red Sox picked up 2 wins and 12 strikeouts in the 1975 World Series.
- Carlton Fisk drilled 4 singles, drew 7 walks, and hit 2 home runs, one of which became legendary, as it sent the '75 Series into a Game 7 showdown.
- Jay Johnstone of the Phillies amassed 7 hits in 9 at bats (two of which were extra-base hits) during the 1976 NLCS.
- The Yankees' Thurman Munson went 9 for 17 against the Machine in the 1976 Fall Classic.

NOTABLE CHANGES FROM 1974 TO 1975
THAT PROBABLY CONTRIBUTED TO CINCINNATI
WINNING A WORLD CHAMPIONSHIP

- Left fielder Pete Rose was shifted to third base, pushing Dan Driessen out of the lineup, to significantly strengthen the bench. The void left by Rose in left field allowed part-time outfielder George Foster to play there full time, which in turn allowed platoon player Ken Griffey to become the everyday right fielder.
- Ken Griffey hit 54 points higher than he had in 1974.
- George Foster hit 36 points higher.
- Second baseman Joe Morgan hit 34 points higher.
- Third baseman Pete Rose hit 33 points higher.
- Gary Nolan and Pat Darcy joined the starting rotation
- Relievers Will McEnaney and Rawley Eastwick were handed the ball with greater frequency.
- The Los Angeles Dodgers scored 150 fewer runs.
- The Oakland A's lost Catfish Hunter and failed to reach the World Series for the first time in three years.

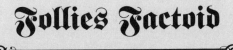

★ Oddly enough, the 1975 world championship Reds hit 11 fewer homers and hurled 212 fewer strikeouts than did the 1974 squad.

NOTABLE CHANGES FROM 1976 TO 1977
THAT MAY HAVE CONTRIBUTED TO CINCINNATI
FALLING FROM CHAMPIONSHIP CALIBER

- First baseman Tony Perez and pitcher Don Gullett left the Reds.
- Dan Driessen was reinserted into the everyday lineup—a move that weakened the bench.
- Jack Billingham's ERA rose from 4.32 to 5.23.
- Center fielder Cesar Geronimo hit 41 points lower.
- Second baseman Joe Morgan hit 32 points lower.
- Gary Nolan started only eight games due to injury.
- Despite the addition of superstar Tom Seaver in midseason, the team's collective ERA rose 0.70.
- The Los Angeles Dodgers scored 161 more runs.

Follies Factoid

⚬❧━━━━━━━━━━━━━━━━━━━━━━━━❧⚬

★ Oddly enough, the 1977 Reds hit 40 more homers and notched 78 more strikeouts than did the 1976 World champs.

THE FIVE REDS FROM THE 70s ALREADY ENSHRINED IN COOPERSTOWN

Sparky Anderson, Johnny Bench, Joe Morgan, Tony Perez, and Tom Seaver.

THE REDS ALL-STAR REPRESENTATIVES FROM THE 1970s

Johnny Bench (10)
Joe Morgan (8)
Pete Rose (8)
Dave Concepcion (6)
George Foster (4)
Tony Perez (4)
Clay Carroll (2)
Ken Griffey Sr. (2)
Tom Seaver (2)
Jack Billingham (1)
Mike LaCoss (1)
Lee May (1)
Jim Merritt (1)
Gary Nolan (1)
Wayne Simpson (1)

TEAM HONORS

During the 1970s, among the twenty-four ballclubs that played ten full seasons, the Cincinnati Reds:
• were 2nd in runs scored
• were 2nd in home runs
• had the 7th best team batting average
and

- were 7th in runs allowed
  but they
- were 1st in saves
- 1st in on-base percentage
- had the fewest passed balls
  and
- were 1st in regular season victories.

IN THEIR DEFENSE

Spanning the decade, only the Baltimore Orioles (.982) managed to post a more impressive fielding percentage than the Cincinnati Reds (.981).

THE REDS GOLD GLOVE AWARD WINNERS DURING THE 1970s
Johnny Bench (8)
Dave Concepcion (5)
Joe Morgan (5)
Cesar Geronimo (4)
Tommy Helms (2)
Pete Rose (1)

KNUCKSIE

In studying the 24-year career of Hall of Fame pitcher Phil Niekro, an interesting fact emerged. The five hitters the longtime Atlanta Brave faced most frequently were all members of the Big Red Machine.

1. Pete Rose (266 plate appearances)
2. Johnny Bench (200)
3. Joe Morgan (200)
4. Tony Perez (174)
5. Davey Concepcion (157)

Tony Perez hit Niekro best, amassing a .313 lifetime batting average to go with a .550 slugging percentage.

Phil Niekro also happened to be the most frequent pitcher that each of these five players faced during the scope of their careers. Additionally, the knuckleballer was also the most frequent career foe for both Dan Driessen and Cesar Geronimo.

REDS POSITION PLAYERS DURING THE 1970s
(100-game minimum per position)

CATCHER
Johnny Bench (1,297 games)
Bill Plummer (302)

FIRST BASE
Tony Perez (764)
Dan Driessen (605)
Lee May (296)

SECOND BASE
Joe Morgan (1,116)
Tommy Helms (297)
Junior Kennedy (147)
Darrel Chaney (106)

SHORTSTOP
Dave Concepcion (1,303)
Darrel Chaney (222)
Woody Woodward (162)
Doug Flynn (106)

THIRD BASE
Pete Rose (618)
Tony Perez (301)
Ray Knight (260)
Denis Menke (253)
Dan Driessen (213)
Darrel Chaney (120)

LEFT FIELD
George Foster (633)
Pete Rose (519)
Bernie Carbo (208)
Hal McRae (111)

CENTER FIELD
Cesar Geronimo (945)
Bobby Tolan (375)
George Foster (276)

RIGHT FIELD
Ken Griffey Sr (734)
Pete Rose (313)
George Foster (162)
Cesar Geronimo (117)
Merv Rettenmund (103)

MUSICAL CHAIRS

1970 Catcher Johnny Bench also played twenty-four games in the outfield, twelve at first base, and one at third base.

1972 Pete Rose shifted from right field to left field, Tony Perez shifted from third base to first base, and George Foster went from center field to the bench.

1973 Right fielder Cesar Geronimo and center fielder Bobby Tolan swapped outfield positions.

1974 Dan Driessen came off the bench to become the primary third baseman.

1974 Catcher Johnny Bench also spent thirty-six games at the hot corner, essentially becoming the team's backup third baseman.

1975 As previously mentioned, Pete Rose shifted from left field to third base. Dan Driessen went from third base back to the bench. George Foster shifted to left field from his role of being a backup center fielder/right fielder.

1977 Dan Driessen became the everyday first baseman.

Reds Factoids

★ Pete Rose logged more games for the 1970s Reds than any other player, despite he fact that he played for the Phillies in 1979.

★ During the decade, including the postseason, Johnny Bench hit exactly 300 homers while George Foster hit precisely 200.

★ Johnny Bench and Davey Concepcion were the only Reds who were around both on Opening Day in 1970 and for the final NLCS game against the Pirates in 1979.

★ The Reds' postseason record during the 1970s was 28-17 (.622). Their regular season record was was 953-657 (.592).

★ Despite playing eight seasons for the Reds, backup catcher Bill Plummer never made it into a postseason game. He watched from the bench as a backup for the appropriately named Johnny Bench.

★ In his three seasons with the post-championship Reds, Tom Seaver compiled a 46-23 record with a 2.82 ERA.

★ Joe Morgan, Pete Rose, and Tony Perez reunited in Philadelphia and became members of the 1983 pennant-inning Phillies.

★ The National League team that fared the best against the '70s Reds was the Chicago Cubs, who tallied a 59-61 record.

★ '70s Reds players Pete Rose, Tony Perez, Tommy Helms, and Ray Knight all went on to manage the ballclub.

THE 25-MAN CINCINNATI REDS TEAM
(1970-1979)

Manager: Sparky Anderson
Honorable Mention: John McNamara

PITCHING STAFF
*(The top five pitchers in games started along with the top five pitchers
in relief appearances) (postseason stats included)*

STARTERS

	Won-Loss	ERA	Strikeouts
Fred Norman	86-65	3.46	876
Jack Billingham	77-64	3.79	626
Gary Nolan	85-49	3.14	666
Don Gullet	95-47	3.03	835
Ross Grimsley	40-27	3.28	246

RELIEVERS

	Won-Loss	ERA	Saves	Strikeouts
Pedro Borbon	63-34	3.30	79	370
Clay Carroll	56-32	2.56	97	331
Rawley Eastwick	22-10	2.47	58	168
Will McEnaney	9-9	3.55	24	97
Tom Hall	18-14	3.19	17	297

POSITION PLAYERS
(The top fifteen Reds in plate appearances)

Position		AVG	HR	RBI	SB
3B/OF	Pete Rose	.312	80	537	86
C	Johnny Bench	267	300	1,033	62
SS	Dave Concepcion	.270	72	542	227
2B	Joe Morgan	.285	155	621	420
1B/3B	Tony Perez	.283	185	737	32
OF	George Foster	.288	200	690	43
CF/RF	Cesar Geronimo	.258	45	345	73
RF	Ken Griffey Sr.	.308	45	316	123
1B/3B	Dan Driessen	.272	77	423	113
CF	Bobby Tolan	.273	35	226	121
1B	Lee May	.266	75	202	4
IF	Darrel Chaney	.206	7	81	19
2B	Tommy Helms	.247	4	97	5
3B	Denis Menke	.214	14	79	1
C	Bill Plummer	.186	12	75	4

48

The All-Dominican Team

◇◇◇

A twenty-five-man dream team that consists solely of players who were BORN in the Dominican Republic (sorry A-Rod and Moises Alou) along with each player's statistics through 2009. (postseason stats included)

Manager: Felipe Alou

THE ALL-DOMINICAN PITCHING STAFF

STARTERS

	Won-Loss	ERA	Shutouts	Strikeouts
Pedro Martinez	219-100	2.93	17	3,154
Juan Marichal	243-143	2.88	52	2,313
José Rijo	119-91	3.22	4	1,635
Ramon Martinez	135-91	3.68	20	1,447
Bartolo Colon	153-103	4.10	8	1,607

RELIEVERS

	Won-Loss	ERA	Saves	Strikeouts
Pedro Borbon, Sr.	70-40	3.49	83	420
Francisco Cordero	33-37	3.18	250	664
Alejandro Pena	60-55	3.07	78	867
José Mesa	83-110	4.38	327	1,067
Armando Benitez	43-49	3.15	293	982

HONORABLE MENTION

Antonio Alfonseca, Joaquin Andujar, José Arredonso, Pedro Astacio, Miguel Batista, Hector Carrasco, José Jiminez, José DeLeon, Octavio Dotel, Francisco Liriano, Carlos Marmol, Guillermo Mota, Al Reyes, Mel Rojas, Ervin Santana, Rafael Soriano, Elias Sosa, Mario Soto, Julian Tavarez, Salomon Torres, José Valverde and Luis Vizcaino

THE ALL-DOMINICAN POSITION PLAYERS

STARTING LINEUP

Position		AVG	HR	RBI	SB
CF	Cesar Cedeno	.285	199	978	552
SS	Miguel Tejada	.289	285	1,185	78
1B	Albert Pujols	.334	366	1,112	61
LF	Manny Ramirez	.313	546	1,788	37
DH	Vladimir Guerrero	.321	407	1,318	175
RF	Sammy Sosa	.273	611	1,674	235
3B	Aramis Ramirez	.286	264	946	15
C	Tony Peña	.261	108	713	82
2B	Julio Franco	.297	175	1,200	282

RESERVES

Position		AVG	HR	RBI	SB
C	Miguel Olivo	.243	96	330	37
1B/DH	David Ortiz	.282	317	1,068	10
2B/SS/3B	Tony Fernandez	.288	95	867	251
2B/LF	Alfonso Soriano	.278	290	760	257
LF	George Bell	.278	266	1,005	67
CF/RF	Felipe Alou	.286	206	853	107

HONORABLE MENTION

CF Matty Alou, 3B Tony Batista, SS Rafael Belliard, 3B Adrian Beltre, 2B Robinson Cano, LF Rico Carty, 2B Luis Castillo, RF Nelson Cruz, 2B Mariano Duncan, RF Juan Encarnacion, 3B Pedro Feliz, SS Rafael Furcal, CF Cesar Geronimo, SS Alfredo Griffin, 1B Pedro Guerrero, RF José Guillen, SS Cristian Guzman, 2B Julian Javier, CF Stan Javier, SS Julio Lugo, RF Raul Mondesi, PH Manny Mota, SS José Offerman, 1B Carlos Peña, SS Neifi Perez, 2B Placido Polanco, LF Luis Polonia, SS Hanley Ramirez, SS Rafael Ramirez, SS José Reyes, 2B Juan Samuel, SS Frank Taveras, 2B Quilvio Veras and SS José Vizcaino

49

Modern Ruins

◇◇◇

For generations, thousands of Red Sox faithful sensed that a curse had been placed upon their boys in red. This belief was bedrock. Too many second-place finishes and Game Seven losses will do that to the sanest of minds.

Much of the fault was laid at the feet of the New York Yankees, who are as hated in New England as any other team in any other place times ten. From 1919 through 2003, Boston teams often managed to be worthy rivals, but the Yankees held the upper hand. In essence, they were to the Red Sox what Chris Brown had been to Rihanna.

But in 2004, David "Big Papi" Ortiz and his merry band of idiots cowboyed up. Their team color was not only pulsing through their veins, on one occasion, it even soaked through Curt Schilling's socks, making the team's moniker gruesomely literal.

Rebounding from a three-games-to-none deficit in the ALCS, this ballclub of destiny diffused the Bombers. It was the most jubilant Boston baseball fans had felt in decades. Their reward was a World Series date with Albert Pujols and the St. Louis Cardinals.

But deep in the pits of their stomachs, weariness remained. Would their beloved Red Sox drop yet another Game Seven in the Fall Classic? The answer probably would have been "yes," except that they swept St. Louis in four straight. Throughout the entirety of Red Sox nation, prayers had been answered, taps ran dry, and glee ran unchecked.

But this victory was especially sweet because the curse seemingly hadn't only ended so much as it got transferred to the Yankees. After all, this time around it had been the Yankees who found themselves on the brink of success only to see it painfully roll through their legs.

Evidence promoting this theory of a curse-reversal continued to mount. After all, just three seasons later, David Ortiz's crew added yet another world championship. As for the once dominant Yanks in 2007, they had to endure their seventh consecutive season of postseason sputtering. Big money just didn't bring champagne celebrations to the Bronx the way it used to.

But in early 2008, fresh hope burgeoned. The foundation was poured for a brand new Yankee stadium and with it, grand designs for future world championships. But one critical detail was overlooked in the construction of this masterpiece: a construction worker by the name of Gino Castignoli.

The very idea of being in the vicinity of this new Yankee Stadium nauseated Gino, a diehard Red Sox fan. In fact, when he was initially given the assignment, he expressed strong reluctance. However, work is work, and he gave in to the union's request. But as Gino diligently labored, he was struck by how funny it could be if somehow a Red Sox jersey could, possibly, be entombed in the foundation of the new ballpark.

The idea was too good to ignore, and so Gino decided to execute his voodoo-tinged prank. When the time was right, as wet concrete poured down into a ground hole, he produced a David Ortiz jersey and dropped it into the mix, where it sank deep into the cold gray soup. In no time, word began spreading that a Red Sox jersey was now a fundamental part of the new Yankee Stadium.

To Boston fans, this story was more than a little amusing, but to Yankee fans, it was akin to terrorism. A white-collar posse of Yankee brass was formed to investigate. Although Gino's planting did not threaten the stadium's structural integrity, the Yankees pursued the matter with comparable intensity.

When the rumor of Gino's prank was verified and after Gino's co-workers helped isolate the general area of the offending jersey, jackhammers met with perfectly smooth concrete.

After five hours of drilling through two feet of solid concrete, the Yankees finally hit payshirt. Beyond the time and stress, the destruction cost them about $45,000. With triumph, the Yankees pulled the now-tattered Ortiz jersey out of the pit as though it were Excalibur from a stone.

Superstition avoided, the Yankees comfortably sighed and went on with their business. Such is the business of baseball.

Follies Factoids

★ During their initial season (2009) in the new Yankee Stadium, the Yankees won the world championship. As for David Ortiz, his numbers mysteriously plummeted, and for the first time in six seasons, he failed to make the All-Star team.

★ The Ortiz jersey went on to sell at auction for $175,100. However, no part of the proceeds went to pay for the construction costs nor did they find their way into the Gino Castignoli retirement fund.

50

Cy Young and Roy Oswalt:
Eleven Degrees of Separation

◇◇

Cy Young and Roy Oswalt never met, nor were they ever together on the same baseball field They were never even alive at the same time.

But, they are inextricably linked all the same...and not just because Roy Oswalt has been a perennial contender for the elite pitching award that is named in Cy Young's honor.
Here's how:

I DEGREE   Both Cy Young and Honus Wagner played in the 1903 World Series.

2 DEGREES   Honus Wagner and Bobby Byrne were both part of the 1909 Fall Classic.

3 DEGREES   Bobby Byrne and Babe Ruth both played in the 1915 Series.

4 DEGREES   Yankees Babe Ruth and Lou Gehrig were part of the 1926 Series.

5 DEGREES   Lou Gehrig and Joe DiMaggio's Yankee team won it all in 1936.

6 DEGREES   Joe DiMaggio and Willie Mays both played in the 1951 Fall Classic.

7 DEGREES   Willie Mays and Reggie Jackson opposed each other in the 1973 World Series.

8 DEGREES Both Reggie Jackson and Mike Scioscia were heavily involved in the 1981 Fall Classic.

9 DEGREES Mike Scioscia and Walt Weiss were each a part of the 1988 Series.

10 DEGREES Walt Weiss and Roger Clemens both played in the 1999 Fall Classic.

11 DEGREES The 2005 World Series featured both Roger Clemens and Roy Oswalt.

Ergo, just eleven World Series players separate the two pitching icons of Cy Young and Roy Oswalt.

For those of you who are coyly wondering if Roy Oswalt is also linked to actor Kevin Bacon, the answer is yes. Both have appeared as guests on *The Late Show with David Letterman.*

As for Cy Young, you might be surprised to know that he is a mere two degrees away from Kevin Bacon. In 1955, an elderly Cy Young appeared as a celebrity guest on the game show *I've Got A Secret* with host Garry Moore. In 1959, Garry Moore acted in a film with screen legend Jack Lemmon, who subsequently appeared in the 1991 film *JFK* with Kevin Bacon.

51

The Designated Chapter

◇◇

Should you walk into a sports pub (outside of Boston or Seattle) and ask who was the best designated hitter of all time, you'll likely start a debate.

We sure wouldn't want you to walk into such a situation unarmed—so below, you will find the lifetime stats for many of the game's greatest DHs. Some of the facts presented here will help make your case.

THE DELUXE DESIGNATED HITTERS

(Note: the following numbers are not career totals; they merely reflect the statistics put up while each player was within the specific roles of designated hitter and pinch hitter)

	GAMES	HITS	HR	RBI	BA
Harold Baines	1,787	1,724	239	1,013	.291
Hal McRae	1,593	1,591	150	854	.292
Edgar Martinez	1,471	1,622	246	1,012	.314
Don Baylor	1,363	1,225	220	821	.259
Frank Thomas	1,353	1,294	271	888	.275
Chili Davis	1,270	1,197	204	765	.281
David Ortiz*	1,213	1,218	275	908	.282
Paul Molitor	1,196	1,458	102	653	.307
Cliff Johnson	977	691	132	489	.263
Brian Downing	926	824	125	421	.269
Jose Canseco	887	860	208	645	.264

* through 2009

ADDITIONAL PLAYERS FROM THE 2000-2009 DECADE

	GAMES	HITS	HR	RBI	BA
Jason Giambi	561	435	106	316	.247
Travis Hafner	753	746	153	525	.285
Mike Sweeney	636	646	81	370	.285
Jim Thome	720	589	161	448	.261

Since the inception of the designated hitter rule in 1973, the American League went on to win twenty-one of the next thirty-six World Series. Some of these champion teams primarily slotted a single slugger into the DH role while other teams preferred to rotate a number of players.

While the American League's superiority shouldn't be credited all that much to the DH, there's no debate that it has helped keep benchwarmers tuned up while also allowing regular defenders the chance to rest their glove without coming out of the batting order. In theory, the junior circuit is a better place to heal an injury, to fight fatigue, or to profit from having an aging slugger in the lineup who is no longer defensively capable—all advantages that the National League does not have at its disposal.

Interestingly, the three consecutive championship teams I played for in Oakland did so under three different circumstances in regard to the DH. We won the first time before the DH era. (Our pitching staff that year had 66 hits including 3 homers).

The second year we climbed the mountain, we did so with one player (Deron Johnson) handling the majority of the DH duties, and in our third championship season, seventeen players revolved through the DH slot (with no one staying there for as many as forty-two games).

There are just different themes for different teams. The following chart lists the primary designated hitters for the first twenty AL champs along with how many games they were plugged into the slot.

YEAR	TEAM	PLAYER	GAMES / DH
1973	OAKLAND	Deron Johnson	107
1974	OAKLAND	Jesus Alou	41
1977	NY YANKEES	Carlos May	53
1978	NY YANKEES	Cliff Johnson	39
1983	BALTIMORE	Ken Singleton	150
1984	DETROIT	Darrell Evans	62
1985	KANSAS CITY	Hal McRae	106
1987	MINNESOTA	Roy Smalley	73
1989	OAKLAND	Dave Parker	140
1991	MINNESOTA	Chili Davis	150
1992	TORONTO	Dave Winfield	130
1993	TORONTO	Paul Molitor	137
1996	NY YANKEES	Ruben Sierra	61
1998	NY YANKEES	Darryl Strawberry	81
1999	NY YANKEES	Chili Davis	141

YEAR	TEAM	PLAYER	GAMES / DH
2000	NY YANKEES	Shane Spencer	33
2002	ANAHEIM	Brad Fullmer	94
2004	BOSTON	David Ortiz	115
2005	CHI WHITE SOX	Carl Everett	107
2007	BOSTON	David Ortiz	140
2009	NY YANKEES	Hideki Matsui	116

But just as the American League seemingly has an extra tool in the box because of the DH, perhaps the National League also has advantages because it doesn't utilize it (save for some interleague games).

First of all, not having to pay for an additional everyday hitter should give them extra money to spend on upgrades elsewhere. Secondly, the NL often ends up looking far more appealing to free agent pitchers since it's much easier to work your way through a lineup that basically has an automatic out at the bottom of it.

Both times that Randy Johnson jumped from the AL to the NL, his ERA improved significantly. The same is true for Roger Clemens. However, when they came back to the AL, their ERAs skyrocketed, even though their win-loss records either stayed similar or improved.

Follies Factoids

★ From 1972 to 1973, with the DH implemented, the American League's collective batting average rose by 20 points (to .259), the league ERA rose 0.75 (to 3.82) and the average team scored 153 more runs.

★ From a fielding standpoint, the average team yielded 3 fewer unearned runs.

★ Both Dave Winfield and Paul Molitor won World Championships with the Toronto Blue Jays while playing as a designated hitter. But they had much more in common as well.
Both ... were born in St. Paul, Minnesota
... played for the Golden Gophers at the University of Minnesota
... made their reputations with 1969 expansion franchises
... collected their 3,000th hit as Minnesota Twins
... collected their 3,000th hit on September 16th
... won the Babe Ruth award
... won the Branch Rickey Award
... never managed to win a league MVP award
... are enshrined in Cooperstown
... had their numbers retired by their original ballclubs
... AND were teammates of Rollie Fingers

Appendix

A. TEN THINGS THAT HAVE DELAYED BASEBALL GAMES

1. EARTHQUAKES
2. BEE SWARMS
3. SKUNKS
4. NAKED FANS
5. HURLED DEBRIS
6. RAIN
7. POWER OUTAGES
8. ILL-TIMED SPRINKLERS
9. SNOW
10. KISSING BANDITS

B. FAMOUS INDIANS

One time Yellowstone spent all night drinking at the Suds Hut in Billings, Montana. It happens. But he was there *with a purpose*, for all through the night he asked those who walked in the door a very important question:
Who are the most famous Indians in history?

Below, you will find the results to his survey.

THE MOST FAMOUS INDIANS OF ALL TIME
(according to patrons at the Suds Hut in Billings, Montana)

1. Bob Feller
2. Injun Joe
3. Mahatma Gandhi
4. Sacajawea
5. Tris Speaker
6. Pocahontas
7. Jim Thorpe

8. Jim Thome
9. The Slumdog Millionaire
10. Tie—Larry Doby and Omar Vizquel
11. Tonto
12. Aishwarya Rai
13. Ricky "Wild Thing" Vaughn
14. Tecumseh (the non-wooden version)
15. Ravi Shankar
16. Chief Joseph of the Nez Pierce
17. Chief Wahoo of the Cleveland Indians
18. Chief Nok-A-Homa
19. Chief Wahoo McDaniel
20. Chief Bender
21. Tecumseh (the wooden version that was on *Cheers*)
22. Tie—Kenny Lofton and Sitting Bull
23. Geronimo
24. The gargantuan Apache Chief
from the *Superfriends* cartoon
25. The old chief from the 1970s television
commercial who cried at litter
26. Lou Boudreau
27. Chief Jay Strongbow of the WWF
28. Eleven-way tie—Joe Charboneau and
each of the ten little Indians from the Agatha Christie novel.
29. Chief Wild Eagle of the Hekawi Tribe
30. Uncas

C. SOME OF THE MORE UNUSUAL FORFEITS IN HISTORY

1883 Providence forfeited a game to Philadelphia in the seventh inning so they could catch a train to New York.

1884 The Wilmington Quicksteps were forced to forfeit a game when they weren't quick enough to arrive at the ballpark on time.

1890 Despite the fact they were leading 18-8, the hometown Brooklyn Bridegrooms were forced to forfeit when they ran out of baseballs after the last one had been hit far out of play, unable to be retrieved.

1891 Umpires awarded a lopsided game to the St. Louis Browns when the Cincinnati Reds willfully allowed eight additional Browns runs to score. This tactic was designed to delay the game to the point that it would have to be called due to darkness.

1894 Cap Anson refused to play on the grounds that he didn't have faith in the veracity of the opposing team's baseballs.

1901 A sold-out game in Cincinnati was called when the fans encroached too far onto the baseball field, eliminating the possibility for play to continue.

1902 Baltimore was forced to forfeit a game because the squad had been purchased by an owner who reassigned too many of their players to another ballclub he owned.

1903 Detroit was awarded a game because Cleveland's Nap Lajoie heaved an "old dirty ball" over the grandstand that the Tigers insisted on using. Cleveland had previously protested the use of the ball to no avail.

1907 Snowball-heaving fans at the Polo Grounds made their way onto the field. When it became apparent there were no police officers to stop them, even more spilled out, pelting everyone in sight, forcing the umpires to call the game.

1913 Johnny "Crab" Evers of the Cubs used stalling to the point that umpires awarded the game to his opponent. One of his tactics included calling someone *from the clubhouse* in as a pinch-hitter even though this player was out of uniform at the time and required time to dress.

1918 Philadelphia fans caused a forfeit when they made it rain on the field with hundreds of seat cushions.

1924 In Detroit, Yankee Bob Meusel stormed the mound after getting plunked in the ribs by the Tiger pitcher. Once order was restored, Babe Ruth stormed in from another angle with his own fists blazing. (Ruth had been thrown at in the at-bat prior). After a few minutes, it seemed order had once again been restored, but Ruth and Meusel took a circuitous route back to the Yankee dugout *via the Tiger bench*. This invasion into the Tiger den incited a major brawl that saw numerous fans storm the field, causing police to get involved as well. The umpires had no choice but to call the game a forfeit in favor of the Yankees.

1942 The Giants had to forfeit a game when hundreds of the math-deficient schoolchildren they were honoring came onto the field *after the eighth inning.*

1977 Despite being in the thick of a September divisional race Earl Weaver pulled his team off the field when umpires refused to remove a bullpen tarp in foul territory that Earl felt was an injury risk to his left fielder. The O's were down 4-0 at the time and the opposing pitcher, Jim Clancy, was dominating them through five innings with a 2-hitter. This forfeit didn't cost them the division, but it was close—Weaver's Orioles finished the year only 2.5 games behind the Yankees.

1995 Dodger fans showered souvenir baseballs onto the field in support of manager Tommy Lasorda, who had been ejected after arguing balls and strikes. This event greatly encouraged the eventual rule of thumb that throwable souvenirs should only be given to fans on their way *out* of the ballpark.

- active as of 2009

D. ANSWER TO NAME THAT PLAYER

Rollie Fingers

Some explanations:
He was born approximately eight miles outside of Toronto.
(Toronto, Ohio)

He was originally signed by Kansas City.
(the Kansas City Athletics)

His teammates over the years included Darrell Evans.
(in Double-AA Birmingham)

He briefly wore the uniform of the Boston Red Sox.
(for three games during the 1976 season—games in which he did not play)
(see Chapter 34 for further details)

Acknowledgments

SPECIAL THANKS

BaseballPrism.com (our sister publication)
Nathan Burton (the Las Vegas headliner)
Rick Bosetti
Howard Cohen
Jerry Coleman of the San Diego Padres
Chris Conroy
Jack Daniels
Keith Dilgard
Giulia Del Priore
Jerry Dowling (for his incredible illustrations)
Lori Fingers
Patrick Gallagher
Carolyn Jevelian
Mac King (for introducing Rollie to Yellowstone)
Allison Lane (the actress)
Josh Peter (Yahoo sports)
ReelSpiel.com (for producing our youtube videos)
George Ritter
The world's finest literary agent, Dr. Neil Salkind
and the staff at Studio B
Ron Santo of the Chicago Cubs
Jimmy Scott and his website:
www.jimmyscottshighandtight.com
Julie Stainer-Loehr
Mike and Dewey at Ideal Baseball Cards in Cincinnati
Rachael Robbins (at RachaelRobbins.com) for her amazing work
as Betty Bombshell in our internet videos
Arnold Topp
and
John Vorperian and his television show:
"Beyond the Game"

ORDINARY THANKS

Jim "Gumby" Gantner

INTERVIEW SOURCES

Bosetti, Rick. Telephone Interview. (July 14, 2008)

WEBSITE SOURCES

ballparksofbaseball.com
baseball-almanac.com
baseballhalloffame.org
baseballprospectus.com
baseball-reference.com
capanson.com
espn.com
hardballtimes.com
howstuffworks.com
kennyrogers.biz
kennys.com/ph
mapquest.com
mlb.com
retrosheet.org
sportsillustrated.com
thebaseballcube.com
wikipedia.com
winningbeyondwinning.org
yahoo.com/mlb
youtube.com

BOOK SOURCES

Castle, George.
    Throwbacks: *Old School Baseball Players in Today's Game*
    (Brassey's 2003)
Fingers, Rollie & Ritter, Christopher "Yellowstone"
    Rollie's Follies (Clerisy Press, 2009)
Kalb, Elliot & Collingsworth, Chris.
    The 25 Greatest Sports Conspiracies of All Time
    (Skyhorse Publishing 2007)
Mead, William B.
    Baseball Goes To War
    (Broadcast Interview Source, Inc. 1998)

ABOUT THE AUTHORS

Hall of Famer pitcher *Rollie Fingers* played seventeen seasons for the Oakland A's, San Diego Padres, and Milwaukee Brewers, winning four pennants and three world championships along the way. He remains one of baseball's most recognizable personalities and makes frequent appearances at charity golf tournaments and fantasy camps across the nation. He currently resides in Las Vegas with his wife, Lori, and their two children.

Rollie is best known for five things: 1) his incisive wit, 2) his devastating slider, 3) his trademark handlebar moustache, 4) his extraordinary skill at golf, and 5) for having won three more world championships than Harmon Killebrew.

Yellowstone Ritter played three seasons for the Our Lady of Angels "Angels" before retiring from the sport to concentrate on his eighth grade studies. Since then, he has written for comedians, television shows, magazines, pharmacists, and for the baseballprism.com website. He visits at least five different stadiums per year, is addicted to barbecued food, and only shaves his beard when the Florida Marlins manage to win five games in a row.

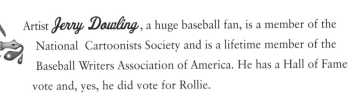

Artist *Jerry Dowling*, a huge baseball fan, is a member of the National Cartoonists Society and is a lifetime member of the Baseball Writers Association of America. He has a Hall of Fame vote and, yes, he did vote for Rollie.

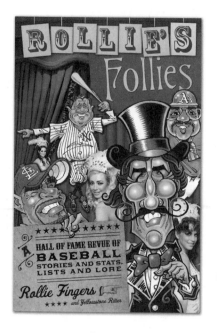

Thanks so much for reading us. Be sure to check out the first book in our critically acclaimed series, *Rollie's Follies*, where you'll find more stories and stats, including:

One-of-a-kind dossiers on Albert Pujols, Rickey Henderson, and Jim Rice

Cy and Ty

The Fallen Smelt

Vince Coleman and the Carnivorous Tarp

The All-Time Lefty Team

Infiltrating the Green Monster

The Japanese Factor

Mickey Mantle, Whitey Ford, and Billy Martin Go Hunting

What Stays In Vegas, Happens In Milwaukee

The Prolific Closers—Decade By Decade

The All-Nineteenth Century Team

Sausage and Presidents

The Oakland A's Dynasty (1972-1974)

The Forgotten Third Baseman

Twenty-One Pitchers Who Could Wield a Bat

A timeline of baseball history that dates all the way back to England in 1085.

Available at rolliesbaseballfollies.com
AND AT FINER BOOKSTORES EVERYWHERE